The Mystery

Of

Prayer Revealed

Julio Alvarado Jr.

The Mystery of Prayer Revealed

ISBN: 978-1492291459

Library of Congress Control Number: 2013923538

Cover art by Roland Pantin

Edited by Bonita Jewel

All Scripture quotations are taken from the Modern King James Version of the Bible, unless otherwise noted.

For information, please contact:

julio@julioalvaradojr.com

Also by Julio Alavarado Jr.

The Mystery of Iniquity Revealed

Coming Soon:

The Mystery of the Kingdom of God Revealed

Contents

Part Three: Prayer Practices

Endorsements

Any relationship is built and maintained by communication. Whether it is a relationship at work or an intimate relationship between a husband and wife, communication is a key element. Without consistent, two-way communication, it is impossible to create or keep a healthy relationship going.

A concept often shrouded in mystery – even within Christianity – is that I, Lord and Creator of heaven and earth, desire to build a close relationship with each of My children. This connection can only be created and maintained through communication with Me.

The avenue of meeting with Me is known as prayer. The majority of My children today consider prayer to be a place where they put forth their concerns, requests, and even demands. Prayer is that, yes, but it is also so much more. Prayer is a sacred meeting place where I wish to not only hear from My children, yet speak as well.

In the book you are about to read, Julio unveils the mystery of prayer, revealing the truth behind My words in the Bible, showing that from the very beginning I AM a God who speaks, who leads, who guides. I AM a God who wishes to be involved in the lives of My children, showing the way to go and speaking of My unique purpose and plan for each one.

Your body was designed by Me to function first and foremost as a house of prayer. Contained within your body is a spirit that is both an extension of who I AM and the means by which I communicate with you. Your soul is the meeting room where the breath of My Spirit yearns to inspire you with truth of who I really AM and who you truly are.

The thoughts that I desire to think towards your mind are purposed to give you knowledge and understanding in order to refresh, inspire and teach you according to the path that I have already predestined for your life.

If you haven't heard My voice today then you haven't truly experienced Me today. Though you may have acquired knowledge about me from other sources, My desire has always been for you to acquire knowledge from Me, personally.

Though My presence can be found everywhere, you will find it the most within you, as you turn your mind toward me in meditation and prayer. You can hear My voice the loudest when you have learned to master the discipline of inner stillness.

Contained within the pages of this book are concepts of prayer that are perhaps unfamiliar to you. As you read this book with a heart and mind open to learning new things and *un*learning some old things, and as you begin to put into practice the new concepts you learn, you will discover our relationship beginning to change. As you quiet your spirit and seek for it to be connected with Mine, you will find the mysteries of life and prayer opening up to you.

Let the information that My son, Julio, has searched out and gathered and made available to you be the catalyst to transform your life and enable you to build your life from the inside out, a life that is led daily by Me through the sacred meeting place of prayer.

Let this book help you discover who I AM ... and who you are ... My child created for a specific purpose and a unique destiny, one that you will begin to discover as you allow Me to speak to you in your times of prayer.

God

Creator of Heaven and Earth

This Book is Dedicated to:

You who believe that there is more to you and your life than what you are currently experiencing and who want to discover that "more."

You who believe that there is more to *God* than what you know ... and that there is more to experience in His presence than what you are currently experiencing.

You who have wondered if you really are a unique individual created by God to fulfill a wondrous purpose.

You who know you have a specific purpose in life but sense something is blocking you from discovering it.

You who know that great power to change and be made anew is within you but you can't seem to turn that power source on and use it to change your life.

You who want to improve your ability to hear the voice of God for your life.

You who have wondered why there are so many religions, denominations and beliefs, with each one affirming to be right.

You who have attended church, are a member of a church or some other type of spiritual organization, and yet have not discovered the full potential of the power of God *within* you.

You who want to learn how to mentally, physically and spiritually position yourself to learn from God personally at the highest-level possible.

You who desire to discover the true "Kingdom of God" experience that you read about in the Bible.

You who are an Apostle, Prophet, Evangelist, Pastor, Teacher, Bishop, Elder, Deacon, Priest, House Church Leader, Kingdom Teacher or Coach, Spiritual Mentor, Advisor, Counselor or Guru who wants to bring positive change and true empowerment to the people you serve.

You who want to simply experience life to the fullest.

Foreword

The Mystery of Prayer Revealed is an erudite, eloquent, and immensely thought-provoking work that gets to the heart of the principles and power of prayer. This book addresses the subject with a profound simplicity that even the least among us can comprehend.

The Mystery of Prayer Revealed is indispensable reading for anyone who wants to understand how to pray effectively. This is a profound, authoritative work which spans the wisdom of the ages and yet breaks new ground in its approach to understanding the very important subject. This book will possibly become a classic in this and the next generation.

This exceptional work by Julio Alvarado is one of the most profound, practical, principle-centered approaches to the subject of prayer I have read in a long time. The author's approach to this timely issue brings a fresh breath of air that captivates the heart, engages the mind, and inspires the spirit of the reader. Enjoy the journey through these pages and be transformed.

DR. MYLES MUNROE

Chairman
Myles Munroe International
International Third World Leaders Association
BFMI

Acknowledgments

This book has been influenced and enhanced by God Almighty and I am eternally grateful that He extended mercy to me through the message in the book, changing the heart and life of a man who was at the end of his rope in many ways.

Lord, thank You for not just saving my life but bringing sanity to my mind, health to my body, and wholeness and completeness to my soul and spirit in the process.

Thank You, God, for showing me what was hindering my ability to accurately and consistently hear Your voice.

Thank You for teaching me how to pray.

Thank You for enabling me to discover, develop, and experience the greatest learning environment, which every believer has access to on the earth today – the place You call "The Kingdom of God."

Thank You, God, for Fathering me and for showing me "The Real me" and "The Real You."

I would also like to thank my editor, Bonita Jewel, for her insights and skills. You have truly been a gem and a Godsend. Thank you once again, Bonita, for partnering with God and me in producing this life changing project. You took all of my writing errors and converted them into a work of art, a picture that speaks a much-needed answer into the human being, the Church, and the world today.

Introduction

Many of Jesus' teachings found in the Bible are understood and applied within the framework of our modern culture and environment. His teachings on prayer are no exception. Many people assume they are thoroughly familiar with the knowledge and wisdom He imparted while He was on earth. Many believe that they have no more to learn or gain from studying how Jesus prayed or taught prayer. This is a serious misunderstanding because it can cause believers to miss so much of what God has in store for their lives.

One of the greatest needs of our time is for people to have an intimate, personal relationship with their Creator – God. More than ever, there is a need for believers to learn *about* God directly *from* Him through the avenue of prayer. Our spiritual journey may begin with us learning about God from other humans, yet at some point there should be what I call *"the transfer of teachers"* where we experience a shift in the way we learn. This transfer is where we make the shift from learning through instructors that God has placed on the earth to learning *directly from God* as our Spiritual Instructor. This will inevitably lead to a life where our "God-consciousness" will lead us towards His plan for our lives. It will enable us to come to know His will more clearly and begin to walk a purposeful path guided by His Spirit.

The greatest lesson we can learn in life is to hear from God through the powerful medium of prayer. Hearing God's voice and receiving His personal instructions will prove to be the answer to so many problems that we face. It will result in us not only receiving His personal direction and guidance, but also in our becoming an answer to problems in the world at large. Sadly, many people never experience this "transfer of teachers" and thus never learn to hear God's voice and receive His plan for their lives.

Why do so many people struggle, including people in the religious and Christian world? It is because although they might know who God is, they have not entered into a place in their relationship with Him where they connect intimately with God and receive His will, counsel, and personal direction. We should be asking why people default to psychics, spiritual gurus, and other spiritual mediums to get in touch with the spirit world and spirituality when they have access to the greatest and most effective teacher within themselves – the Spirit of the living God. This living connection with God is a foundational element of prayer.

Without this connection, however, something is missing from our prayer life and from our relationship with God, which results in a lot of questions and misunderstandings about prayer. I'd venture to say that every person asks, at some point in time, "Does God really hear our prayers?" We make statements to other believers such as, "I will pray for you" or, "Our prayers are with you," yet are we really praying for others? Or are these just comforting words that have little to no effect?

Many people struggle to believe in God or decide that there is no God because they fail to receive answers to their prayers. This could occur for a variety of reasons, but often the unanswered question of, "Why didn't God answer my prayer?" leaves someone with less faith to ask the next time around.

How long should it take to get an answer from God once someone prays for something? Does God truly answer with "Yes," "No," or "Wait," as traditional teachings on prayer tell us? Or could it be that the reason our prayers don't carry the power they should potentially have – the awesome power that we read and hear about – is because traditional religious teachings and practices have distorted God's original purpose and application of prayer?

Many people practice prayer as a mere ritual with no bearings in their day-to-day world; others pray out of hope that something will happen when they pray. Still, there are many vague and mysterious aspects to prayer so that even those who often approach the throne of grace wonder if they're really getting everything they can out of prayer.

Perhaps one of the primary reasons that prayer is a mystery to so many today is that the majority of Christians are getting their knowledge, understanding and application of prayer doctrines and techniques from humans instead of from God Himself. This disconnection from the true Source of prayer leaves us with many questions:

What is prayer?

When should someone pray?

Is there a specific or proper way to pray?

Does prayer work?

The real question is not *whether* prayer works. The real question is, do we truly *understand* the art of prayer and do we know *how* it works?

My search to understand prayer came from a growing need to enter a deeper relationship with God. After over 20 years of Christianity, I felt that I did not know or understand God as I should. As I began to study prayer from a definitive root-word perspective, I was shocked at what I discovered. Delving into information on the original practice of prayer forced me to peel away layer upon layer of former teachings that I had been exposed to and some practices that I had implemented as a result.

For instance, many prayer meetings I have attended consisted of one-way communication with God. I have to admit that I now question the true motive for some of those meetings. Sometimes I felt as though the group was begging God for land, buildings, or finances, and quoting scripture as though they were twisting God's arm to give them what they wanted. In most of these meetings it was "all talk," with people praying yet not positioning themselves to hear from God.

Even in my own prayer life, if I were to put a number on it, I would say that 98% of my prayer time was spent talking and maybe 2% trying to listen to God. As I studied the origins of prayer and biblical communication with God, I realized that I had it completely backwards.

The purpose of this book is to introduce prayer from a new perspective – the overlooked and forgotten perspective of *hearing from God*. Prayer is a misunderstood skill that is meant to be one of the most powerful and exciting benefits of a believer's life.

Jesus – the greatest Teacher on prayer – introduced another Teacher before He left the earth. This was the same voice that taught Jesus to pray: the Holy Spirit. The Holy Spirit within us is meant to be our *primary* instructor on prayer. When we allow ourselves to be instructed by men and women without seeking God personally to teach us about prayer, we miss so much of what God has ordained for our lives, because we never hear it spoken from His lips.

> *"And* **He taught***, saying to them, Is it not written, 'My house shall be called the house of prayer for all nations?' But you have made it a den of thieves"* [Mk. 11:17].

Could this be the condition of the modern church? We line up numerous activities that have nothing to do with prayer, such as bingo, raffles, and fundraisers. The church has also become a place where people try to launch or enhance their personal businesses and agendas. Why did Jesus call the religious people of His day "thieves"? Could it be that they deviated from the primary purpose of the synagogue being a house of worship, a house of prayer? That primary purpose was – and is today – to teach personal connection to God through the art of prayer.

The primary purpose of churches should be to teach those in their congregations to hear the voice of God for themselves. Otherwise, the church will be comprised of spiritual babies. Spiritually, they will remain like children who never mature to the point that they can stand on their own two feet. They will stay dependent on others to "feed" them when the voice of God through the Holy Spirit is available to all who believe.

Why don't all nations call churches houses of prayer? It is time that we transform the church to become what God initially ordained it to be. It is time that we understand the original intent and purposes for prayer and begin to use its awesome power to shape our lives and to change the world.

How to Use this Book

Though I am well aware that what you are about to read will likely contradict and/or cause you to question prior teachings on prayer, I am also aware that many believers are looking for more depth in their knowledge of prayer. If you are one of those who are not satisfied with a surface understanding of prayer, please keep reading.

This book contains numerous passages of Bible scripture to validate the unique perspective I have gained on "the mystery of prayer." All information within this book has been well researched from sources that delve into the root understanding of words and concepts. Direct translations from original Hebrew, Greek and Aramaic will enable you to grasp the subject matter more clearly.[1]

Rather than filtering this information from the perspective of traditional, religious or denominational teachings, I recommend

---

[1] Note: Some concepts or definitions are repeated in more than one chapter. This is because certain ideas are brought out in different ways depending on the chapter's unique content; any repetition is for the purpose of aiding in full understanding of the concept.

that you delve into studying the scripture for yourself. Also, bring this information before God in prayer. Ask for His guidance and open your spirit to hear what He says about how to connect with Him. The things you learn just might change your life.

In no way is this book intended to speak negatively about any denomination or belief. This book is not purposed to *offend* anyone, but to *defend* all believers by helping them discover what hinders their ability to hear the voice of God clearly and consistently.

The purpose of this book is to provide you with vital information about prayer, to strengthen your personal connection with God, and empower you to fulfill your God-given purpose in life. At the same time, I am aware that the spiritual life and experience of readers will vary greatly. If some of the chapters or concepts are difficult to understand at first glance, I encourage you to study and review them repeatedly. After taking the time to study, reflect and pray, I am confident that the subject matter will not only make sense, but will begin to transform your perspective on prayer as well.

To the skeptic, the curious, and those that are hungry for more, I encourage you to keep an open mind as we journey together to explore prayer from a root-word understanding and examine the prayer life and practices of Jesus in depth.

This book is not intended to be a "doctrine" on prayer. It is simply a tool to expand your knowledge and understanding of prayer in a way that transcends traditional religious teaching. Truth be told, though this book may change how you view and practice prayer, I cannot stress enough that *the ultimate teacher on prayer is God Himself* through the Holy Spirit of Truth. Very few people have been taught to pray by God Himself; again, this "transfer of teachers" is a key to spiritual development.

Jesus, when He was on earth, set aside all that was taught to Him through His rabbinical education and positioned Himself to be taught by God on how to pray. The knowledge and guidance

He received from His Father gave Him direction, guidance, power, and strength to fulfill His destiny and change the world.

This book will help to introduce you to the Holy Spirit of Truth and position you, like Jesus, to receive guidance and instruction directly from Him. The summary after each chapter will enable you to review what you have just read. The recommended applications will encourage you to use this information and start making immediate changes in your life. Pull out your highlighter and mark the quotes that speak to you; take additional notes if necessary. Do whatever you need to ensure this isn't just another "good read," but a life-changing event.

Just a disclaimer at the beginning: this is not a normal book. If studied and applied according to God's personal leading in your life, *The Mystery of Prayer* has the potential to change your life forever!

PART ONE

THE FRAMEWORK OF PRAYER

CHAPTER ONE:

The Border Crossing

"A border is defined as 'a line that separates two geographical areas.' I have discovered that it is also a place that connects two areas. The first area is the environment where I was naturally conceived; it is the world where I 'do life.' The second area is the place where I 'get life' – where I meet with God."

– Julio Alvarado Jr.

I have had the privilege of traveling to a few countries beyond the United States. There are some common things that I experience whenever I cross a border. Besides the change in scenery and people, I am often fascinated by the different customs, food, language and laws. The diversities between my country and theirs add to my overall experience in life after I have visited these foreign lands.

A Daily Crossing

I liken my time of Morning Prayer to crossing a border into another country. When I purpose in my mind and heart to hear from God during those moments, I experience changes similar to that of entering a new country. In the spiritual environment of prayer, I receive nourishment from God Himself through His Word. I also experience firsthand the spiritual laws that He uses to create order in my life. In this "prayer environment," I am exposed to the customs by which God wants me to live. In this environment, instead of English, Spanish, Hebrew, Arabic, or Italian – which are the languages of the countries that I have visited – I experience the language of God, which is Truth.

This unique environment sometimes known as the realm of prayer is the "secret place" that Jesus talked about [Matt. 6:6, 18], where the mysteries of the Kingdom are revealed to us. This is not a place that we travel to physically, but rather mentally and spiritually, by entering the prayer environment. When I position my heart and spirit in this manner, I experience what the following passage of scripture says is available:

> *"If then you were raised with Christ, **seek those things which are above,** where Christ is sitting at the right hand of God. **Be mindful of things above,** not on things on the earth"* [Col. 3:1-2].

Though the passage tells us to seek things above, I have discovered that this "place" is the environment of the Kingdom of God. It comes from above, yet it is also within you. It is not some out-of-body experience where you find yourself floating off to a realm "above." It is a place that God has already created within your spirit. If you position your heart towards Him, God meets with you in this place. It is literally an extension of the Kingdom of Heaven, where God originally created you before He created the foundations of the world [Eph. 1:3-4].

This may seem foreign even to many who pray; it was a foreign place to me for over 20 years of traditional Christian life. Though I was exposed to some teachings stating this fact, I don't remember anyone teaching about how to get there or how the process works. All I knew was that I wasn't experiencing God in prayer at this level. I knew I had the Spirit of God within me, yet I was still praying as though I was trying to make contact with

God through some type of external connection. Connecting with God was like an outside element rather than a true part of my heart and life.

Inside God's Heart

This revelation came to me one morning while I was in prayer. God expressed a thought to me. I heard Him say to my heart, "Julio, I want to take you to a place that you have never been before."

I immediately thought, "Location." I assumed God was going to direct me to another job, city, ministry or church. Yet I have learned that when God speaks, it is okay to ask Him questions. We don't have to settle for just a word or two from God. As His beloved children, we have the right to question Him for the details of His guidance for our lives. In fact, He wants us to ask Him for clarifications when we're not sure of the way to go; He desires to lead and guide us every step of the way.

When I began to ask Him where He was going to take me, God simply said, "I want to take you inside of my heart." I left my Morning Prayer session in shock. I thought that I had been at that place all along. After all, I had been a born-again believer for years. That morning I had two reactions. First, I felt as though someone had punched me in my stomach and knocked the air out of me. Second, I felt as though I was being indicted for a crime I didn't even know I had committed.

Both of these reactions have taught me two major lessons. First of all, my breath needed to be knocked out so that I could be inflated and inspired by the breath of God – the only breath that truly brings life. The other lesson was that, in one sense, I *was* breaking the law. I was breaking one of the greatest laws that a human could ever break. I wasn't truly seeking after or loving God with my whole heart although for many years I thought that I was. Though my intentions and efforts were sincere, God had exposed me to the life-changing reality that, even as a Christian believer, I was living a lie in many aspects.

In other words, like Moses, I was attempting to "cross the border" of prayer and approach God on Holy Ground with my sandals on. God had no problem with Moses wearing sandals; the issue was what they symbolized. Under Moses' sandals was soil from his natural environment, the place he was used to walking. In Moses' interaction with God, God revealed his unique purpose, which was to be a deliverer. This was the reason that Moses' life was spared not just once, but twice – at his birth and again when he slew an Egyptian. God had been preparing him for this all his life. The request from God that he remove his sandals symbolized that he could no longer walk in the same natural environment; Moses had been sanctified and set apart for a special purpose [Ex. 3:5].

We can't continue to walk towards God in the condition we are normally in; we need to remove anything from the soil of our heart that doesn't line up with the original purpose for which we were created. I had been approaching God in the manner that I assumed was correct instead of allowing Him to instruct me personally on how He wanted me to approach Him. I wasn't open to Him asking me to "remove my sandals." My mind needed a major shift. I had to realize that I was misguided in my walk with Him because of my misunderstanding and misapplication of prayer.

Once Moses approached the presence of God in obedience, he was no longer required to remove his sandals. The Bible didn't say that he approached Pharaoh barefoot or led the Israelites across the Red Sea without sandals on. Once he began walking in the purpose of what he was sanctified and ordained to do, Moses was no longer asked to take off his sandals.

Before that insightful moment in my life, much of my understanding of God came from traditional church teachings. Though some of these teachings added value to my life, I am sorry to say that much of what I was taught had been influenced with worldly fundamentals and traditions. *"Beware lest anyone rob you through philosophy and vain deceit, according to the tradition of men, according to the elements of the world, and not according to Christ"* [Col. 2:8]. In many cases, I was instructed according to the philosophies of men rather than from the reference point of Christ – which is the only, anointed and authorized voice of the Kingdom of God. In the area of prayer, the Holy Spirit of Truth (Christ) is the greatest prayer teacher to which any of us could ever be exposed.

That was the day I began to experience "the transfer of teachers" [Jn. 16:13]. I determined to no longer follow my own understanding of prayer or the teachings of my past. I needed to position myself before God alone so that He could teach me how to pray. What I have learned has completely revolutionized my personal prayer life. It has introduced me to a "Kingdom mindset" and a relationship with God that filled a void I thought could never completely be filled. He has exceeded and continues to exceed my expectations.

In the following scripture, Job asked two very important and key questions: "What is the Almighty, that we should serve Him? And what profit should we have if we pray to Him" [Job 21:15]. The word "pray" in this verse is the Hebrew word *pâga*.[2] According to ancient Hebrew, this word is defined as "to meet or to encounter." Job was asking, "What is the purpose of meeting with or encountering God?" In other words, he was asking, "What purpose does prayer have?"

My "border crossings" in the realm of prayer have introduced not just one, but *multiple* reasons to encounter Him as well as multi-faceted purposes for prayer. They all lead to one primary reason and purpose: *to experience God by receiving His will and fulfilling it every day*. This purpose has become my life's passion.

Though there are many reasons for prayer, I have discovered that one primary reason for my personal prayer time with God

---

[2]   *Strongs* #6293: AHLB#: 2592 (V)

is so that I can manifest the wholeness of God towards humanity. I can only accomplish this when I enter the realm of prayer not to speak, but rather to *listen* to the voice of God. Our prayers are meant to be more like that of young Samuel in the Bible, when he said to God, "Speak, Lord, for your servant is listening" [1 Sam. 3:9].

When we take time to hear from God and receive His thoughts and plans for our lives, we begin to take on more of His divine nature. We can only accomplish this through our desire and efforts to be one in spirit with Him. Since our original existence came out of God, it stands to reason that in His presence is the one place that we will be truly complete and whole. This is a concept that Jesus touched on in His prayer:

> *"And I have given them the glory which You have given Me, that they may be one, even as We are one, I in them, and You in Me, that they may be made perfect in one; and that the world may know that You have sent Me and have loved them as You have loved Me"* [John 17:22-23].

The word *"one"* in this verse is defined as *"to be of the same, to repeat or to be synchronized."* What Jesus was saying could be reworded as, *"Let them be the same as you are; let them repeat your presence by being synchronized with you."* Have you ever played that game where two people stand facing each other and one tries to mimic the exact movements of the other? This is a great analogy; we are meant to synchronize ourselves to or mirror the movements of God in our own lives.

Crossing the border from a traditional understanding and application of prayer to a true "Kingdom style" of prayer gave Jesus the ability to make such profound statements as, *"The Son can do nothing of Himself but what He sees the Father do. For whatever things He does, these also the Son does likewise"* and, *"I do nothing of Myself, but as My Father has taught Me, I speak these things"* [John 5:19b, 8:28b].

Traditionally, a border is defined as "a line that separates two geographical areas." I have discovered that it is also a place that *connects* two areas. The first area is the environment where I was naturally conceived; it is the world where I "do life." The second "area" is the place where "I get life," where I meet with God; it is the place where I was originally conceived in spirit. What I experience on that side of the border determines how I live my life on this side according to the daily instructions that He assigns me.

An in-depth study of the word "border" according to *The Ancient Hebrew Lexicon* revealed to me a few other interesting definitions for this key word.[3] It is described as *"a place where another language (truth) is spoken"* [Deut. 32:1-4]. It is also described as *"a threshold, an entrance, or the start of something"* [2 Cor. 5:17]; *"a storehouse or a place of gathering and a place of feeding or nourishing"* [Gen. 48:15, Eph. 1:3]; and *"a place where heavy rain occurs"* (rain or water is a metaphor for the spoken word of God) [Deut. 32:1-4, Isa. 55:10]. It is also distinctly described as *"a place of repair or reconstruction where something is healed or perfected"* [Matt. 5:48]. Another unique perspective of "border" is *"a place of augmenting where increase, expansion and building are experienced by what is added to it"* [Prov. 24:1-5, Ps. 139:16]. This last perspective fascinated me due to the connection it had to what I have been experiencing as a result of viewing my prayer life from a "border crossing" perspective. As I have begun to build my life from the inside out, my purpose has been augmented and I find my vision is increasing and expanding according to God's plan for my life.

King David prayed to God:

"My frame was not hidden from You, When I was made in secret, And skillfully wrought in the lowest parts of the earth. Your eyes saw my substance, being yet unformed. And in Your book they all were written, The days fashioned for me, When as yet there were none of them" [Psalms 139:15-16 NKJV].

---

3   Border = AHLB#: 1339-(A, C, E, L) : 1448-C (d1) : 2467 (lb)

What I have been experiencing – and capturing through journaling my times of prayer – is that God is actually reading to me the details of the book of my life. Through my traditional Christian experience, I didn't even realize this "book" existed; yet I have discovered it in Scripture and through the mouth of God.[4]

It has been in this place of prayer through crossing the border that I have truly discovered the Author, Biographer and Narrator of the Kingdom book of my life [Heb. 12:2]. This is the volume that contains the will of God for my life [Heb. 10:7]. It is my personal Word (Logos) that I am supposed to flesh out into the world. [More on this "book" will be covered in a later chapter.]

A Time to Listen

I have tried numerous prayer techniques over the past 24 years. There were times when I used prayer books to guide me. There were times when I used a "prayer wheel" that divided my prayer time into sections such as: thanking and praising God, pleading with God for specific petitions using a written prayer list, singing to God, confessing known sin and asking for forgiveness, praying in tongues, and praying through the Scriptures.

Though I'm sure that God honored my attempts and met with me at the level of knowledge that I had about prayer, I have to admit that these prayer sessions turned into a kind of ritual. Many times I had the feeling that I didn't get through to God as I should have. During those years, many of my prayer requests went unanswered, which led me to believe that either I was praying incorrectly or that God was not pleased with me. Much of my knowledge about prayer was based on what I read

---

[4]   This concept will be full explained in the pages to come.

in books about prayer or teachings on prayer while in church settings.

It wasn't until that I began to study the prayer life of Jesus and other key people in the Bible that the light went on for me. One of the first things I realized is that when someone had an encounter with God – which is what prayer really is – *God was the one who did almost all of the talking*. My prayer practice had been the opposite of this. In the past, I would do all the talking with little or no listening.

When I began to adopt this approach to prayer, my times of connecting with God, and the quality of the connection, changed drastically. At times I even received almost a guided tour of what God wanted me to see – His vision for my life. I had finally crossed the border into the true environment of prayer and my life has never been the same.

This is what Moses did. When he stepped toward the burning bush, he crossed over into a new dimension of experiencing the voice of God. He was exposed to the truth of God's plan for his life. Moses came to understand his purpose and mission, as well as receive remedies to all of his excuses. This never would have occurred had he not removed his sandals and crossed over to holy ground.

We can't walk towards God and discover a new connection with Him while still walking with the same contaminated mindsets and practices that we have carried throughout our lives. When you come in contact with the voice of God, you have a choice to actively walk towards His plan for your life, or to turn aside and go the other way. When you choose to follow God's plan, you discover what you were created for and ordained to be, and you are sanctified to follow that plan. God will then begin to work in your heart and spirit, removing anything from your life that might hinder you from fulfilling His will.

The first two verses of Colossians Chapter three describe an atmosphere that transforms the Kingdom of God within you:

"If then you were raised with Christ, seek those things which are above, where Christ is, sitting at the right hand of God. Set your mind on things above, not on things on the earth." As you "seek those things above," you are constantly discovering and developing God's detailed plan and purpose. The next step is then deploying that purpose in the world around you. You receive detailed instructions on how to become an answer to a world problem.

The Breath of God

When I cross over my personal border to experience prayer at this level, it is as though I am breathing air from the environment of Heaven. The word "Spirit," as it relates to God, comes from the Hebrew word *Ruach*. This word has three primary definitions: "wind, breath and mind." When I cross over to this place of prayer, it is as though I'm being inspired or inflated with the breath of God, which contains His mind (doctrine) for my life. As a result of this inspiration, His influential wind of words blows me into the direction that He desires me to walk.

Our souls are designed to be inspired by the breath of God. In the beginning God breathed into Adam and he became a living soul. This should not be a one-time event. On a spiritual level, we should experience this every day of our lives. This is why many believers are suffocating spiritually. They are kept *physically* alive by oxygen but they are *spiritually* dormant. They lack inflation by the breath or truth of God; this results in them being blown around by winds of doctrine that do not originate in God [Eph. 4:14, 2 Tim. 4:3].

By God's grace and according to His leading, I am learning how to hear the voice of God and see the plan He has for my life, as well as speak and do the works assigned to me according to the same training that Jesus had [Jn. 5:17-19, 6:45, 8:28]. This exact same training is available for every believer because the exact same Trainer is available to everyone who believes in Jesus Christ. As you open your heart to the Spirit of God by crossing the spiritual border into a place where you can hear God's voice, you will receive His specific instruction for your life.

Before I received the revelation from God that He wanted to take me inside His heart, I didn't even know this place was accessible. Yet as I studied the life of Jesus, I began to understand that it was a place that He went morning by morning so that He could experience the tongue/language of truth for His life. God wants to do the same for each one of us as we discover the environment of true prayer for ourselves. It is the place where Heaven meets earth – the closest we can get to Heaven while we still walk in this world.

As you begin to hear God's words of truth for your life, you will discover the will of the Lord. In other words, you will enter the place that contains the blueprints for your life that can then be converted into a truth-print that will enable you to live for God's glory. God wishes to give you a specific plan that is purposed to reprimand, correct, instruct, and complete you so that you may produce the predestined works of God [2 Tim. 3:16-17].

In the past, I used my mind for lustful imaginations, desires, and dreams that did not originate in God. Yet here in this place I get a daily dose of instructions that clarifies God's purpose for my life. Now I am learning to use my imagination accurately by allowing it to be painted with the strokes of God's words.

Step beyond the Border

Following are some descriptions of what this "secret place" has been for me, *and what it can be for you.* Step beyond the borders of our realm into the environment of true prayer ... and meet with God today:

- It's the place where I'm learning how to become true worshipper according the spirit and truth of God and not of man [Jn. 4:23-24].

- It's the place where the blindness of ignorance was removed from my life and true sight – through the vocabulary of God – introduced my purpose.

- It's the place where I receive answers to all that is wrong with me, and remedies on how to correct those things.

- It's the place where I am discovering "The Real Me" and "The Real God."

- It's the place where I was first born in spirit form before I was naturally born on the earth.

- It's the place where my obedience to what I hear from the Lord determines when (or whether) I will hear from Him again.

- It's the place where Heaven talks and this earthen vessel listens as it receives the treasure of God's Words stored in Heavenly places – Words purposed to prosper me according to His will [Eph. 1:3].

- It's the place where I learn to eat from the tree of life and am told where the tree of knowledge of good and evil is planted in my life and warned not to go there.

- It's the place where I am trained on enemy awareness and tactical procedures to keep him under my feet.

- It's the place where I learn to be perfect as my Father in Heaven is perfect [Matt. 5:48].

- It's the place where God reveals to me the mysteries (secrets) of the Kingdom for my life [Lk. 8:10].

- It's the place where true spiritual intelligence is revealed.

- It's the place where I become "pregnant" with ideas from God that I must "birth" into the world.

- It's where I'm introduced to the most accurate scripture "Interpreter" that the world has ever known – the Holy Spirit.

- It's the place where God instructs me how to accurately build my life from the inside out through the key components of righteousness, peace and joy [Rom. 14:17]. [5]

What can this place of true connection with God through prayer be for you?

- It's the place where you find out just how much you are like God, your Father in heaven.

- It's the place where you are connected to the "Golgi Apparatus" of your spirit – where God's memories and character are transferred to you.[6]

- It's the place where you can come as you are, but because of what you are exposed to, you will not leave as the same person.

- It's where you experience "the secret place" – physically and internally, where God's secrets are revealed [Matt. 6:6, 13:11, Lk. 8:10].

- It's the place where you discover your "cross" and learn to carry it accurately and faithfully [Matt. 10:38].

---

[5] This will be the topic of the next book in this series, the working title of which is "The Mystery of the Kingdom of God Revealed."

[6] Covered in my first book *The Mystery of Iniquity Revealed*, Chapter five.

- It's where you give God permission to search you to find anything wicked or out of order in your life [Ps. 139:23-24].

- It's a truth environment where you find hidden answers and discover mysteries.

- It's the primary meeting room between Spirit and flesh on the earth.

- It's where you discover why you were created.

- It's the place where purpose is given to you and where vision is strengthened.

- It's the place where you need to go on a regular basis if you want to be a world changer.

- It's the place that you can receive accurate and proper Fathering, no matter what your personal experiences are or were with your earthly father.

- It's the place where deep calls unto deep [Ps. 42:7].

- It's a place where you will experience the greatest sense of awe possible in this world.

- It's a place of cleansing and nurturing, refreshing and renewal.

- It's a place where all uncertainties are removed.

- It's a place where faith is distributed, purpose is revealed, and vision is shown.

- It's a place of thought exchange.

- It's a place where you bring your questions and receive God's solutions.

- It is a place where you receive a pattern or blueprint for removal of your sins.

- It's the most crucial time of your day.

- It's the place where you experience Truth at its purest level.

- It is the most organic and "holy-istic" (holistic) place on the earth.

In this environment of truth, the absence of iniquity is a non-negotiable requirement [Deut. 32:4], yet the grace of God receives us where we are at and works with us to bring us to where we need to be.[7] Through my time "across the border," I'm learning to live in the spirit. My life is becoming more based on what I see and hear with the inner eyes and ears of the spirit as opposed to using my five natural senses.

This meeting place with God is the greatest learning environment in the world. In fact, I prepare for this meeting the night before by going to bed early so that I can be prepared to receive from my "Teacher" the following morning [Isa. 50:4-5]. My times in prayer have become the highlight of my day. It has also come to be the most productive and best part of my day. I often find myself getting up anywhere between one and six hours earlier than I normally would so that I may cross over to this place where I know I will experience God in many wonderful ways.

I pray that this "secret place" will become the same for you. It's not your home away from home. It is your *true home*. It is the home within your heart, the place where God will renew your mind and purpose if you allow Him to do so.

---

7   The topic of "iniquity" was covered in full in my previous book "*The Mystery of Iniquity Revealed*" and it will be reviewed in later chapters of this book as well.

CHAPTER SUMMARY:

- As you "cross the border" and enter the spiritual environment of prayer, you receive nourishment from God Himself. You also experience the language of God, which is Truth.

- The environment of the Kingdom of God comes from above, yet it is within you already.

- We can't continue to walk towards God in the condition we are normally in; we need to remove anything from the soil of our heart that doesn't line up with the original purpose for which we were created.

- Jesus Christ is the greatest prayer Teacher.

- There is one primary purpose for prayer: to experience God by receiving His will for your life and then fulfilling it every day.

- As you open your heart to the Spirit of God by crossing the spiritual border into a place where you can hear God's voice, you will receive His specific instruction for your life.

APPLICATION:

1. Do you feel like you always approach God in the same manner? Today, stop and ask Him how He wants you to approach Him in prayer.

2. Have you ever asked, "What is the purpose of meeting with or encountering God?" or "What purpose does prayer have?" Now that you have read this chapter, write down your answers to these two questions.

3. As you continue to read this book, you will have the opportunity to come in contact with the voice of God. Make the choice now that you will actively walk towards His plan for your life. Determine to discover what you were created for and ordained to be, and to follow that plan.

4. Ask God to help you step beyond the borders of this realm into the environment of true prayer and meet Him today.

CHAPTER TWO:

Pre-Prayer Instructions

"In approaching God in prayer, failing to prepare our minds and hearts as sacred ground will produce failure to receive the answers that we need from the sacred places of God's mind, heart and tongue."

– Julio Alvarado Jr.

As mentioned in the introduction, many of Jesus' teachings have been so fully integrated into our culture and religious denominations that people suppose they are thoroughly familiar with them and have nothing more to gain from studying the Bible, specifically the Gospels.[8] The trouble with most interpretations of Jesus' teachings is that they have not been approached from a root-word perspective, which hinders us from understanding the uniqueness of Jesus' words and perspective. We might have a lot of information, but we miss much of the depth of what He lived and taught while He was on earth.

Prayer was one of the most important themes that Jesus taught. I have been exposed to many books and other resources on prayer. Though some of these resources contained good information and lessons from the authors' personal experience,

---

[8] The biblical New Testament books of Matthew, Mark, Luke and John are often called the "Gospels" which is translated as "Good News."

in some cases the teachings did not at all line up with how Jesus taught His disciples to pray. We must grasp this foundational subject of prayer if we wish to effectively connect with God and receive His direction and guidance for our lives.

Jesus' multi-topic lecture that began with "The Beatitudes" includes the first of two teachings that Jesus gave on prayer.[9] The second teaching is recorded in Luke 11:1-4 in a more private setting. It came as a result of one of His disciples asking, "Lord, teach us to pray." Some Christians believe that these prayer lessons were the exact same event, as they carry similarities. In looking at the scenarios that led up to each prayer lesson, however, it is clear that they were two separate events. The first one was taught to a large group that followed Jesus [Matt 4:25, 5:1-2] and the second came after Jesus had one of His own personal prayer sessions [Luke 11:1].

It is interesting to note that Jesus' disciples didn't ask Him how to cause the blind to see, the deaf to hear, or even how to raise the dead. It is apparent that after following Jesus for a while and witnessing the awesome miracles Jesus performed that His disciples connected the power to the prerequisite: prayer. The request to learn how to pray came as they realized that Jesus consistently prayed before His miracles took place. Any spiritual leader should first of all model Jesus' style of prayer and then teach others this same "Art of Prayer" that Jesus taught His disciples.

Jesus would not have taught His disciples something that He wasn't practicing personally. Some key points to validate this is the fact that Jesus said He only spoke what He heard the Father speak and only did what He saw His Father do. Jesus' prayer life was according to the will of His Father [See Jn. 5:19, 6:38, 8:26, 28]. We have to remember that Jesus was an earthly model – a "Kingdom Replica" – for us. We who claim to serve God should model our lives after Jesus, including His instructions and example on prayer.

---

[9]   The Beatitudes are found in Matthew Chapters five through seven.

Jesus' first prayer lesson, as He spoke to the multitude, included an important aspect of prayer, what I will call "pre-prayer instructions." If we accurately understand these instructions, we will then be able to apply and fulfill Jesus' true purpose and power in prayer.

Pre-prayer Instruction #1

"But you, when you pray ..." [Matt. 6:6a].

The phrase "when you pray" leaves room for assuming that prayer can be done whenever we wish; however, it is important to note that Jesus experienced prayer on a daily basis ... and primarily in the morning.

"He awakens Me morning by morning, He awakens My ear to hear as the learned" [Isaiah 50:4b].

The word "by" is probably the most important word in this key scripture. It signifies that He prayed every single day, "morning by morning." The morning is a time that seems especially sacred and set apart for meeting with our God and Savior.

Pre-prayer Instruction #2

"... go into your room, and when you have shut your door, pray to your Father who is in the secret place; and your Father who sees in secret will reward you openly" [Matthew 6:6b NKJV].

To "go into your room" denotes going to a private place where no physical distractions are present. This would exclude what many today consider prayer sessions, such as praying in the car, at church, in a corporate setting, in small groups, or any other environment that does not consist of only you and God. Though

I am not discrediting these types of prayer settings (Jesus did promote "two or three gathered together" in His name [Matt. 18:20]), it must be clear that Jesus taught and demonstrated a prayer life that was absent of distractions, including the presence of others.

According to Ancient Hebrew thought and practice, the instruction to go into your room – or "closet" as the King James Version of the Bible states – and to shut the door has a two-fold meaning. It meant going to a place absent of *external* or physical distractions; it also meant going to a place free of any *internal* or mental distractions. This internal "secret place" is referred to as the *cheder*,[10] the inner chamber within the mind where we meet with God.

This is the place within the mind where information is transferred to you and where you are rewarded with the knowledge and understanding of the mysteries of the Kingdom of God that Jesus referred to [Matt. 13:11, Lk. 8:10]. This is the reason that Jesus always went to a place that was not only absent of *physical* distractions but where His *mind* could also be cleared in order to receive the thoughts of God for His earthly life.

"Now in the morning, having risen a long while before daylight, He went out and departed to a solitary place; and there He prayed" [Mark 1:35 NIV].

"And when He had sent them away, He departed to the mountain to pray" [Mark 6:46 NIV].

"So He Himself often withdrew into the wilderness and prayed" [Luke 5:16 NIV].

---

[10]   *Strongs* #2315: AHLB#: 2150 (N)

Pre-prayer Instruction #3

"And when you pray, do not use vain repetitions as the heathen do. For they think that they will be heard for their many words. Therefore do not be like them" [Matthew 6:7-8a NKJV].

It was a custom in Jesus' time to recite the same prayers repeatedly. In the Luke 11:1-3 account of Jesus' teaching on prayer, His disciples asked, "Lord, teach us to pray."

Jesus said in response, ""When you pray, say ..." and He went on to teach what is commonly known as "The Lord's Prayer." He wasn't telling His disciples to repeat those exact words. The word "say" comes from the Greek word *Legō*, which is defined as *"a discourse of discussion."* In other words "say" meant "let the discussion be about." Jesus never intended it to be prayed in a repetitious mode as many believers use it today.

The word "vain" that Jesus used in this key pre-prayer instruction is the Hebrew word *rîyq*, which is defined as "empty of contents or of original purpose."[11] What God is looking for in true prayer is not *many* words, but the *right* words – words that have content and purpose that originate from His will.

"Now this is the confidence that we have in Him, that if we ask anything according to His will, He hears us" [1 John 5:14 NKJV].

The most effective prayer that we can pray is the one that comes from a place where God tells us what to pray for! This realm of prayer is foreign to many due to teachings that come from denominational beliefs or the practices, traditions, and philosophies of men rather than from the true Kingdom perspective that Jesus taught.

---

[11] AHLB#: 1456-M (N)

The most accurate way to pray according to the will of God is to hear His will from His mouth. God the Father has insight and foreknowledge that should determine what we should petition Him for in our prayers.

Pre-prayer Instruction #4

"Therefore do not be like them. For your Father knows the things you have need of before you ask Him. In this manner, therefore, pray" [Matthew 6:8b-9a NKJV].

Jesus is actually saying, "Do not pray for your needs." This instruction conflicts the traditional religious teachings on prayer, which brings up the question, "If we are not to pray for needs, what should we be praying for?" We discover the answer to this question by studying Jesus' teachings found in Matthew 6:19-34 and Luke 12:22-34, mentioned earlier. The reason we are not to pray for needs God already knows about is made clear in the following key statement from Jesus:

"But seek first the kingdom of God and His righteousness, and all these things shall be added to you" [Matthew 6:33 and Luke 12:31].

From where, or from whom, should we be learning how to pray? Should we be learning this life-changing activity from traditional religious beliefs, philosophies and denominations of men, or from the words of Jesus and the Holy Spirit of Truth? God's Holy Spirit is ordained to be our primary instructor and will lead us to spiritual maturity in prayer as we seek after true understanding. It is for this reason that we must explore the depth of Jesus' pivotal statement to pray "in this manner." This phrase is often interpreted from the Greek word *houtō*, and is traditionally defined as "in this way."[12]

---

[12] *Strongs* G3779

The original Hebrew word that would have been used for the word "manner" is *kên*. According to the *Ancient Hebrew Lexicon of the Bible*, this word has a very powerful definition. It means "the opening of a seed." It goes on to further explain that "when the seed opens, the roots begin to form the base of the plant by going down into the soil. The plant rises out of the ground forming the stalk of the plant. A tall tree can only stand tall and firm because of the strong root system which supports it."[13] Jesus often used agricultural terms to explain Kingdom principles, such as in the pivotal parable of "The Soils."[14] The importance of understanding what Jesus was originally conveying through this parable is reflected in the following words:

> *"And He said to them, 'To you it is given to know the mystery of the kingdom of God. But to those outside, all these things are given in parables'"* [Mark 4:11].

> *"And He said to them, 'Do you not know this parable? And how then will you know all parables? The sower sows the Word'"* [Mark 4:13-14].

The "seed that is sown" and the "opening of this seed" are both referring to what should be happening with the words that come from His mouth. They are purposed to build a root system that produces a "Tree of Righteousness" [Isa. 61:3]. The seed comes from God's "Tree of Life" [Prov. 11:30, Rev. 2:7, 22:2] and is meant to produce an exact replica. This agricultural narrative describes one whose life structure is planted, nurtured and upright, causing them to produce fruit. We are purposed to serve others; the strength and power to do so originates from a Kingdom-of-Heaven environment. The Kingdom of God is planted within us. We discover, develop and deploy it through the framework and architecture of The Lord's Prayer [Lk. 17:21]!

---

[13] *Strongs* #3653: AHLB#: 1244-A (N)

[14] The parable of "The Soils" a parable about prayer, which we will explore in a subsequent chapter.

Defining the word "pray" that Jesus used in His teaching on prayer will help us understand the full scope and power of the prayer that Jesus practiced and taught His disciples. God desires for us to avail ourselves of this same power today.

"Palal" is the original root word from which all scriptural references to prayer originated. Prior to the block letter Hebrew script of today, Hebrew writings were communicated by drawings of specific items. Depending on how these pictures were combined, readers would have a root understanding of what was being communicated. This form of communication is called Paleo Hebrew, which means "Ancient Hebrew." Writings of Paleo Hebrew have been found in many archeological discoveries, some dating back to over 4,000 years ago. The great historical finding of the ancient scrolls found in the Qumran caves of Israel in 1948 – known as the Dead Sea Scrolls – contained scrolls written in Paleo Hebrew. These pictures were similar to ancient Egyptian picture writings (Hieroglyphics), also discovered on walls and artifacts at many archeological sites.

Paleo Hebrew uses a total of 22 pictorial drawings. Some Hebrew Rabbinical schools today use "Word Wheels" – teaching resources derived from Paleo Hebrew – to teach original Hebrew understanding of Biblical scriptures. These Word Wheels are believed to be the most accurate study tool available to obtain a deeper understanding of original Hebraic words in the Bible. Paleo Hebrew is the origin of some of our modern-day alphabet. In the Hebrew culture, it is known as the *alef bet*, which are the names for the first and second letter of the Hebrew alphabet, "A" and "B". The Modern Hebrew word for pray – *pâlal* – is derived from two of these 22 original pictographic letters.[15]

In Paleo Hebrew, vowels as we know them today were not used. The pictographic script of *pâlal* would have read "PLL" – pronounced *Pey Lamed Lamed. Pey* was pictorially illustrated as a mouth. *Lamed* was pictorially illustrated as a shepherd's staff,

---

[15] For a list of sites where the charts of the ancient Hebrew script can be viewed, please see Appendix I.

which represented authority; and as a tongue, which represented language or speech.[16] Combined, we find the original definition of prayer: "one authority speaking to another authority" [17]and "to speak the tongue of tongues."[18]

In others words, the original understanding of prayer paints a scenario of a meeting where one authority (God) speaks to another authority (you); the dialogue spoken at these prayer sessions is known as the "language of languages" or "the speech of speeches." Truth is the language of God. When He speaks; all that comes out of His mouth is truth. Prayer is communication between God and you; the purpose of it is to speak the truth of truths. When God speaks to you, each word is a truth. When these words are combined into sentences, they form the truths for your life.

Since truth is the language of God, it is the substance that is required for what I call "Higher Learning." This was the language and type of speech that was consistently present during Jesus' earthly prayer life:

> *"The Lord GOD has given Me the tongue (language) of the learned, that I should know how to speak a word in season to him who is weary. He awakens me morning by morning, he awakens my ear to hear as the learned"* [Isaiah 50:4].

This was the reason that Jesus constantly made such statements as, "I tell you the truth" and "I only speak what I hear My Father speak" [See Jn. 8:45, 12:49-50]. It doesn't matter if you hear the voice of God in English, Spanish, French, Hebrew, Greek or whatever language that you are most familiar with; when God speaks to you, it is truth. He is a God of Truth [Deut. 32:1-4]. The primary purpose of *emet* – the Hebrew word for truth – is "to

---

[16] AHLB#: 1380

[17] Seekins, Frank T. *Hebrew Word Pictures: How Does the Hebrew Alphabet Reveal Prophetic Truths*. Phoenix, AZ: Living Word Pictures, 2012.

[18] This is not to be confused with the speaking in tongues or what is commonly referred to as praying in the spirit. This is a topic that we will explore in a subsequent chapter.

nurture or feed and support the covenant or agreement" that God has with you. According to ancient Hebrew thought, truth nurtures and strengthens a blood covenant. It is also described as the substance required for "the passing of skill or strength to the next generation."[19]

The greatest example of the passing of skill and strength to the next generation is found when Jesus stated, "As I hear my Father speak, I speak" [John 8:28, 12:49-50, 14:10]. Though many put this statement in the context of what Jesus spoke to others, I believe that Jesus exercised this same principle during His times of prayer. It was a Father passing skill and strength to His Son through the substance of truth. To put it another way, Jesus was constantly positioning Himself to receive the inspiration or breath of truth through the words spoken to Him; He then exhaled back to God words and actions based off the instructions of this truth. This type of prayer is foreign to many religious people today, including many Christians.

This level of prayer is also connected to the vital principle and practice of "worshiping in spirit and truth" that Jesus mentioned to the Samaritan woman in John 4:23-24. In other words, you honor and worship God by breathing back to God the truth He has inspired you with or breathed into you. You exhale back to God – in the form of your words and your works – those things that God has inspired you to say and do. This in essence is the purest form of Spirit-and-Truth worship.

Jesus taught within the culture and general mindset of the place and time He lived. Linguistically, this means He spoke within the framework of Hebrew and some Aramaic. The English versions of the Bible do not give us the same depth of meaning of many of these original words because the English language is limited compared to ancient Hebrew and Aramaic (as are many other languages). A good example of this would be the word "love" in the Bible. Depending on where it is used, it could have up to six different meanings in Hebrew; in English, the closest

---

[19]   AHLB#: 1290-C (N2)

we can get to the original meanings is by using the single word "love."

Though Jesus taught The Lord's Prayer, you will not find it being prayed anywhere in the Bible by Jesus' disciples or the believers that followed them. The reason for this is that it was never meant to be used as a vain repetition. After Jesus' resurrection, He taught His disciples things that pertained to the Kingdom of God within them, which would soon be activated by the Holy Spirit.

> *"I made the first report as to all things that Jesus began both to do and teach until the day He was taken up, having given directions to the apostles whom He chose, through the Holy Spirit; to whom He also presented Himself living after His suffering by many infallible proofs, being seen by them through forty days, and* speaking of the things pertaining to the kingdom of God" [Acts 1:1-3].

It would be safe to surmise that a major part of Jesus' 40-day teaching – between the time He rose again and the time He ascended to the Father – included training on the purpose and function of the Holy Spirit of Truth: to help them discover, develop and deploy the Kingdom of God that was within them into the earth [Jn. 16:12-15]. Twice in The Lord's Prayer, Jesus mentions the Kingdom of God, showing the importance of focusing on building this kingdom during our times of prayer. How do we accomplish this? As we examine the The Lord's Prayer by delving into it phrase by phrase, we will come to understand that, rather than it being a prayer to repeat word for word, it is meant to be both a lifestyle and an approach for listening to the voice of God. Looking at key words from this prayer and their original definitions through a root-word perspective will deepen our understanding of prayer. It will align our view of this vital topic to be more in line with what Jesus originally intended when He answered the disciple's request, "Lord, teach us to pray."

In the next few chapters, we will delve into The Lord's Prayer that Jesus taught from a root-word perspective and begin to understand it in a new way. Though this prayer lesson is found in both Matthew and Luke, we will use Matthew's account since it contains more details overall:

> *"In this manner, therefore, pray: Our Father in heaven, Hallowed be Your name. Your kingdom come. Your will be done in earth as it is in heaven. Give us this day our daily bread. And forgive us our debts, As we forgive our debtors. And do not lead us into temptation, But deliver us from the evil one. For Yours is the kingdom and the power and the glory forever. Amen"* [Matt. 6:9-13 NKJV].

As we progress in true spiritual growth and development, our prayers should transform. Rather than us speaking to God, our prayers should eventually result in us hearing more from God in times of prayer. God's plan, spoken into your life, will give you understanding and faith for the things that you are meant to ask from Him. These requests will always be in alignment with the purposes that He has preordained for your life. In other words, God is not obligated to provide for your self-imposed will and purposes [Eph. 2:10, 1Jn. 5:14]. He will, however, send His Holy Spirit of Truth to guide you towards accomplishing His perfect will and plan for your life. Prayer is the primary medium by which you are able to hear and see this predestined purpose.

CHAPTER SUMMARY:

- Jesus' prayer life was an earthly model for us. Jesus experienced prayer on a daily basis, primarily in the morning.

- Jesus' instruction to go into your room or "closet" meant going to a place absent of external and internal distractions.

- What God is looking for in true prayer is not many words, but the right words. The most effective prayer that we can pray is the one that comes from a place where God tells us what to pray for!

- Truth is the language of God. True prayer is communication between God and you; the purpose of it is for God to speak to you His truth.

- The Lord's Prayer was never meant to be used as a repetitive prayer; it is meant to be a lifestyle and an approach for hearing the voice of God.

APPLICATION:

1. The strength and power to live a purposed life of service to others originates from living in a Kingdom-of-Heaven environment. Ask God to help you enter this environment daily through prayer.

2. As we progress spiritually, our prayers should transform to hearing more from God rather than just speaking to Him. What are your prayers primarily comprised of? If it is mainly *speaking* to God, take time to stop and *listen* to His voice today.

3. As prayer is the primary medium by which you are able to hear and see God's perfect will for your life, how often do you take time in personal and undisturbed prayer? Think about how you can make prayer a part of your daily schedule.

CHAPTER THREE:

Hallowing the Father

> *"A failure to understand the depth of "The Lord's Prayer" keeps us from perceiving and experiencing the depths of the mind of God."*
> *– Julio Alvarado Jr.*

"Our Father in Heaven"

In Jesus' opening instruction of The Lord's Prayer, He established His and our origin by using the word "Our." He did not say "my Father" or "your Father," but clearly stated "Our Father" – implying that we originated from the same source that He did.

The word "Father" that Jesus used here is the Hebrew word "*Ab.*" Jesus was not referring to a physical male parent. He was referring to His and our original source of creation, our life source and sustainer: God. The Hebraic concept conveyed here is that this "Father" has no human origin. He is a Spirit that has always existed. Ancient Hebrew thought describes a *Father* as "the strength of the house."[20] This Father provides not only the strength but also the support and structure of the house. This

---

[20] *Strongs* #1: AHLB#: 1002-A (N)

may seem to describe a male parent or head of a household, yet the deeper understanding would define "the house" as your body – a temple of God's Spirit [1 Cor. 6:19].

By starting the prayer with "Our Father," Jesus wishes to establish within us a mindset where God the Father is accepted as our origin of existence. He has infused His living Spirit into you. God desires to inspire and govern your mind! This is the reason why Jesus stated, *"And call no one your father on the earth, for One is your Father in Heaven"* [Matt. 23:9]. Jesus was not saying that you cannot call your biological dad your father. The deeper meaning is that your biological father is not your original source of existence. Your biological parents made you, but God *created* you.

This understanding enables us to view Heaven as not only an external place where we will go when this life is over, but more importantly as an internal place where we meet with and are trained by God [See Ps. 25:4-5, 86:11, 119:12, 26, 66, 135, 143:10]. This is a heavenly realm or environment that exists within you, the "secret place" where the Spirit of God desires to teach you. It is "the Kingdom of God within you" that God's Spirit wishes to activate. This is where God begins to reward you with the mysteries of the Kingdom, which we will discuss further in this chapter.

> *"He who dwells in the secret place of the Most High shall abide under the shadow of the Almighty"* [Psalms 91:1].

Since the Spirit of God is within, the secret place is not a place where we merely go to in prayer and leave at the end of a prayer session; this heavenly environment is ordained to be the primary reference point from which we walk *throughout the day*. It sets the tone for a God-consciousness that lasts all day. Unfortunately, this concept is foreign to many Christians.

To put it another way, this continual God-consciousness should be as real as every breath that we breathe: "As long as my breath is in me, and the spirit of God is in my nostrils" [Job 27:3].

We often take our natural breathing for granted and forget to recognize that it is the very practice that keeps us alive. Just so, we take for granted the God-consciousness to which we have access. Being mindful of this God-consciousness, this heavenly environment, throughout our day gives us access to being Fathered through a true spiritual life as God designed it.

Hallowed be Your Name

The word "hallowed" is *qâdash* in Hebrew. In this case it is defined as, "to set someone apart for a special purpose."[21] In order to fully understand what is set apart for a special purpose here, we must take a look at the Aramaic translation of "Our Father in Heaven" and "Hallowed be your name." The Aramaic version of this phrase follows:[22]

Abwoon d'bwa*shm*aya (Our father who art in heaven)

Nethquadash *shm*akh (Hallowed be thy name)

Within the contents of both Aramaic phrases are the letters "*shm*." This is the Hebrew and Aramaic root word for "Name" as it relates to the "Father" and His divine being as God. This is important because "*shm*" is part of the root of the word "Heaven." In other words, the "Name" comes from Heaven.

The Modern Hebrew word for "Name" as it relates to God is *Shêm*. *Strong's Concordance* defines *Shêm* as "authority and character." The *Ancient Hebrew Lexicon of the Bible* describes "Name" or *Shêm* as it pertains to God as "breath" or "wind." It further goes on to explain that the "name" of an individual (in this case, God) is more than just an identifier but is descriptive of His character. It further describes the breath or name of God as "a sweet aroma that originates in heaven."[23]

---

[21] *Strongs* #6942: AHLB#: 2700 (V, H)

[22] For a full version of "The Lord's Prayer" in Aramaic, please see Appendix 2.

[23] *Strongs* #8034: AHLB#: 1473-A (N), (B)

In ancient Hebrew thought, a primary purpose of God – who was known as "The Name" – was "what destroyed chaos." Someone who truly functions in the Name of God has access to the breath, wind, or voice of God from Heaven that destroys any form of disorder, chaos or confusion.

A Jewish ruler named Nicodemus recognized Jesus as a teacher who came in the Name of God in that He destroyed chaos and confusion through the signs and wonders that Nicodemus had evidently witnessed or heard about:

> *"This man came to Jesus by night and said to Him, 'Rabbi, we know that You are a teacher come from God; for no one can do these signs that You do unless God is with him'"* [Jn. 3:2].

In reply, Jesus began to describe to Nicodemus what set Him apart from other teachers and what the requirements were in order for someone to function like Jesus functioned.

> *"The Spirit breathes where He desires, and you hear His voice, but you do not know from where He comes, and where He goes; so is everyone who is born of the Spirit"* [John 3:8 MKJV].

When one is born of the Spirit, they are at first unaware where this wind or voice comes from. As a believer matures in experiencing the voice of God, they eventually become familiar with its origin because they come to understand two key descriptions of the voice of God: water and spirit. It is important to keep in mind that water (a metaphoric description of the spoken word of God) cleanses and nourishes, and spirit gives life. Through water and spirit, the Name of the Lord is proclaimed.

Examples of these facts are found in the following scriptures.

Water:

*"Give ear, O heavens, and I will speak; And hear, O earth,
the words of my mouth. Let my teaching drop as the rain,
My speech distill as the dew, As raindrops on the tender
herb, And as showers on the grass. For I proclaim the name
of the LORD: Ascribe greatness to our God"* [Deut. 32:1-3]
[See also Ps. 119:9, Isa. 55:10-11].

Spirit:

*"It is the Spirit who gives life; the flesh profits nothing. The
words that I speak to you are spirit, and they are life"* [Jn.
6:63] *[See also Job 33:4].*

Jesus told Nicodemus, "You must be born again," stating
that if someone was not born again, they would not be able
to see or enter the Kingdom of God. Traditionally, this has
been taught to mean that if someone is not born again, they
will not enter in Heaven when they die. Yet Jesus said that the
Kingdom of God is within you [Lk. 17:21]. Was Jesus making
this statement to describe a future event or a current result?
In order to understand what Jesus meant, we must explore
what He meant by "see" and "enter."

*"Jesus answered and said to him, 'Most assuredly, I say to
you, unless one is born again, he cannot **see** the Kingdom
of God'"* [Jn. 3:3].

*"Jesus answered, 'Most assuredly, I say to you, unless one is
born of water and the Spirit, he cannot **enter** the Kingdom
of God'"* [Jn 3:5].

The word "see" that Jesus used here is *yâda* in Hebrew. As
it relates to the kingdom, this word is described as "having an
intimate relationship with an idea or an experience through
knowledge that is gained through visual observation."[24]

---

[24] *Strongs* #3045: AHLB#: 1085-L (V)

Jesus was a "Father impersonator." Being born again is the portal that gives you the ability to mimic God the Father through the works that He has ordained for your life. This is what Jesus was describing in the following passage:

"Then Jesus answered and said to them, 'Most assuredly, I say to you, the Son can do nothing of Himself, but what He sees the Father do; for whatever He does, the Son also does in like manner. For the Father loves the Son, and shows Him all things that He Himself does; and He will show Him greater works than these, that you may marvel'" [Jn. 5:19-20].

In these verses, Jesus explained how He practiced ongoing vision at the purest level possible, which is accessible to a mature Kingdom-minded believer today.[25]

The word "enter" that Jesus used is the Hebrew word *yâshab*, which is very complex and rich in meaning. It is defined as "a place of dwelling that is returned to."[26] Other forms of this key word describe this place of dwelling as a place that you have to "cross over into" in order to gain access to things beyond your normal environment. As you will recall, the first chapter of this book is titled "The Border Crossing" and speaks of this necessary spiritual crossing-over. In that place, you will "perceive vision" in order to experience your preordained purpose. Jesus was not describing a physical location. He was describing a kingdom mindset that is experienced within you. In essence, we are meant to return to the place where it all started!

We were first conceived and born in the mind of God [Eph. 1:3-4]. This reality is foreign to many believers and non-believers alike, yet understanding this point is critical in learning to hear the voice of God personally and to experience the Kingdom of God within you. Being born again in the flesh has

---

[25] This is a concept that I will explore in the next book in this series titled *The Mystery of the Kingdom of God Revealed*.
[26] *Strongs* #3427: AHLB#: 1462-L (V)

nothing to do with being born in the spirit. Though traditional religious teachings tell us that this conversation between Jesus and Nicodemus meant that one must be baptized with water, a deeper study from an original Hebrew and Aramaic perspective provide a deeper meaning and application of what Jesus meant by the term, "You must be born again."

In some translations of the Bible, instead of the term "born again" you will see "born anew" or "born from above." The *Accurate New Testament* version of the Bible states it this way: "You must be birthed downward." Some of the ancient Aramaic texts express it as, "You must return back to the place where you were first born!"

The term "born again" implies that you must have been birthed before. For anything to happen "again," the same thing must have taken place before. Did Jesus indicate to Nicodemus that he must be born again in the flesh? This is what Nicodemus thought, but Jesus quickly ruled that out by saying, "What is born of flesh is flesh and what has been born of spirit is spirit" [John 3:6]. When you discover the reality that you were first born in a spirit form before you were naturally born as a human being, this revelation introduces you to the "The Name" (breath, wind, or voice) of God in an intimate way that will release the true power of God for your life.

In reference to Jesus, we read, "He is the image of the invisible God, the firstborn over all creation" [Col. 1:15]. The word firstborn used here is defined as "the beginning of a time" and "the beginning of a position."[27] God created us in spirit form before the foundations of the world were ever created [Eph.1:3]. Biblically, over 6,000 years of human history is recorded. Spiritually, you are over 6,000 years old. When you were conceived in the mind of God in spirit form, your existence and position in Him began according to God.

---

[27] *Strongs* #7223: AHLB#: 1458-D (ej)

We normally measure our time or existence from the moment that we were naturally conceived or birthed into this world. God sees our origin of existence well before this. He sees back to the time where our position and power began as an offspring of God. We have the opportunity to be reconnected to this awesome origin through the spiritual adoption process of becoming born again ... or more accurately stated, becoming acquainted with where we were *first born* [Rom. 8:15, Eph. 1:5].

It is imperative to understand the significance of this reality because this is where The Name of God (identity, authority, character and breath) was originally applied to our lives. It is where our mindset has to return in order to properly "hallow the Name of God." In other words, we honor the Name of God when we understand our true spiritual origin in Him.

The Relationship of Baptism and the Name of God

Jesus told His disciples something that I believe is one of the most misunderstood and misapplied scriptures in the Bible. It is the mandate of the Great Commission:

> *"Go therefore and make disciples of all the nations, baptizing them in the name of the Father and of the Son and of the Holy Spirit"* [Matt. 28:19].

This passage was not intended to simply be a formula of words spoken over a believer at a baptismal ceremony; it was intended to bring a death of the former ways of thinking and a rebirth into new thought and purpose. This is necessary in order to experience unity with God through an immersion and saturation with teachings from God Himself that are purposed to cause you to function in the Name of God.

The key to understanding the core of what baptism ultimately signifies is revealed in an in-depth examination of Jesus' baptism:

"When He had been baptized, Jesus came up immediately from the water; and behold, the heavens were opened to Him, and He saw the Spirit of God descending like a dove and alighting upon Him. And suddenly a voice came from heaven, saying, 'This is My beloved Son, in whom I am well pleased'" [Matt. 3:16-17].

There are three primary keys that we must capture from this vital portion of scripture.

1. Jesus was baptized in water (a natural cleansing and nourishment medium) by His prescribed and authorized forerunner, John.

   This ceremony signified a type of outward burial process. Water baptism originated in and was practiced as a part of the rabbinic Jewish culture before Jesus mandated it as a part of the Great Commission. It was an outward act performed in front of witnesses, a symbolic gesture signifying a type of burial. Inwardly, it signified a cleansing of a former lifestyle, which included the doctrines of former teachers. It was intended to be the starting point of a new life and a submission to the authority and teaching of the person that was baptizing them. This was a part of Jewish customs and was traditionally considered a law.

   The concept of baptism or immersion by water originated in the days of Moses and Aaron, when God gave instructions on ceremonial cleansing and washing of the priests when the priesthood was first set up [Exodus 29]. The baptism hallowed or consecrated and set the priests apart for a special dual purpose. One purpose was to serve as mediators between God and the people. The other purpose was to experience the identity or Name of God at a presence-to-presence level. At this level, they experienced a presence of God that contained His identity, authority and character.

Fundamentally, they were experiencing "spiritual" air – His breath and words that came from Heaven. This is where the concept of "Hallowing the Name" was originally conceived. It was one name (the human) experiencing another Name (God). In other words, the priests were positioning themselves through a natural cleansing process to remove any external impurities in order to experience the authority, teachings and purity of God.

This is exactly what Jesus did as He was baptized by John the Baptist. Jesus, as priest, submitted Himself to John's authority and teaching on the Kingdom, which were established by the Name of God. This introduced Jesus into His earthly ministry. John the Baptist was a type and shadow of someone that you submit to, such as a pastor or teacher. This individual should serve as a helper, mentor, or forerunner for your life.

2. The heavens were opened to Jesus and the Spirit of God descended upon Him.

     The Holy Spirit is the inner cleansing agent and helper that leads you to experience a daily burial of self-will. It then begins to activate the details of the Kingdom of God as it pertains to God's will for your life, just as it did for Jesus. This event represents the Holy Spirit – God's authority on the earth – coming into your life. Proof that you have received the Holy Spirit is that it begins to lead you into a process of transformation according to what God has ordained for your life.

     "But the Helper, the Holy Spirit, whom the Father will send in My name, He will teach you all things, and bring to your remembrance all things that I said to you" [Jn. 14:26].

3. Jesus received the Father's affirmation as a result of this outer and inner baptism.

He was now baptized under the immersion and authority of God, which is where the Name (the identity, authority, character and breath) of God became fully operational in His life. In essence, from this moment on, Jesus began to breathe the continual cleansing and nurturing of the environment of heaven.

Today, this represents God the Father constantly affirming you. As you submit yourself to the Spirit of the Father, you begin a maturation process where your primary authorized Teacher – the Holy Spirit of Truth – begins to lead you to function in the likeness, image and Name of God. We receive affirmation from our Father as we discover, develop and deploy the Kingdom of God that is within.

Once this process develops and becomes fully operational, you begin to experience *"the transfer of teachers"* spoken of earlier. You go from being baptized through the immersion of natural water by another human being (who should be your earthly teacher) to being internally baptized through a continual immersion of the water of the Word that can only come from the breath or mouth of God.

Jesus' baptism serves as a model for our lives. Nowadays, people are baptized in many different ways. The pastor or priest quotes scripture or follows some type of scripted ceremony, which concludes with saying, "I baptize you In Jesus Name" or "I baptize you in the Name of the Father, the Son, and the Holy Ghost." In these ceremonies they sprinkle you with water, pour water over you, or submerge you completely. There is much debate amongst Christian believers on whether to baptize in "Jesus Name" – as the disciples did in the book of Acts – or in the "In the Name of the Father, the Son and the Holy Ghost," which Jesus mandated in the great commission. Scripturally both of them were applied. My suggestion is that if this is an issue, why not use them both?

The importance is not which one is correct, but what they both signify. The verbal application contains no power or magic in itself. The primary purpose of baptism is ultimately to experience being taught by the Godhead of the Father, the Son (Jesus), and the Holy Spirit. Otherwise, we are guilty of taking on the Name of the Lord in vain.

Personally, I have been baptized by water three times in my life: first as a baby according to Catholic tradition, then when I was 11 years old at a Baptist church because the other kids were doing it. Finally, as a 26-year-old adult, I was baptized in a Pentecostal church. In all three of these, I was either sprinkled with or immersed in water. Scriptures were quoted over me. I was baptized with the words "In Jesus Name" and "In the Name of the Father, and of the Son and of The Holy Ghost" spoken over me. In none of these three cases, however, did anyone truly explain to me what I was doing. They did explain to me what the organization's beliefs and practices were as they related to baptism. In essence, I was baptized a sinner and came out of these ceremonies a wet sinner.

After my baptism as an adult, I experienced some positive changes in my life. I joined the church where I was baptized and was taught by the pastor who baptized me. Prior to this, I was an alcoholic, a drug addict, and I struggled with pornography and sexual immorality. I had a lot of other problems in my life, which I wrote of in detail in the first book of this series. Through this pastor's ministry I learned a lot of good things that improved my way of living, yet I still had internal struggles. I also carried the constant thought that "there has to be more to God than this" in the back of my mind.

It wasn't until I experienced a true inner baptism of Jesus' Name that I began to experience the "more to God than this" experience, which ultimately led to a "more to me than what I see" experience. Through an intimate immersion with God's presence, I finally began to discover a God that was more real than anything I experienced before, which led me to discover my true origin in Him.

What does it truly mean to be baptized in "Jesus' Name" or "in the Name of The Father, the Son and The Holy Ghost"? It means that your soul should constantly be taught by the triune Godhead that functions as one from Heaven.

> *"For there are three that bear witness in heaven: the Father, the Word, and the Holy Spirit; and these three are one"* [1 Jn. 5:7].

You don't need to be baptized multiple times. It all boils down to one baptism where your faith and knowledge has to come through the teachings of the Godhead [Rom. 10:17].

> *"There is one body and one Spirit (the Holy Spirit), just as you were called in one hope of your calling; one Lord (The Word-Jesus), one faith, **one baptism**; one God and Father (the almighty God) of all, who is above all, and through all, and in you all"* [Eph. 4:4-6].

For most people, "baptism" is a word that has been limited to a water immersion ceremony according to traditional church practices. Though it may start as a physical ceremony, baptism should lead to an internal baptismal ceremony that should be happening every day of your life [Ps. 119:9, Eph. 5:26]. The inner spiritual immersion is designed and purposed to keep your mind clean and pure so that you can be continually synchronized with the mind of God. His Name is then manifested in your life through the purposes that He has established for you.

Natural water baptism should eventually lead to Spiritual baptism, which is also known as the baptism of the Holy Spirit. The Holy Spirit of Truth exposes you to the water of the Word that is purposed to cleanse and nurture you in order to teach you how to "Hallow the Name of God." Concerning Jesus' baptism, John the Baptist stated:

> *"I indeed baptize you with water unto repentance, but He who is coming after me is mightier than I, whose sandals I am not worthy to carry. He will baptize you with the Holy Spirit and fire"* [Matt. 3:11].

To be baptized with fire is a Hebrew metaphor that describes an inner immersion ability to receive the Spoken Word of God (Truth) that functions as a purification process to remove iniquity as part of the maturation process in your life where you are ultimately justified and righteous as God is. *[See also Deut. 4:6]*

"A God of truth and without iniquity, just and right is He" [Deut. 32:4b KJV].

"'Is not My word like a fire?' says the LORD" [Jer. 23:29a].

This is what is metaphorically described in the following scripture:

"When the Day of Pentecost had fully come, they were all with one accord in one place. And suddenly there came a sound from heaven, as of a rushing mighty wind, and it filled the whole house where they were sitting. Then there appeared to them divided tongues (languages), as of fire, and one sat upon each of them. And they were all filled with the Holy Spirit and began to speak with other tongues (languages) as the Spirit gave them utterance" [Acts 2:1-4].

These people were endowed with a language that was foreign to them but was understood by the receiver. The recipient understood their words, as they came from God; they were clear messages with interpretations of truth that came from God [Acts 2:6-11].

John the Baptist's statement, "I indeed baptize you with water unto repentance," also carries a depth of meaning that we must understand in order to properly connect with the Name of God. This point is further stressed in Peter's key instruction to repent and be baptized in the name of Jesus Christ:

> *"Then Peter said to them, 'Repent, and let every one of you
> be baptized in the name of Jesus Christ for the remission
> of sins; and you shall receive the gift of the Holy Spirit. For
> the promise is to you and to your children, and to all who
> are afar off, as many as the Lord our God will call'"* [Acts
> 2:38-39].

The word "repent" is traditionally defined as, "to express
sorrow, to change one's mind or to think differently." Further
study of this key word reveals what you need to change your mind
to in order to think differently. The Hebrew word for repent is
shoov. It is defined as "a turning back to a previous state or place
of dwelling."[28] According to ancient Hebrew thought, to repent is
to destroy a way of thinking that has taken you captive in order
to return to a place of thinking where freedom is present. From
an Aramaic perspective, the word for repent is *tab*. It is defined
as, "to return to the place of your original existence" which is
back into the mind of God.

A further study of Peter's key statements reveals a hidden
secret that remains unknown to many believers today. Though
the gift of the Holy Spirit is God's promise to you, it is purposed
to reveal "a promise" to you. The word "promise" that Peter used
here is *epaggelia* in Greek. It is defined from a Greek perspective
as, "an exposition, a declaration, an announcement, a message
and a sum." The Holy Spirit is a messenger that delivers to you
the sum total of your life through declarations He announces to
you.

The original Hebrew root word perspective of this word
illuminates the origin of these declarations. The Hebrew words
that define the promise are *pârâshâh* and *sêpher-siphrâh*.
Pârâshâh is defined as "an account that is spread out as an
event." *Sêpher siphrâh* is defined as "a book" that is "evidence."[29]
Sêpher siphrâh comes from the Hebrew root word *sâphar*.[30] It is

---

28 *Strongs* #7725: AHLB#: 1462-J (V), I.
29 *Strongs* #5612: AHLB#: 2500 (e1): *Strongs* #6575: AHLB#: 2644 (N1)
30 *Strongs* #5608: AHLB#: 2500 (V)

described as an event that is announced through "the spreading apart of thoughts in order to understand and make clear" this "book of evidence." It is also described as the book that one must learn from. If that was not enough, this process is described as, "what is rehearsed to you by a mode of showing and telling."

> *"Howbeit when he, the Spirit of truth, is come, he will guide you into all truth: for he shall not speak of himself; but whatsoever he shall hear, that shall he speak: and he will shew you things to come. He shall glorify me: for he shall receive of mine, and shall shew it unto you. All things that the Father hath are mine: therefore said I, that he shall take of mine, and shall shew it unto you"* [Jn. 16:13-15 KJV].

In other words, the "gift of the Holy Spirit" becomes *the* Promise that delivers a promise – which is the script for your life. God's Name is all over it because He authored it! The Holy Spirit introduces you to the promise of God. This promise of God is access to your personal book that He has prescribed for your life.

A main purpose and function of the Holy Spirit of Truth is to read books. He reads the book that has already been prescribed and prewritten for your life! In a way, the Holy Spirit is God's librarian and transcriber.

> *"Your eyes saw my substance, being yet unformed. And in Your book they all were written, The days fashioned for me, When as yet there were none of them. How precious also are Your thoughts to me, O God! How great is the sum of them"* [Ps. 139:16-17].

This "book" is your life. In other words, it is the document that contains the thoughts of God for your life, which becomes your life's curriculum. It enables you to live according to God's design! This book – though it is *about* you – has been authored by God! By fulfilling this book, you are functioning in the identity, authority, character, and Name of God.

Because God created you, He is obligated to provide you with the details of your life. These details will always be from a reference point of truth that will help you function in the Name of God. Otherwise we are spiritually Fatherless and will function as illegitimate offspring – also known as bastards. We will have the tendency to function as bastards if we don't take time to hear the account of the promised book on our life.

Jesus also had such a book on His life.

"Then I said, 'Lo, I come in the volume of the Book it is written of Me to do Your will, O God'" [Heb. 10:7].

Many people have been baptized in water and received the gift of the Holy Spirit, but have failed to take the next step of receiving information that reveals the promised book of their life. This comes through experiencing the inner baptism that identifies us with the Name of God. Jesus mandated what He experienced in order for others to experience the same:

"And Jesus came and spoke to them, saying, 'All authority has been given to Me in heaven and on earth. Go therefore and make disciples of all the nations, baptizing them in the name of the Father and of the Son and of the Holy Spirit, teaching them to observe all things that I have commanded you; and lo, I am with you always, even to the end of the age Amen'" [Matt. 28:18-20].

Believers are initially baptized by another human, someone who may also serve as their teacher in the beginning stages of their conversion process. Eventually, the believer should develop into a disciple or student of God. This occurs when she or he learns to hear the voice of God and is taught primarily by the Holy Spirit of truth. This is why it is vital to learn to hear the voice of God; otherwise you will always limit yourself to the knowledge and teachings of a human being. As good as this teacher may be, the highest form of learning, knowledge and teaching should eventually come from God Himself.

The word *observe* that Jesus used in this crucial mandate is the Hebrew word *shâma*[31]. It is defined as "to hear intelligently." It is described as "a careful hearing as well as responding appropriately in obedience and action." Your observance, combined with a high level of diligence, will enable you to spiritually perceive what the Holy Spirit is reporting to you.

Regeneration – True Spiritual Life

Regeneration is an authentic result of one who is baptized in the name of God and is born again. *Re*generation from a scriptural standpoint is to be born of God. It is to return to the place where you were first born in spirit form. Mankind in regeneration becomes related to God by spiritual birth and therefore becomes god-kind.

Regeneration is the beginning of spiritual life in God. It becomes the basis upon which true predestined life is built. One who is not born again cannot see or experience the fullness of the Kingdom of God that is within them. Even those that claim to be born again, if not properly trained, will not be able to perceive the spiritual mysteries or secrets about their life that Jesus referred to [Matt. 13:11, Mk. 4:11, Lk. 8:10].

It is imperative for born again or regenerated persons to fully understand what they have attained through their new birth experience; otherwise their experience will become nothing more than a traditional religious event. A regenerated person is exposed to the spiritual genes and Name of God the Father, from whom he originated before being introduced into this world.[32] This is where spiritual adoption by God takes place [Rom. 8:13-17]. Spiritual adoption has present and eternal benefits. It has the potential to remove any false doctrinal teachings that you

---

[31] *Strongs* #8085: AHLB#: 2851 (V)

[32] This will be further explored in my next book in this series titled *The Mystery of the Kingdom of God Revealed.*

may have been exposed to, which are replaced with the doctrine of true Kingdom life that comes from the mouth of God. Spiritual adoption is the catalyst that introduces you to the pure spiritual and genetic coding of God, which has the power to genuinely influence the soul of man. It removes the curses of iniquity that have been transferred from the biological birthing process. Biologically, the location where iniquity is transferred is known as the Golgi Apparatus.

In humans, the Golgi Apparatus are protein cells found next to the nucleus that holds the DNA. The Golgi Apparatus is responsible for directing the molecular "traffic" of information and life experiences. This information – in the form of protein in the cells – travels to the brain and throughout the brain in the vein and nerve systems, which affects the thought process of an individual and his or her overall identity. The Golgi Apparatus is designed to collect and store behaviors, histories and memories that are then transferred to the next generation through the conception process by way of the protein in the male's sperm. During the process of conception, the blood type, structure and content of the blood – including the Golgi Apparatus – is birthed in the child's DNA.

Once you are genuinely born again by way of spirit and water – the spoken word of God – and are baptized into the Name of God, you are introduced to the genes of God. The spiritual genes of God the Father are transferable, just as natural human genes are. The blood of Jesus, which came from God the Father, contains the power to re-engineer and rewrite the DNA (Dynamic Named Ability) for your life.[33] In other words, you get the Golgi Apparatus of God, which contains "traffic" of truth information – the genes, character, behaviors, histories, and the very memories of God Himself – as they relate to the life that He has already seen about you and that make you just like Him! This is the secret of what

---

[33] This reality is also explored in my first book of this series titled *The Mystery of Iniquity Revealed* in chapter 13: "The Blood, the Water and the Spirit" and chapter 14: "The Iniquity Removal Process."

made Jesus so "Father-conscious" and caused Him to "Hallow the Name" of God in all that He said and did.

In essence, when Jesus said, "You must be born again," He meant that we naturally function according to the genes of a natural father, and that needs to change. When we come to know the truth of who Jesus is, we need to start functioning according to God's genes. This is a level of experiencing God that many believers are unfamiliar with. I used to be one of them. When we fail to understand the true depth and application of hallowing the Name of God, we cannot receive access to the full measure of abiding in God.

Being born again has been turned into a traditional religious concept and event rather than a spiritual rebirth. It is meant to be the starting point of understanding where you originally came from and the introduction of how you are supposed to function in life. The original and true purpose of being born again is to experience a death of your current way of thinking in order to return your mind back to where it originally came from so that you can experience the identity of God and the fullness of His Kingdom within you.

> *"If then you were raised with Christ, seek those things which are above, where Christ is, sitting at the right hand of God. Set your mind on things above, not on things on the earth. For you died, and your life is hidden with Christ in God"* [Col. 3:1].

"For you died" is referring to your carnal way of thinking, which must die in order to reveal a life that is "hidden with Christ in God." In order to begin the process of Jesus' mandate to "Seek first the Kingdom of God and His righteousness" [Matt. 6:33], we must discover that life which is "hidden with Christ."

When scriptural passages (such as Jesus' conversation with Nicodemus and Jesus' teaching on The Lord's Prayer) are taught from the philosophies, traditions and denominational doctrines of men, they are often taught simply as portions of scripture to be memorized, traditional religious events to be observed, and prayers to be repeated instead of life-changing experiences that will set us on a new path in life [Col. 2:8]. The believers' experience with God then becomes paralyzed and their capacity to experience true transformation is hindered.

Jesus said that Kingdom of God is already within you. In other words, the wind that comes from the Kingdom of Heaven needs to invade and activate your inner being through a cleansing that is purposed to reveal the character of God within you. As you begin to understand how you are made in the image and likeness of God, the end result is renewal and restoration. You are taken back to your original place in the Name (identity and character) of God.

A deeper look into this key word (Name) divulges that one who is not experiencing this Name or Breath is "desolate, resulting in being a place of ruin." If that were not enough, it further describes this condition of desolation as "one in horror or in astonishment because they are dried up in the inside."[34] This was my condition. Though I was a believer and I practiced traditional religion, I was completely dry on the inside. I knew that there was more to me than what I was experiencing in life. When we are dried up in the inside, it is a result of not getting the water of the Word that can only come from the mouth of God [See Deut. 32:1-2, Hosea 6:3, Isa. 55:1-11]. I had a vast amount of Bible knowledge, but my dryness came from me not hearing the voice of God telling me the story of my life. This was due to my lack of understanding the original purpose for prayer.

As we saw earlier, the word "hallowed" is *qâdash* in Hebrew. It is defined as "to set someone apart for a special purpose." From an original Hebraic and Aramaic perspective, hallowing the Name requires a focused and disciplined meditative mindset in order to properly set apart "The Name" or presence of God so that He can fulfill His special purpose within you. The special purpose that God fulfills through the framework of The Lord's Prayer is to inspire you with His preordained will for your life.

---

[34] *Strongs* #8034: AHLB#: 1473-A (B)

He will also give you information on anything that is hindering this process from being accomplished.

Hallowing the presence of God carries a responsibility of the person who is praying at this level, to discipline themselves mentally, spiritually and physically. From the Aramaic understanding of "hallowed" – which is the word *nethquadash* – there comes an assignment and responsibility of outer and inner discipline. This discipline is taught through an agricultural presentation. The lesson conveyed in this process of hallowing the mind is portrayed as one who is bending towards the ground to ensure that nothing will hinder the special seeds about to be sown. Those seeds are special because they contain the true purposes for the individual's life. We must remove and release any clutter that keeps our minds busy and distracted when we are attempting to position ourselves to come in contact with the presence of God. We need to take on an inner posture of stillness and silence in order to hear and receive the "seeds" of the still, small voice of God.

"The preparations of the heart belong to man, but the answer of the tongue is from the Lord" [Proverbs 16:1].

As mentioned before, this is the secret place that is prepared in order to experience oneness with God. It is a place where you receive the intelligence of God as it pertains to your life. From an ancient perspective, it is viewed as a nuptial chamber, a place where mutual desire is fulfilled and where birthing begins. It is also described as a workshop to envision the ideas of God in order to reproduce and create the purposes of God.

The Name of God is proclaimed to us first by God Himself through His instructions that inform us how to function in His identity, authority and character. We must understand this before we can truly proclaim the power of the Name accurately before others.

In order to properly "Hallow the Name," you must understand where this concept came from, what it means, and its primary purpose – which is to enable you to function in the image and likeness of God. Once you do so, you are introduced to the Kingdom of God within you, and thus empowered to introduce to the world a true manifestation of the Kingdom of Heaven on earth. This leads to the next portion of the prayer that Jesus prayed and taught.

CHAPTER SUMMARY:

- Someone who truly functions in the Name of God has access to the breath, wind, or voice of God from Heaven that destroys any form of disorder, chaos or confusion.

- All humans were first conceived and born in the mind of God. We honor and "hallow" the Name of God when we understand our true spiritual origin in Him.

- Water baptism is intended to be the starting point of a new life. It represents a death to ones former way of thinking and living in order to experience a newness of thinking and life that is introduced through the Holy Spirit-God's authority on the earth.

- The primary purpose of baptism is to ultimately experience being taught by the Godhead of the Father, the Son (Jesus) and the Holy Spirit.

- The highest form of learning, knowledge and teaching should eventually come from God Himself.

- The original and true purpose of being "born again" is to "die" to your current way of thinking in order for your mind to return to its place of origin so that you can experience the fullness of the Kingdom of God within you.

APPLICATION:

1. The "secret place" referred to in the Bible is meant to be a heavenly environment in which you operate *throughout the day*, not just at a certain time in your day. Reflect on whether your moments spent in prayer are singular times that you don't "take with you" throughout the day. If so, ask God to help you change your mindset so that you can commune with God throughout the day.

2. God has penned a unique "book" for your life. It is the document that contains the thoughts of God for your life, which is meant to become your life's curriculum. Ask the Lord to give you a glimpse of that "curriculum" today.

CHAPTER FOUR:

His Kingdom, His Will

> *"The greatest learning environment – which you have access to on the earth today – lies within you. Jesus called this environment 'The Kingdom of God.' It's an educational system where only one student (you), and one Teacher (The Holy Spirit of Truth) are allowed to attend."*
>
> – Julio Alvarado Jr.

"Your Kingdom Come"

Now that you have prepared your inner self to clearly hear and receive the words of God, you are ready to experience the greatest learning environment possible. Jesus clearly stated that the Kingdom of God has been appointed to you and that it is within you [Lk. 17:21, 22:29]. What is so important about His statements is that there was also a Kingdom within Him; it was the reference point from which He did life while on earth as a man. It is therefore important that we understand and apply the term "Kingdom of God" from an inward domain.

The word "Kingdom" that Jesus used in His prayer lesson from a Greek perspective is commonly known as the word *basileia*. According to *Strong's Concordance and Thayer's Greek Definitions*, it is defined as "royal power, dominion, to rule, or a realm."[35] From the Greek perspective the word "Kingdom" is commonly viewed from *outer-realm* perspective where the dominion, rule and royal power of that particular kingdom are expressed *on the earth*.

The Hebrew word that would have originally been used here is *mamlâkâh*. From an ancient Hebrew perspective, *mamlâkâh* is first experienced inwardly *within the inner-realm of the Kingdom of God* of the human being first, through information and instruction that is communicated before it is expressed as an outward manifestation. The Hebrew root word of *mamlâkâh* is *mâlak*; its primary definition is "a messenger who is purposed to deliver counsel as the will from the one that rules."[36] The messenger in this case that delivers such information is the actual voice of God, which is biblically known as the Holy Spirit of Truth.

In other words, in Jesus' prayer lesson "your kingdom come your will be done" was intended to mean "let your counsel come that contains your will to be done."

This is how Jesus personally experienced this portion of the prayer lesson that He taught in His prayer life. He first experienced kingdom counsel through the disbursement of information and instruction inwardly within the realm of the Kingdom of God that was within Him then He manifested it outwardly after being informed and instructed how to do so.

The inherent environment of the Kingdom of God that is within the human being is a learning environment that already exists within you. It is purposed to receive this level or type of information. The term "Kingdom of God" that Jesus used in His earthly ministry as it relates to the realm within the human being

---

[35] *Strongs* G932
[36] *Strongs* H4467, H4427

where God's influence takes place is anciently known as the *Bet Hammelekh* which is described as the "House of Counsel" and the *Medinot Malkhut,* which is described as "the province and jurisdiction of the Lord that is purposed to restore a righteous life."[37]

These ancient and original concepts of the Kingdom of God as an inner-learning environment that has been inherently placed within every human being will be further explored in the next book of this series in order to maximize its original understanding, application, purpose and reason for which Jesus mandated all of humanity to "Seek first the Kingdom of God and His righteousness" as your life's first and foremost priority [Matt. 6:33].

A simple etymological word study of the word "Kingdom" from its Hebrew equivalent *"mamlâkâh"* from an English perspective reveals that it is a compound word. The first word is "King" – defined as a ruler whose purpose is to function as "a counselor." The second word is "dom," is a key suffix that is defined as "a state of being" that is governed by the counsel of the King.

As it relates to God, the purpose of this counselor is to place or set "a state of being" of a higher-level of consciousness than what is ordinarily experienced that comes directly from the mind of God. When we combine the definitions of both *King* and *dom*, we get "a counselor that comes to introduce a higher consciousness that comes from the mind of God." This higher consciousness is the thoughts and ways of God for your life that cannot be naturally attained but must be spiritually perceived.

> *"For My thoughts are not your thoughts, nor are your ways My ways," says the LORD. "For as the heavens are higher than the earth, so are My ways higher than your ways, and My thoughts than your thoughts"* [Isa. 55:8-9 NKJV].

---

[37] *Strongs* #H1004: AHLB#: 1045-M (N), *Strongs* #4082: AHLB#: 1083-M (k1)

"But the natural man does not receive the things of the Spirit of God, for they are foolishness to him; neither can he know them, because they are spiritually discerned" [1 Cor. 2:14].

Another way of viewing "Your Kingdom come" is to see it as the province of the mind of God that desires to influence you in order to create an area of activity within you where His thoughts are converted into His ways, resulting in you being Kingdom-minded and Kingdom-personified! This was the pinnacle of one of the most profound statements that Jesus made when He stated, "Seek first the Kingdom of God and His righteousness" [Matt 6:33a]. His statement was one of life prioritization and purpose, yet it still remains one of the most misunderstood and misapplied scriptures in the Bible.[38]

Someone who chooses to experience the fullness of the Kingdom of God is one who accepts His ruler-ship as God and King from a position of counselor. It is one who chooses to remain under His power, authority and consciousness. In other words, when a person refuses, disregards, or fails to hear the consulship of His rule, they no longer experience the benefits of His power, authority or consciousness. The Kingdom of God is the domain and counsel of God that exposes you to His consciousness. The counsel of God is the voice of God; His domain is the only place where His consciousness can remain! It is impossible to experience the full essence of the Kingdom of God if we do not listen to His voice. He cannot establish His domain or allow for His consciousness to continually rest in a place where His advice or counsel is not taken.

From an Aramaic perspective, the word Kingdom is *malkuthakh*. It is known as the "I can" and the "You said." It is a word rich with meaning, described as the highest quality of ruler-ship possible, one that introduces God's counsel through principles that guide us towards a life of unity with the ruler. Originally, the concept of an inner Kingdom included a

---

[38] This will be the topic of my next book in this series titled *The Mystery of the Kingdom of God Revealed.*

preparation of a sacred place within the mind that was viewed as a nuptial chamber. This is where a covenant is consummated with God by allowing the thoughts of God to be conceived. It is where we are impregnated with creativity to foster and insure that the ideas of God are birthed into the world. The guiding instruction and principles we receive from God produce a sense of urgency to turn the guiding principles into the manifested visions of God.

When you partake of this relational intercourse with God, His course of life enters your course of life and they join to become a single course of life. Achieving such a vision allows you to experience your full potential through oneness with God.

"Your Will be Done On Earth as it is in Heaven"

The word "will" from a Greek perspective is *thelēma*, defined as: "one's determination, choice, or desire which has a specific purpose."[39] It is a will announced through an oral decree that comes from a written record or chronicle. This chronicled recording was called a *râtsôn*. In ancient times these writings were inscribed and recorded on tablets called potsherds which were basically broken pieces of pottery where the will of a King was transferred from one region to another by way of a messenger. The tablets of the Ten Commandments were considered *râtsôns* as they were God's written will that was announced orally to others.[40]

The Hebrew term that would have originally been used here for the word "will" is *'ălîylâh ălilâh*. This word is described as "an exploit or act of God that is purposed to affect others." The *Ancient Hebrew Lexicon of the Bible* describes this exploit or act of God as a work that is produced as a result of you being yoked

---

[39] *Strongs* #G2307
[40] AHLB#: 1455-H (j)

to one who already has the eye of knowledge and experience.[41] In the Hebraic and other cultures, when they would train oxen to plow a field, they always yoked an experienced ox with an inexperienced one so that the knowledge of the older ox would influence the inexperienced ox for future work. We are meant to yoke ourselves to the Holy Spirit of Truth who has foreknowledge of our experiences because He has already seen them take place!

King David described this process we he stated, "Thy testimonies also are my delight and my counselors" [Psalms 119:24 KJV]. The word "testimonies" here is the Hebrew word *'êdâh*, which is described as the repeating of an account or what a witness recounts as a result of an event that is seen. This event is further described as, "a meeting that takes place at an appointed time and place that is repeated again and again."[42] The word "counselors" in this passage is the Hebrew word *'êtsâh* which is defined as, "firm advice and purpose that results in uprightness which is a descriptive of one who is righteous or high-minded."[43]

> *"Where no counsel is, the people fall: but in the multitude of counselors there is safety"* [Prov. 11:14 KJV].

The "multitude of counselors" in this passage of scripture is not a reference to a multitude of people who give you advice, as traditionally taught. It is a direct reference to the multitude of counseling sessions that we can experience by positioning ourselves before The Counselor – The Holy Spirit of Truth – on a daily basis.

The "Daily Bread" that Jesus mentioned in His lesson on prayer were daily provisions of counsel meant to fulfill God's preordained will and purposes for your life. If the counsel is accepted and followed through, it keeps you in a righteous (kingdom-minded) position. You are guaranteed success as your life is going in the right direction. In order for God's "will to be

---

[41]   *Strongs* #H5949: AHLB#: 1357
[42]   *Strongs* #5713: AHLB#: 1349-A (N1), (J), (L)
[43]   *Strongs* #6098: AHLB#: 1363-L (V)

done on earth as it is in heaven," you must hear, receive, and then enact what is already witnessed about you in heaven.

> *"Your eyes saw my substance, being yet unformed. And in Your book they all were written, the days fashioned for me, when as yet there were none of them"* [Ps. 139:16 NKJV].

> *"However, when He, the Spirit of truth, has come, He will guide you into all truth; for He will not speak on His own authority, but whatever He hears He will speak; and He will tell you things to come"* [John 16:13 NKJV].

Even Jesus had a book on His life that He was constantly being exposed to, which was His daily bread so that He might fulfill what was prescribed for His life. This spiritually nourished Him and gave Him a consistent preciseness in every deed, thought, and action.

> *"Then I said, 'Behold, I have come in the volume of the book that is written of me to do your will O God'"* [Heb. 10:7 NKJV].

The ultimate outcome of this portion of the prayer lesson should be a life of harmonious movement that includes natural discipline in all areas in order to see God's will being done through us. We need to set our thoughts and actions to the tune of His will so that it may be done "on earth as it is in heaven."

From an Aramaic perspective, the word "will" is *sebyana*, which is defined as "an inner agreement that leads to a manifestation." As the knowledge of God's will is revealed to you, it should eventually go beyond just the mental or idea stage. The goals that you make, derived from what God reveals to you, are designed to synchronize you as a partner with God in ensuring that His will is fulfilled on the earth. This mindset will enable you to stay focused and to rule out any activities that do not originate from the mouth of God. In essence, it is the fulfillment of your functioning as an answer to a problem in this world.

There is something that God needs solved through you. Are you up to the challenge? You can be, if you are faithful to allow His will to become your own.

"Give us this Day our Daily Bread"

The term "daily bread" in this portion of the prayer lesson is very rich in meaning. It is obvious that He wasn't talking about a daily provision of natural bread. It was a figure of speech that Jesus' audience was very familiar with, which was an expression of God's provision of manna that came from Heaven to feed the Israelites while they were in the wilderness [See Ex. 16:15, Ps. 78:23-24].

> *"This is the Bread which came down from Heaven, not as your fathers ate the manna, and died; he who partakes of this Bread shall live forever"* [John 6:58].

The manna from God came in an unprocessed form described as similar to the coriander seed. It had to be processed in order to turn it into a consumable type of corn bread. The Israelites called it manna, which meant "What is this?" It wasn't that they were not familiar with turning other types of grain into edible foods but the "What is this?" had more to with them having to work to process what God gave them [Ex. 16:31].

When God speaks, it comes metaphorically in the form of seed. If we are to produce the potential of what the seeds contain, we must work at it. Today people are still asking, "What is this?" People are looking for answers to deficiencies that they are facing. In response, God provides words that, like seeds, must be planted within you and then processed through His further instructions. It is from these words that true faith should originate [Rom. 10:17]. The words that are spoken to you must go beyond just the belief stage. They must be coupled with works in order to bring about the potential of what is within the seed of His word. Otherwise, the seed remains dead until the works bring it to life [Jam. 2:14-18].

> *"Though He had commanded the clouds from above, and had opened the doors of the heavens; and had rained down manna on them to eat, and He gave them of the grain of the heavens. Man ate the food of the mighty; He sent them meat to the full"* [Ps. 78:23-25].

The word "grain" in this passage is *dâgân*, a natural description of grain such as wheat or corn. Interestingly the *Ancient Hebrew Lexicon* defines and illustrates *dâgân* as "a fish's tail moving back and forth to propel its movement" or "what causes the back and forth moving of the foot" –describing what you do when you are walking.[44] The spiritual concept here is that once you consume and process the seed of God's heaven-sent word, its nutrients provide the energy for movement and the direction for you to walk. Jesus describes Himself as this type of grain when He said, "I am the bread of life," and "For the bread of God is He who comes down from Heaven and gives life to the world" [Jn. 6:33, 48].

To further understand the depth of such statements, let's examine a fuller version of the message that He was conveying:

> *"I am the Living Bread which came down from Heaven. If anyone eats of this Bread, he shall live forever. And truly the bread that I will give is My flesh, which I will give for the life of the world"* [John 6:51].

In this passage, Jesus describes this bread as His flesh. The word "flesh" that Jesus used here is the Hebrew word *basar*, which is commonly defined as "the skin and muscle or the whole of the person." In the *Ancient Hebrew Lexicon of the Bible, basar* also describes "someone who brings good news," which is the definition for the word *gospel*. When Jesus made statements about the need to "eat His flesh," He was literally saying, "eat my

---

44 *Strongs* #1715: AHLB#: 1072-A (m)

gospel." His statement was not a cannibalistic announcement that one must eat His natural flesh.

When Jesus taught His disciples to pray [Matt. 6:11 and Luke 11:3], the statement "Give us this day our daily bread" was a specific reference to receiving a daily diet of words that came from the environment of Heaven. These words therefore become the gospel or good news specifically for our lives, which we are then supposed to "flesh out" through our actions for the benefit of others. Therefore, to receive this "daily bread" is to consume the gospel or spiritual bread (the word of truth) that causes us to experience inner growth so that we may learn how to walk in the will and the Spirit of God in order to "flesh out" and fulfill His purposes. We need to discover and develop a spiritual appetite where the only thing that satisfies us is what comes out of the mouth of God.

> *"But He answered and said, "It is written, 'Man shall not live by bread alone, but by every word that proceeds out of the mouth of God' "* [Matt. 4:4].

Lachma is the Aramaic word for "bread." Within this word are the letters *HMA*, which is the Aramaic root word for wisdom. From an Aramaic perspective, spiritual bread that comes from God is the building material known as knowledge. Once processed, this knowledge produces understanding. When we apply this understanding to our lives, we produce in our lives the structure that God has ordained for us through the wisdom of God.

> *"Through wisdom a house is built, and by understanding it is established; and by knowledge the rooms shall be filled with all precious and pleasant riches. A wise man is strong; yes, a man of knowledge increases strength"* [Prov. 24:3-5].

From the Aramaic perspective, *lachma* causes inner growth or increase that produces the vision of possibilities only accomplished through a building partnership with God.

CHAPTER SUMMARY:

- If we want to experience the fullness of the Kingdom of God, we must accept His ruler-ship as God and counselor of our lives, as well as remain under His power, authority and consciousness.

- We are meant to yoke ourselves to the Holy Spirit of Truth who has foreknowledge of our life's experiences because He has already seen them take place!

- In order for God's "will to be done on earth as it is in heaven," you must hear, receive, and then enact what is already witnessed about you in heaven.

- When God speaks, it comes metaphorically in the form of seed. If we are to produce the potential of what the seeds contain, we must work at it.

- When Jesus taught His disciples to pray, the statement "Give us this day our daily bread" was a specific reference to receiving a daily diet of words that came from Heaven. These words become the gospel for our lives, which we are then supposed to "flesh out" through our actions for the benefit of others.

APPLICATION:

1. A quote from this chapter states, "There is something that God needs solved through you. Are you up to the challenge?" Meditate on those words and take time to record your thoughts and answer to this. If you are not satisfied with your response or your current level of faith, start asking God to change your heart and desires.

2. Spiritual bread that comes from God is the building material known as knowledge, which is meant to be processed to produce understanding. As you apply this understanding to your life, it will become the "structure" God has ordained for your life to be. Mentally draw a picture of the current "structure" of your life. Use your imagination. Then, mentally draw a picture and visualize the structure that you *want* your life to become.

PART TWO:

CONCEPTS OF PRAYER

CHAPTER FIVE:

Our Debts and His Forgiveness

"Forgiveness is the debt that must be paid in order to restore the offender and you back to your original states of being."

– Julio Alvarado Jr.

"Forgive us our Debts as we Forgive our Debtors"

In this portion of the prayer lesson that Jesus taught, we are introduced to one of two primary hindrances not just to prayer but also to our relationship with God and others. The root word for "forgive" used here is *sâlach*, simply defined as "to pardon someone and to lift someone out of debt."[45] The Luke 11:4 version of Jesus' prayer lesson uses the word "sins" and Matthew's account uses the word "debts." It is therefore important that we look at both of these words to get a full understanding of what Jesus meant by this teaching.

---

[45] *Strongs* #5545: AHLB#: 2482 (V)

The Hebrew word for "debts" used here is *nâshâh*. It is described as "an act of deception against someone else that causes oppression."[46] It is what puts negative pressure on a relationship. The root word for "sin" in Luke's account is *châṭâ'*, which has the common definition, "to miss the mark." It is further described as "a cord that binds someone," which restricts them from being free.[47]

To summarize, the phrase "forgive us our debts (or sins)" is to ask God to pardon us of any act that we have committed against Him or others. The phrase "as we forgive our debtors" or "as we forgive everyone who sins against us" carries a sense of prioritization with it. "As we forgive" implies that we first forgive others so that God can duplicate the same type of pardon toward us, otherwise we will remain restricted from experiencing freedom from the trespass, sin or offense that was committed. This was at the heart of Jesus' following words:

> *"For if you forgive other people when they sin against you, your heavenly Father will also forgive you. But if you do not forgive others their sins, your Father will not forgive your sins"* [Matt. 6:14-15].

To not forgive someone is similar to a having a financial debt that accumulates interest the longer you hold it. In essence, you carry a burden that accumulates, causing you to bear a weight that you were never designed to carry. Instead of lifting that burden from yourself and others through God's love – which contains freedom – it creates an environment of imprisonment.

From the Aramaic perspective, forgiveness or a cancellation of debt was considered a gift and one of the highest expressions of love that one could give to someone guilty of an offense – whether intentional or not. From their point of view, forgiveness was considered "restoring individuals back to their original state of being." This has been one of the greatest lessons of

---

[46] *Strongs* #4859: AHLB#: 1320
[47] *Strongs* #2398: AHLB#: 1170-E (V)

forgiveness that I have personally accepted and practiced to set me free from anyone who has hurt me.

To restore the individuals back to their original state is to view them in the state where they were first created in the mind of God before the foundations of the world. In other words, we see them in that place where they were without sin. In their original state of being, they were sane, whole, and perfect – just like God. One who is insane is not in their right mind. A right mind is one that operates from the reference point of the mind of God. In my life, I have had to forgive many people who committed acts against me, either intentionally or unintentionally. Otherwise, I would have remained bound. I have also had to ask others to forgive me for wrongful acts – intentional and unintentional – that kept them bound.

Three of these were men that seriously hurt me. The first of them was my biological father, who fell short in many ways of properly parenting me. My father never told me that he loved me. I tried to reach out to him numerous times in my life in order to try to establish some form of healthy father-and-son relationship, yet with every attempt I walked away disappointed.

The second man was a former pastor whom I loved and looked up to who said some very hurtful things towards my wife and me once we made a decision to leave his church. I cried that evening after our meeting with him and it took me a long time to fully recover.

The third man that I had to learn to forgive was "me." For a long time, I constantly tormented myself with past mistakes that I committed against others and myself. Though I verbally asked God to forgive me, I still wasn't experiencing true freedom from my past mistakes.

In all three of these cases, none of us were in our right mind. My father acted the way he did due to a lack of proper parenting skills and duplicating how he was raised. My former pastor did what he did due to the fact that he also wasn't properly spiritually fathered, which caused him to be underdeveloped as a shepherd in the ministry. This was the reason he responded from a place of immaturity and hurt. I failed to properly forgive myself due to the fact that I chose to mentally rehearse time and again the wrongful acts that I had committed towards others and myself.

The greatest demonstration of forgiveness is found in Jesus' final moments of life on this earth. As He was nailed to a cross for crimes He did not commit and hung there for the sins of mankind, He said, "Father, forgive them, for they do not know what they do" [Luke 23:34a]. Had He not forgiven them for what they did to Him, He would have remained bound by the acts that were committed against Him. It was that act of forgiveness before His last breath that introduced Him to His next breath where He once again found Himself in His original state of being, which is the primary definition of one who is truly redeemed.[48] It is difficult to restore someone to *his or her* original state of being if we are not familiar with *our* original state of being.

When someone isn't truly Kingdom-minded, he or she will not convey behavior that is rooted in "God-love," traditionally known as "agape" love. The original Hebrew word for the God kind of love is *ahav*, defined as "the father revealed."[49] Whenever we fail to forgive like God desires us to and like Jesus did while on this earth, we fail to reveal the core nature of God, which is love.

When someone does me wrong in any way, especially intentionally, what I do to help me completely forgive them is simply declare them temporarily insane. If they were operating in a sane mind according to their original state of being – in the mind, image and likeness of God – they wouldn't have done what they did to me. I consider these offenders "ministers" as they are in a sense training and helping me to produce a "love walk" in life. This helps me to treat them according to who they

---

[48]   AHLB#: 1372

[49]   Seekins, Frank T. *Hebrew Word Pictures: How Does the Hebrew Alphabet Reveal Prophetic Truths?* Phoenix, AZ: Living Word Pictures, 2012.

are *supposed to be* and not who they are today. It helps me to understand them and to cancel any debt of sin or trespasses that they have committed against me.

Taking on this mindset helps me release the burden of carrying an offense that I have no business carrying. It also puts me in a position to pay another type of debt towards them. I now understand that I am designed to carry a debt that I will never pay off – that of continually revealing and sowing the nature of God into their lives. In doing so, I become the primary benefactor. The law to love creates order in my life and helps me understand my original state of being.

"Owe no one anything, except to love one another; for he who loves another has fulfilled the Law" [Rom. 13:8].

"Do not Lead us into Temptation but Deliver us from the Evil One"

In this portion of the prayer lesson that Jesus taught, we are introduced to the second hindrance to not only prayer but also our relationship with God and one another. From a Greek and English perspective, the opening words "and do not lead us into temptation" imply that God somehow tempts us do wrong. This is not the case at all as that would violate the following scripture:

"Let no one being tempted say, I am tempted from God. For God is not tempted by evils, and He tempts no one" [James 1:13].

From a Hebrew and Aramaic perspective, "do not lead us into temptation" means that God cannot tempt you to do wrong or evil because it goes against His position on sin. From the Hebrew and Aramaic perspective, "do not lead us" can be more accurately understood to mean "do not allow us to be tempted." The following verse proves that this is God's desire:

"No temptation has taken you but what is common to man; but God is faithful, who will not allow you to be tempted above what you are able, but with the temptation also will make a way to escape, so that you may be able to bear it" [1 Cor. 10:13].

God will always provide a way of escape, often through His instructions pertaining to that temptation. If we position ourselves to hear His voice, He will always provide the way of escape.

To further understand where the temptation to do wrong or evil originates, the Scriptures point to two primary sources. The first source is of course the Devil himself, who is known as the tempter. Satan literally has no power as long as we know that our true identity is in God and are hearing from God and obeying His instructions [Matt. 4:1-3]. Truth be told, the Devil can be one of the best catalysts for spiritual growth and development.

Satan is a tempter. The word tempter also means tester, a device used to test the functioning of something. The Devil is a device that comes to test the functioning of the Kingdom within you![50] If you fail the test, you don't know who you really are and thus will not know how to function in your true Kingdom identity, an identity that automatically brings an awareness of how to overcome the Devil's tactics. As long as you're functioning in the image and likeness of God, the Devil's tests will fail every time.

When we speak of evil, we must distinguish between spiritual evil – which comes from Satan – and moral evil – which comes from the condition and intention of a person's heart through their self will. The second and most powerful source of temptation is the human mind. Instead of focusing on the Devil as the only source of evil, we must also focus on the primary enemy – the one within ourselves.

---

[50] *Strongs* #5254: AHLB#: 1314-H (V); The topic of the Satan's influence, will be further explored in my next book in this series titled *The Mystery of the Kingdom of God Revealed.*

"Let no one being tempted say, I am tempted from God. For God is not tempted by evils, and He tempts no one. But each one is tempted by his lusts, being drawn away and seduced by them. Then when lust has conceived, it brings forth sin. And sin, when it is fully formed, brings forth death" [Jam. 1:13-15].

In order to understand this more clearly, let's go back to the first biblical accounts mentioning evil:

"And out of the ground the LORD God made every tree grow that is pleasant to the sight and good for food. The tree of life was also in the midst of the garden, and the tree of the knowledge of good and evil" [Gen. 2:9].

The question often asked is, "Why would God plant something that was evil in the garden for Adam and Eve to be tempted?" The answer is in one simple word: choice. They could have chosen to follow the one simple instruction that came from the mouth of God, yet they chose to follow advice that came from the mouth of Satan – described as a serpent, which is a Hebrew metaphor for an enemy [Gen. 3:1-5].

"And the LORD God commanded the man, saying, "Of every tree of the garden you may freely eat; But of the tree of the knowledge of good and evil you shall not eat, for in the day that you eat of it you shall surely die"' [Gen. 2:16-17].

God gave them clear instruction to not eat from the tree yet they chose to do evil by allowing themselves to be led into temptation, thus choosing not to accept the way of escape that God provided for them. Adam and Eve allowed a voice other than God's to pervert what God said. Through that single act, they opened three doorways through which come all forms of sin, disobedience, rebellion, destructive living, spiritual death and impotency. When humans disobey God's instructions for their lives, they face the same result. These three doorways are known *as the lust the flesh, the lust of the eyes and the pride of life* [See 1 Jn. 2:13-17].

This was the demise of Adam and Eve's unhindered relationship with God. They failed to obey the original source of truth and as a result fell to the temptation of the father of lies and worldly influences – the Devil himself:

> *"And when the woman saw that the tree was good for food [lust of the flesh], and that it was pleasing to the eyes [lust of the eyes], and a tree to be desired to make wise [the pride of life], she took of its fruit, and ate. She also gave to her husband with her, and he ate"* [Gen. 3:6].

The keys to understanding what worldly influences are not designed for your life are found in the mouth of God. Only God can renew our minds to help us achieve the ultimate level of God-consciousness and understand the perfect will of God.

> *"And do not be conformed to this world, but be transformed by the renewing of your mind, in order to prove by you what is that good and pleasing and perfect will of God"* [Rom. 12:2].

The tree of the knowledge of good and evil in the garden of Eden is a representation of the spiritual cancer called iniquity, which is what Lucifer (the Devil) was originally guilty of [Ez. 28:15 KJV].[51] Good and evil do not mix, nor can they coexist according to God. Good is defined as "something that functions properly."[52] Evil is defined as "something that is dysfunctional."[53] Evil is anything or anyone that is not functioning according to its original purpose. It is something functioning out of the will of God.

---

[51] This is the topic of my first book in this series titled *The Mystery of Iniquity Revealed.*

[52] *Strongs* #2896: AHLB#: 1186-J (N)

[53] *Strongs* #7451: AHLB#: 1460-A (N)

The Tree of Life in the garden is a representation of truth, which is always good and is free from the perversion of evil. Someone who is functioning in a state of truth has knowledge of what is evil but never makes the choice to ingest it. The tree of life is the breath of God, free of iniquity, which contains the words that come from His mouth. As long as you consume them through spiritual gestation, you will become just like Him. In other words, one cannot eat from both trees.

> *"Then the LORD God said, 'Behold, the man has become like one of Us, to know good and evil. And now, lest he put out his hand and take also of the tree of life, and eat, and live forever'"* [Gen 3:22].

Two important trees grew in the Garden of Eden: the tree of the knowledge of good and evil, which resulted in spiritual death through disconnection with God; and The Tree of Life, which represented God's continual provision through the fruit of His words that lead to eternal life.

Also present in the Garden of Eden were two spiritual fathers. One was the Devil – the "father of lies" [Jn. 8:44]. His mission is to foster you with lies that steal, kill, and destroy your original identity, purpose in life, and relationship with God through perversion [Jn. 10:10]. He will encourage you to eat from the tree of the knowledge of good and evil through his subtle tactic of iniquity.

The other is God – the Father of Truth [Jn. 1:14]. The true Father's mission is to endow you with truth, with knowledge that continually sustains, strengthens and reveals the secrets of the Kingdom that He has placed within you so that you can experience life more abundantly. He will encourage you to eat from The Tree of Life, which will always keep you God conscious.

Spiritually, these two trees still exist. The question that we need to seriously ask ourselves is, "Which tree am I eating from?" Your answer determines who is fathering you.

Jesus' statement in His prayer lesson, "And do not lead us into temptation but deliver us from the evil one," is a principle straight from the Garden of Eden. God's constant provision of instruction and wisdom will show you where the Devil is crouching at the door of your life trying to tempt you to do wrong so that he can "father" you and rule your life [See Gen. 4:7, Prov. 3:6-7, Matt. 26:41, Luke 22:40, 1 Pet. 5:8, 1 Jn. 5:18].

CHAPTER SUMMARY:

- The phrase "as we forgive our debtors" carries a sense of prioritization; we must forgive others so that God can pardon us, otherwise we will remain restricted from experiencing freedom from the trespass, sin or offense.

- Forgiveness is one of the highest expressions of love that we can give to someone guilty of an offense. Forgiveness is restoring an individual back to their original state of being.

- When someone isn't truly Kingdom-minded, they will not convey behavior that is rooted in "God-love," traditionally known as "agape" love.

- One source of temptation is the Devil, who is known as the tempter. The Devil is a device that comes to test the functioning of the Kingdom within you.

- The second and most powerful source of temptation is the human mind.

- All forms of sin, disobedience, rebellion, destructive living, spiritual death and impotence come through three doorways: the lust the flesh, the lust of the eyes and the pride of life.

- Evil is anything or anyone that is not functioning according to its original purpose and thus functioning out of the will of God.

APPLICATION:

1. If forgiveness is one of the highest expressions of love that we can give, is there someone in your life to whom you feel you owe forgiveness? Remember that forgiveness will not only restore individuals back to their original state of being, but it will also restore you to right standing with God.

2. We have a "debt" of love towards others. We are meant to reveal and sow the nature of God into people's lives. If you feel this is not a focus in your life, pray and ask God to change your heart and reveal to you how you can repay this "debt."

CHAPTER SIX:

God's Kingdom

> *"If you have not chosen the Kingdom of God first, it will in the end make no difference what you have chosen instead."*
>
> – William Law

"For Yours is the Kingdom and the Power and the Glory Forever and Ever"

Some scholars familiar with the ancient scriptures question whether the doxology of this line was part of the original prayer that Jesus taught. Those that disagree with its originality believe that this line was added later in order to bring a harmonious ending that would link back to the start of the prayer, since traditionally it was repeated over and over again. For this reason, this last line is not included in some biblical translations.

Matthew's version contains the line but Luke's version does not, yet this is the case of many of the other teachings of Jesus according to the varied recordings of the four books of Matthew, Mark, Luke and John – known as the synoptic Gospels. Combined, these four books give different views of similar events that, once put together, give a synchronized, broader view of the events that took place.

I have chosen to include this line due to the following scripture, since there is no doubt or debate as to whether *this* was a part of the original scriptures. This passage encompasses the full scope of the purpose of The Lord's Prayer and God's desired outcome when we pray it. It also describes how Jesus demonstrated it through His life while on the earth:

> *"All Your works shall praise You, O LORD, and Your people shall bless You. They shall speak of the glory of Your king-dom, and talk of Your power, to make known to the sons of men His mighty acts, and the glorious majesty of His kingdom. Your kingdom is an everlasting kingdom, and Your dominion endures throughout all generations"* [Ps. 145:10-13 NKJV].

We have already defined the Kingdom of God as a domain within each of us who believe in Christ. It is a Kingdom that was appointed to Jesus and has been individually appointed to every human being that is washed by the blood of the Lamb. It is, in essence, a part of our original home deep within us, as we originally came from the realm of the Kingdom of Heaven. This Kingdom functions to introduce a higher consciousness that comes from the mind of God.

The Holy Spirit of Truth is your personal counselor that activates the consulship of God within you by transferring information from the mind of God into your mind. It introduces the thoughts and ways of God that cannot be naturally attained but must be spiritually perceived. When you allow God consulship over your life, you can then access the power of God. This is a power that God shares with you once you have an authentic encounter with Him. He will begin to help you understand your original identity in Him. An example of this is found in the story of Jacob's life and encounter with God, which is filled with deep insights.

The highlights of Jacob's story can be found in Genesis Chapter 25, verses 19-34. Jacob's life began with his mother Rebekah being informed by God that she had two nations within her womb:

"And the LORD said to her: 'Two nations are in your womb, two peoples shall be separated from your body; one people shall be stronger than the other, and the older shall serve the younger'" [Gen. 25:23 NKJV].

The firstborn son always had the birthright – special privileges from the father which included a double portion of the estate as an inheritance. In other words, the favor of the father was always given to the firstborn son as a legal continuation of the family. This prohibited a father from playing favorites among his sons by trying to give the birthright to anyone other than the firstborn [See Deut. 21:15-17]. This is important because the same principle applies today. Every human was first conceived and birthed in the mind of God before the foundations of the world.

"Blessed be the God and Father of our Lord Jesus Christ, who has blessed us with every spiritual blessing in the heavenly places in Christ, just as He chose us in Him before the foundation of the world, that we should be holy and without blame before Him in love, having predestined us to adoption as sons by Jesus Christ to Himself, according to the good pleasure of His will" [Eph. 1:3-5 NKJV].

The mystery of God's will in terms of the inheritance of spiritual blessings for our lives can only be revealed through the mouth of God.

"Having made known to us the mystery of His will, according to His good pleasure which He purposed in Himself." In Him also we have obtained an inheritance, being predestined according to the purpose of Him who works all things according to the counsel of His will" [Eph. 1:9, 11 NKJV].

Another major principle that we must capture from Jacob's encounter with God is not that his name was changed from Jacob to Israel; the important thing is *what these names mean*. The name Jacob means "a heel holder," which is description of what happened at his birth when he grabbed his twin brother Esau's heel [Gen. 25:26]. The significance of this event of Jacob grabbing the heel of his older brother parallels another event when Jacob deceived his brother Esau of his birthright [See Gen. 25: 29-34]. In other words, the grabbing of the heel symbolizes the second born (your natural birth) hindering the walk and birthright of the firstborn (your spiritual origin and birth).

This is a portrait of our natural or physical birth hindering our true spiritual beginning. Only our spiritual beginning gives us access to our birthright in God. We can't experience the power of God until we get access to our "first birth environment," which contains the information that we need to prevail with God. Jesus was naturally born (second birth) on the earth but was spiritually conceived in the mind of God (first birth). This principle applies to us as well.

To further the understanding of Jacob's encounter with God as it relates to our life, we must also understand the words "power" and "prevail" from a root-word perspective in the following passage:

> *"And He said, Your name shall no longer be called Jacob, but Israel; for like a prince you have power with God and with men, and have prevailed"* [Gen. 32:28 NKJV].

The word "power" that is used here is *sarah*. According to the *Ancient Hebrew Lexicon of the Bible*, it describes "what is corrected by making a change in direction through instruction or chastisement." It further illustrates this power as "the turning of the head of the child or student into a particular direction." The result of this is also described as "one who has access to a government that has power through the legislation or body of laws by which they allow themselves to be governed." This is a description of the government or system of the Kingdom that

Jesus frequently talked about during His earthly ministry and that was prophesied about Him [Isa. 9:6-7]. It further describes this power as "one who has authority" and describes this person as "a ruler or king and a lord," which validates the term "Lord of lords and King of kings" [Rev. 19:16].[54]

In other words, you don't experience the power of God unless you allow your life to be pointed in a specific direction by receiving words of instruction from the King of Kings that become the laws for your life. Your obedience to these "laws" from the mouth of God will position you to a place of authority, enabling you to experience the power of God as a son (or daughter), a king and a lord.

The word "prevailed" in Jacob's encounter with God is the Hebrew word *yakol*. It describes one who has truly prevailed through three unique perspectives. First, it describes one who has prevailed with God as "a person who is a vessel who is now complete, perfect, whole and full of content." Second, it describes this person as a bride (the bride: you) that is added to a man (the Bridegroom: Jesus) in order for the bridegroom to be complete. Third, it describes someone who has prevailed with God as a vessel or whole human that functions as "a god or king" because they are a container full of "water" – a metaphor for "the spoken word of God." This "vessel" is designed to provide others with what they need to be whole or complete![55] This is what Jesus was describing when He said:

> *"He who believes in Me, as the Scripture has said, out of his heart will flow rivers of living water. But this He spoke concerning the Spirit, whom those believing in Him would receive; for the Holy Spirit was not yet given, because Jesus was not yet glorified"* [Jn. 7:38-39].

When someone is in a covenant with God, they partner with Him to live out their preordained purpose for the benefit of

---

[54] *Strongs* #8280: AHLB#: 1342-H (V), A(M,H)
[55] *Strongs* #3201: AHLB#: 1242-B, H, J, L

others. In doing so, they become an answer to a world problem. This is what Jesus did. Fundamentally, this is the process that Paul describes in the following scripture:

"And we know that all things work together for good to those who love God, to those who are the called according to His purpose. For whom He foreknew, He also predestined to be conformed to the image of His Son, that He might be the firstborn among many brethren. Moreover whom He predestined, these He also called; whom He called, these He also justified; and whom He justified, these He also glorified" [Rom. 8:28-30].

According to this passage, we must love God according to the standard that Jesus set forth in the following key passage: "And you shall love the Lord your God with all your heart, and with all your soul, and with all your mind, and with all your strength. This is the first commandment" [Mk. 12:30]. This is a wholehearted, lifelong commitment where you are clearly hearing from God, which results in an alliance and covenant where you and God become one.

Second, the word "called" in this passage is the Hebrew word *miqrâ*. It is defined as "an individual that is called out for a special purpose." It describes this process as "an encounter or meeting where a scroll or document is read" to you![56] This document is the book that God has already written about you that is read to you daily in segments!

The information that is read to you causes you to be fully informed so that you can function in the likeness and image of His Son. When God speaks to you according to this level, He informs you how you are equipped to fulfill the purposes that He has established. This results in you becoming glorified. The Hebrew word used here for "glorified" is *kâbêd*, which is defined as, "someone that is heavy in the weight of wealth, abundance,

---

Strongs #4744: AHLB#: 1434-E

importance and respect."[57] In essence, you have full access to the spiritual blessings that can only be found in heavenly places [Eph. 1:3].

Don't Speak It; Live It

Learning The Lord's Prayer from a root-word perspective introduced me to a greater understanding of its purpose. It has introduced me to the greatest prayer teacher in existence: The Holy Spirit of Truth. It has introduced me to my original source of existence, my true identity in Christ, my preordained purpose, the vision that God has for my life, and the mission He is calling me to live out every day. As I take time to not only pray, but also to live this prayer, I receive instructions from God that help me maximize my purpose and fulfill my mission in life in order that I may be an answer to a world problem. In other words, this prayer opens my heart and life to the reason why God created me.

Jesus never verbalized this prayer; He *lived* the prayer every day of His earthly existence, and this is what we are meant to do as well. You see no one else in scripture praying the prayer either because they understood what He said from a root-word and cultural standpoint. Jesus' disciples lived their lives according to the prayer He taught by listening and receiving God's truth for their lives and enacting it day by day. This is what enabled them to change the world and establish the original intent of Christianity throughout the earth. It is what will enable us also to change the world around us and establish God's Kingdom "on earth as it is in heaven."

---

[57] *Strongs* #3513: AHLB#: 2246 (V)

CHAPTER SUMMARY:

- The mystery of God's will and your true inheritance of spiritual blessings can only be revealed from the mouth of God.

- Only our spiritual beginning gives us access to our birthright in God. We can't experience the power of God until we get access to our "first-birth" environment.

- Living our lives according to the prayer Jesus taught by listening and receiving God's truth and enacting it day by day will enable us also to change the world around us and establish God's Kingdom "on earth as it is in heaven."

The Lord's Prayer that Jesus taught is...

- A call to "pray without ceasing" (1 Thess. 5:18).

- A learning environment that starts in the morning and is demonstrated throughout the day.

- A level of prayer that requires complete God-consciousness.

- Where God becomes your primary prayer partner.

- Not something that was intended to be quoted, but is rather meant to be the framework and structure of your very life.

- A prayer that introduces you to your origin of existence and the reason why God created you.

APPLICATION:

1. When we enter a covenant with God, we can partner with Him to live out our preordained purpose for the benefit of others. Have you ever considered that your life is meant to be an answer to a problem in this world? Take time to consider your personal interests, skills and talents, and how God might want to use them to make a difference in the world today.

2. Learning to truly understand The Lord's Prayer introduces us to our original source of existence, our true identity in Christ, our preordained purpose, and the mission God is calling us to live out every day. Determine that this prayer will not be a vain repetition in your life, but a prayer framework that leads you to understanding and following God's specific plan for your life.

CHAPTER SEVEN:

The Parable of the Sower – A Parable of Prayer

> *"Do you not understand this parable? How then will you understand all the parables?"*
> – Jesus Christ

We discern the spiritual depth of godly things more through the influence of the Holy Spirit than from the teachings of others. Parables that have a spiritual meaning or application require more than intellectual knowledge. They require spiritual intelligence that can only come from the Holy Spirit of Truth.

The primary purpose of the "Parable of the Sower" is to reveal the mysteries or secrets of the Kingdom of God. This disqualifies any human from being the revealer of these secrets, since these mysteries originate in God. His Holy Spirit of Truth is the only one authorized to reveal such information regarding your personal life. Understanding this key parable unlocks the understanding to all other parables, including the "parable" of life!

One of the primary functions of parables – a reason unknown to many – is that they help us *un*learn one thing in order to learn something else. In a sense, the parables that Jesus taught are purposed to mend or untangle something that is out of order within us in order to restore us to our original condition or state of being. Jesus taught in parables because they challenge us to seek beyond traditional thinking in order to grasp the depth of their spiritual meanings. The foundational parable that brings this reality to life is The Parable of the Sower.

The Parable of the Sower is also known as "The Seed and the Sower" and "The Parable of The Four Soils." It can be found in Matthew 13:1-23, Mark 4: 1-20 and Luke 8:4-15. It is the most important parable that Jesus taught. According to Jesus' statement, understanding all of the other parables hinged on understanding The Parable of The Sower:

> *"And He said to them, "Do you not understand this parable? How then will you understand all the parables?"* [Mk. 4:13]

Traditionally, we are taught that this parable applies when someone is being taught the Word of God such as in a church service, Bible study, discipleship course, or class setting. An in-depth study of The Parable of The Sower reveals that this parable is actually purposed to reveal an environment where God Himself is speaking or teaching.

Parables are comparison lessons. They are designed to engage not just our human intellect but also our spiritual intelligence because they require the spirit of man to interact with the Spirit of God. Parables are mysteries that reveal the secrets of life. They synchronize you with the mind of God. Similar to a blue tooth device that pairs with a phone – making them one – when you pair yourself with God, you become Pair-able with God. The Kingdom of Heaven, where God resides, and the Kingdom of God that is within you now become one in communication capabilities!

The Hebrew word for "parable" is *mâshal*, which is traditionally defined as, "a byword or comparison of things." A deeper look into *mâshal* from an ancient Hebrew perspective reveals a much deeper meaning. Key words that describe the purpose for *mâshal* (parable) are "governor, dominion, power, reign and rule." From this perspective, this parable introduces you to the ability to hear the "governor" for your life – a reference to the Holy Spirit.[58] The purpose of the seed – a metaphor for the spoken word of God in this parable – is to show you who is meant to teach and rule your life's purpose (God).

At its core, the seed – the spoken word of God – gives you the details as to why you were created; it reveals to you how you are meant to become an answer to a problem that God has predestined for you to partner with Him to solve. Understanding parables also enables you to know the dominion that you are to have in life.

Jesus exemplified the soil of "good ground." This was the life He lived while on earth. We see the result of the seed of God's Spoken Word falling on good ground in Jesus' own life through the following statement that He made:

> *"I can do nothing of My own self. As I hear, I judge, and My judgment is just, because I do not seek My own will, but the will of the Father who has sent Me. If I bear witness of Myself, My witness is not true. There is another who bears witness of Me, and I know that the witness which He witnesses of Me is true"* [Jn. 5:30-32].

Discovering what is hidden within the parable of The Sower can become the catalyst to the greatest strength for your life. The opposite is also true; failure to discover what is hidden may lead to a life of unnecessary experimentation, frustration and hopelessness.

Jesus' disciples questioned Him as to what this parable of The Sower meant and why He taught in parables. The disciples, like many people today, would have preferred simple, plain and practical answers. They were confused as to why Jesus would use this style to teach. His answer to them came in a statement

---

[58]   *Strongs* #4912: AHLB#: 2359

that unlocks the mystery of true spiritual growth, development, and awareness:

> *"And when he was alone, they that were about him with the twelve asked of him the parable. And he said unto them, Unto you it is given to know the mystery of the kingdom of God: but unto them that are without, all these things are done in parables: That seeing they may see, and not perceive; and hearing they may hear, and not understand; lest at any time they should be converted, and their sins should be forgiven them"* [Mk. 4:10-12 KJV].

Jesus' statement was not intended to mean that only the disciples were entitled to such exclusive information. Jesus was training the disciples on how to use their inner ears and their inner eyes, which are the senses of the spirit. Jesus validated this key principle when He said, "That seeing they may see, and not perceive; and hearing they may hear, and not understand" [Mk. 4:12]. True spiritual perception and understanding can only be attained as we use our inner senses of hearing and seeing.

From a biblical perspective the Greek word for mystery is *mustērion*. The Hebrew word for mystery is *raz*.[59] Both words are simply defined as "a secret," yet not just any secret. They were described as secrets revealed to someone who goes through a process of initiation. This process of initiation was exposure to the Holy Spirit of Truth. The revelation of these secrets is referred to as "initiated knowledge." This is the reason Jesus made the conditional statement: "Unto you it is given to know the mystery of the kingdom of God: but unto them that are without, all these things are done in parables." The disciples were constantly exposed to the Spirit of God through Jesus, yet many others who heard Him speak did not have this same exposure. Their knowledge or spiritual intelligence could only be acquired through personal experiences with God, not through ordinary educational processes. The mysteries of God can only be revealed through the Holy Spirit.

---

[59] *Strongs* #7328: AHLB#: 1444-A (N)

Learning about the Kingdom from human teachers will not enable you to learn about the *secrets* of the Kingdom. These are secrets that can only be revealed to you by God Himself through His Holy Spirit of Truth.

Parables are what I call "seek material" and "spirit trainers" that give insight to our inner eyes and ears. Parables attach spiritual eyes and ears to what God really wants to tell and show us. They push us to seek from His mouth those things that God has hidden. They are purposed to reveal a depth of knowledge and understanding that doesn't come from an earthly resource. They provide us with details that help us fulfill the mandate to "Seek first the Kingdom of God" [Matt. 6:33].

The key word "know" in Jesus' vital statement of "Unto you it is given to *know* the mystery of the kingdom of God" begins to unlock the parable's meaning, which is to reveal the mystery of the Kingdom within you.

The Hebrew word used here for "know" is *yada*. It is the root word for "knowledge" and is described as, "knowledge that can only be disbursed and perceived through an intimate experience and relationship." It is also defined as, "an appointment or a meeting with a witness that is repeated over and over again."[60] The witness in this case is God Himself! According to ancient Hebrew, this experience is called "the door of the eye." It is the intimate and personalized knowledge that God has already witnessed for your life. It is also described as "knowledge that is gained by visual observation."[61]

This is the type of knowledge that Noah received once "Noah found grace in the eyes of the Lord" [Gen. 6:8]. Noah received knowledge and instructions that came from the mouth of God to build an Ark, which had already been seen by God before it was built. This ark saved Noah and his families' lives from the flood that cleansed the earth of evil. Grace is the portal for truth. Without grace, parables can't be revealed. Grace is actually a

---

[60] *Strongs* #3259: AHLB#: 1349-L (V)
[61] *Strongs* #3045: AHLB#: 1085-L (V)

manifestation of the voice of God. It expresses the favor of God for your life in that it introduces to you the good ground He would have you experience. The instructions that God disburses to you relay what He has predestined for you to do. As you follow and obey, the fruit gets multiplied so that others can benefit from your life!

From a Hebraic perspective, "to know" is not a reference to intellectual knowledge acquired through studies; it is rather to experience knowledge through the process of having an intimate relationship with God. This results in God sharing the secrets of His ideas with you, and the things that He has already seen for your life. From the ancient Hebraic perspective, this is what they call "intelligence." I call it "spiritual intelligence." True spiritual intelligence is based on facts that originate from the mind of the Author of life.

Let's now examine some of the key points of this pivotal parable.

"And he taught them many things by parables, and said unto them in his doctrine" [Mk. 4:2 KJV].

Jesus taught no "original" material. All of His teachings came from God:

"Jesus answered them, and said, My doctrine is not mine, but His that sent me. If any man will do his will, he shall know of the doctrine, whether it be of God, or whether I speak of myself" [Jn. 7:16-17 KJV].

Let's examine the origin of the word "doctrine" to understand why Jesus said this about His doctrine.

"Give ear, O ye heavens, and I will speak; and hear, O earth, the words of my mouth. My doctrine shall drop as the rain, my speech shall distil as the dew, as the small rain upon the tender herb, and as the showers upon the grass" [Deut. 32:1-2 KJV].

The previous passage is the first mention of the word "doctrine." In Hebrew, it is the word *leqach*. It is described as "a learning that comes from the speech of the one teaching."[62] Jesus implied that His learning and teaching came from hearing the speech of God. Though Jesus would have gone through approximately 25 years of being trained by Rabbis through the Jewish education system, what He taught did not come from their doctrines. He even warned many to beware of the doctrine of the religious leaders of His day [Matt. 16:12].

This is the reason why Jesus made the pivotal comment in The Parable of the Sower: "so that seeing they may see, and not perceive and hearing they may hear, and not understand" [Matt. 13:14, Mk. 4:12, Lk. 8:10]. It wasn't that His audience was deaf or blind; they heard and saw His teachings. The point that Jesus was making was that this *type* of learning couldn't be received through our physical eyes and ears. This type of learning must come from the ability to be able to perceive the Master Teacher – God Himself – through the voice of His Spirit.

"For this people's heart is waxed gross, and their ears are dull of hearing, and their eyes they have closed; lest at any time they should see with their eyes, and hear with their ears, and should understand with their heart, and should be converted, and I should heal them" [Matt. 13:15].

The term "waxed gross" describes those who have a hardened heart. It is a condition that desensitizes one's ability to accurately discern God's presence and hear God's voice in their lives. To be waxed gross is also a metaphoric expression that means "to make stupid or to render the soul dull or callous." A hardened heart is known as *avah* in Hebrew. *Avah* is one of the key words describing "iniquity." It is defined as "one who is perverted or twisted in their actions," which comes as a result of not having the right frame of mind.[63]

---

[62] *Strongs* #3948: AHLB#: 2319 (N)
[63] *Strongs* #5753: AHLB#: 1511-J (V)

Iniquity renders us unable to be sensitive to the presence and voice of God. It is what Lucifer – whom we now know as the devil – was originally guilty of and what he uses today to desensitize the minds of people without them even knowing it.[64] Iniquity is the primary reason why many people today fail to either discover or fully develop the inner ears and eyes of the spirit man, resulting in dull hearing and spiritual blindness.

A crucial detail about this key parable is that the Sower is sowing *His* seed, not seed that belongs to another [Lk. 8:5]. This seed is the doctrine (learning or teaching) that comes from God [Mk. 4:2]. The seed is the Spoken Word of God [Lk. 8:11]. According to Matthew's account, this word is specifically "the word of the Kingdom" [Matt. 13:19]. In all three accounts of this parable, the word "Word" is the Greek word *Logos*. *Logos* is *Sêpher Siphrâh* in Hebrew. It is the narrative account for your life that is based off the book of your life that God has authored. When Jesus stated, "The sower sows the word" [Mk. 4:14], this specific "word" is the voice of God delivering information to you that comes from your personal Kingdom book. This is the book of your life that reveals the Counsel of God or Kingdom that is within you [Lk. 17:21], which you are supposed to flesh out and live as a true story.[65]

The mysteries are the secrets that God established for your life from before the foundations of the world:

"That it might be fulfilled which was spoken by the prophet, saying, I will open my mouth in parables; I will utter things which have been kept secret from the foundation of the world" [Matt. 13:35].

Let's now examine the four types of soil and Jesus' interpretation of each one, seeing how they relate to prayer from a hearing perspective.

---

[64] The vital topic is covered in my first book in this series titled *The Mystery of Iniquity Revealed*.

[65] This concept will be explored further in the next chapter.

The Wayside:

"A sower went out to sow his seed: and as he sowed, some fell by the way side; and it was trodden down, and the fowls of the air devoured it" [Lk. 8:5 KJV]. *[See also Matt. 13:4, Mk. 4:4.]*

JESUS' INTERPRETATION:

"And these are those by the wayside, where the Word is sown. And when they hear, Satan comes immediately and takes away the Word that was sown in their hearts" [Mk. 4:15]. *[See also Matt. 13:19, Lk. 8:12.]*

Though many view the good soil as the most important soil, special attention needs to be given to the significance of the soil that fell by the wayside. This is the seed that Satan makes a priority to immediately attack. His entire focus is to make sure that what has been sown in you does not grow. He uses his covert tactic of iniquity to accomplish this.

The phrase "trodden down" is crucial in understanding the wayside soil. From a Greek perspective it means to "reject with disdain."[66] According to *Thayer's Definition of Greek Words* it means "to treat with rudeness and insult, to spurn and treat with insulting neglect."

Remember that this seed is specifically "the word of the Kingdom," which Jesus stated is already planted inside of you. To "trod down" means to step on something and consider it worthless. When you reject it and consider it worthless, you are essentially giving Satan permission to steal its true meaning and application away from you because you consider it of no value.

---

[66] *Strongs* G2662

FROM A HEARING PERSPECTIVE:

Many people are not looking to receive information *from* God in prayer. A primary reason for this is that few people know that they *can* receive this information and guidance directly from God through prayer. Instead of quieting themselves to listen to the Father, they use prayer as a tool or medium to tell God what they need. This leads to one of the biggest problems on how prayer is taught. Many teach on *what to say* when we pray instead of teaching on *how to hear* and *what type of information we should hearing about* when we pray. Sadly, this causes us to reject, from the very beginning, what God wants to tell us because we don't even stop to listen to Him. We can rectify this fundamental problem by coming to understand the original purpose for prayer: *to hear from God in order to fulfill the purpose of why He created us.*

In my opinion, the greatest lesson that all humanity needs to learn is to *hear the voice of God.*

The Stony Ground:

"And some fell upon a rock; and as soon as it was sprung up, it withered away, because it lacked moisture" [Lk. 8:6 KJV]. *[See also Matt. 13:5, Mk. 4:5.]*

The word "moisture" from an English and Greek perspective is defined simply as "dampness." From a Hebrew perspective, however, it holds a much deeper meaning. First of all it is related to the Hebrew word *yuval*, which is defined as "a stream."[67] Yet it is also defined as the Hebrew word *shemets*, defined as "a whisper."[68] This describes what the Bible refers to as "a still, small voice," found in First Kings 19:12. It is also described as "a stream of water that emits a sound." In other words, this

---

[67] *Strongs* #3105: AHLB#: 1035-L (o)
[68] *Strongs* #8102: AHLB#: 2852 (N)

"moisture" is the sound of God's voice; it is a whisper that should be constantly flowing like a river, otherwise the seed of the word will not take root within you. This is what Jesus was alluding to when He made the statement, "out of your belly shall flow rivers of living water" [Jn. 4:10, 7:38]. It is a metaphor for the voice of God speaking to you.

JESUS' INTERPRETATION:

"And these are those likewise being sown on stony places; who, when they hear the Word, immediately receive it with gladness. But they have no root in themselves, but are temporary. Afterward when affliction or persecution arises for the Word's sake, they are immediately offended" [Mk. 4:16-17]. *[See also Matt. 13:20-21, Lk. 8:13.]*

Understanding the term to "have no root in themselves" unlocks what Jesus was conveying in this statement. The phrase describes those who have no true sense of their spiritual origin and as a result make themselves barren. The word "root" is the Hebrew word *kên*. Someone who has this root "has a firmness in any situation." *Kên* is illustrated in the agricultural expression of "an opening of a seed."[69] In other words, since you originally came out of the seed of God, the root system causes you to grow into what the Bible calls "a tree of righteousness" [Isa. 61:3]. Your root system will build a base that will enable you to accurately deal with anything that tries to come against you.

FROM A HEARING PERSPECTIVE:

The phrase "but are temporary" describes one who is spiritually immature or underdeveloped. They have perhaps heard the voice of God but haven't acquainted themselves with the consistent practice of learning to hear the voice of God.

---

[69] *Strongs* #3653: AHLB#: 1244-A (N)

From an Aramaic perspective, the seed that falls on stony or rocky ground illustrates a couple of other interesting perspectives. The word "rock" is translated as *sua*.[70] It is defined as a verb or action that "causes a stop up or obstructs something." From the Aramaic perspective, metaphorically this rock is "what causes the closing of the senses of the heart" which are the inner eyes and ears of your spirit.

The Thorns:

"And another fell among the thorns, and the thorns grew up and choked it, and it yielded no fruit" [Mk. 4:7]. *[See also Matt. 13:7, Lk. 8:6.]*

JESUS' INTERPRETATION:

"Now the ones that fell among thorns are those who, when they have heard, go out and are choked with cares, riches, and pleasures of life, and bring no fruit to maturity" [Lk. 8:14]. *[See also Mk. 4:18-19, Matt. 13:22.]*

Thorns represent anything that hinders our ability to hear the voice of God. Jesus described these hindrances in three specific categories: cares, riches, and pleasures of life. Examining many of the prayer requests today, we find that they fall under one or more of these categories.

FROM A HEARING PERSPECTIVE:

Cares are defined as burdens or distractions.[71] They describe anything that will cause you to be distracted from hearing

---

[70] All Aramaic references are sourced from: Payne, Smith R., and Smith J. Payne. *A Compendious Syriac Dictionary: Founded upon the Thesaurus Syriacus of R. Payne Smith*. Winona Lake, IN: Eisenbrauns, 1998.

[71] *Strongs* #3052: AHLB#: 1094-N

the voice of God. They solicit your attention, resulting in you becoming defocused. These "cares" become the focal point of your prayers. Examples of these are: financial burdens, the day's agenda, your physical tiredness, or even legitimate needs that you may have. You may be saying, "But I am supposed to ask God for what I need from Him." Or you may be wondering, "Didn't Jesus say that I can ask for anything in His name?"[72] Let's carefully examine Jesus' words in the following scripture:

> *"Therefore do not worry, saying, 'What shall we eat?' or 'What shall we drink?' or 'What shall we wear?' For after all these things the Gentiles seek. For your heavenly Father knows that you need all these things. But seek first the kingdom of God and His righteousness, and all these things shall be added to you"* [Matt. 6:31-33].

A Gentile is a foreigner. Today this describes someone who doesn't know his or her Godly origin. When we find ourselves asking for these types of things in prayer, we fail to understand that since we came out of God, He has to provide for us as long as we are truly seeking first the Kingdom God and His righteousness. To seek first the Kingdom of God and His righteousness is literally the primary purpose for prayer.

RICHES:

In this passage, riches are described as "external possessions." It represents "the idea of continually looking toward something of interest."[73] The greatest thing that should prosper in our lives is the Kingdom of God within us, which is an internal possession that culminates in fulfillment of the purpose for which you were created.

Seeking riches is focusing more on prospering financially or materially than on the Kingdom of God. Many of today's teachings on prosperity focus more on prospering externally as

---

[72] We will explore this topic in a subsequent chapter.
[73] *Strongs* #1952: AHLB#: 1106-J (N)

opposed to prospering internally through discovering the riches of the Kingdom of God and finding our preordained purpose. Jesus stated, "For where your treasure is, there will your heart be also" [Matt. 6:21]. Praying for riches or prosperity exposes ignorance as to the true purpose of prayer and ultimately the true purpose of life.

Many of these types of prayers cater to the mindset of covetousness: "The more possessions I have, the more I am blessed by God." I have seen prayer taught in this way, using scripture to portray God as some type of Santa Clause or Genie in that, "If I've been good or if I rub you the right way or quote the right scriptures, you have to bless me." Examples of this would be praying for finances or business success. Jesus said that it is harder for a rich man to enter the Kingdom of heaven than for a camel to enter the eye of a needle. The story of the Rich Young Ruler comes to mind in conveying this point [Matt. 19:24, Mk. 10:17-27]. Not everyone is preordained to be rich with earthly possessions or finances, but each of us is preordained to seek first the Kingdom of God. As we do so, God will add to our lives those things that we truly need.

PLEASURES OF THIS LIFE:

The word "pleasures" that is used here is described as "what keeps someone from being able to distinguish between thoughts." It is also defined as "what is meditated on." In other words, it is what preoccupies the mind.[74] These types of prayer requests keep us from experiencing the thoughts and ways of God for our lives.

> *"For as the heavens are higher than the earth, so are My ways higher than your ways, and My thoughts than your thoughts. So shall My Word be, which goes out of My mouth; it shall not return to Me void, but it shall accomplish what I please, and it shall certainly do what I sent it to do"* [Isa. 55:9, 11].

---

[74] *Strongs* #2940: AHLB#: 2236; *Strongs* #7879: AHLB#: 1330-M (N)

"For I know the thoughts that I think toward you, says the LORD, thoughts of peace and not of evil, to give you a future and a hope" [Jer. 29:11].

Examples of these prayers are "bless me club" prayers, which are any type of prayer that ask for things focused solely on our earthly existence and that make our lives comfortable. These types of prayers and this manner of thinking are a primary reason that many prayer requests go unanswered. They are prayer requests that miss the mark of God's intended will for your life. "You ask and do not receive, because you ask amiss, that you may spend it on your pleasures" [Jam. 4:3].

Knowing the will of God for your life is the key to having your prayers answered. This knowledge can only come from His mouth. Prayers that align with the will of God for our lives are guaranteed to be answered.

"Now this is the confidence that we have in Him, that if we ask anything according to His will, He hears us. And if we know that He hears us, whatever we ask, we know that we have the petitions that we have asked of Him" [1 Jn. 5:14-15].

THE GOOD GROUND:

"But other seed fell on good ground and yielded a crop that sprang up, increased and produced: some thirtyfold, some sixty, and some a hundred" [Mk. 4:8]. *[See also Matt. 13:8, Lk. 8:8.]*

JESUS' INTERPRETATION:

"But he who received seed on the good ground is he who hears the word and understands it, who indeed bears fruit and produces: some a hundredfold, some sixty, some thirty" [Matt. 13:23]. *[See also Mk. 4:20, Lk. 8:8.]*

In a natural agricultural environment, good ground is soil absent of any substance or predators that would hinder the full growth potential of the seed. It is also rich in nutrients and has access to clean oxygen, consistent rainfall and sunlight to aide in the growth process. In other words, the lower environment – the soil – has to be in a healthy condition in order for the soil to receive the nutrients that come from the upper environment. All of these natural elements create good ground, the environment needed for unhindered growth and maximization of the seed's potential.

In essence, the air, rain, and sun speak to the ground and seed, saying, "As long as you have the right conditions, I'm going to give you what you need to build a healthy root system in order to fully produce what is inside of you." In a spiritual environment, these same principles apply.

The key to understanding the original lesson and intention of this monumental parable is found in Jesus' words, "good ground." From an Aramaic perspective, the word "good" is the word *taba*. It is defined as "what is ripe, mature and fit for a particular purpose." Its root understanding points to something that maintains its integrity and health by an inner growth that is in harmony with what surrounds it: the identity and the spoken word of God.

From a Greek perspective, the word "good" used here is *kalos*, defined as "what is excellent, genuine, approved and worthy."[75] From a Hebrew perspective, the word "good" is connected to the two key words, *kavod* and *Shêm. Kavod* is defined as, "someone that is heavy in honor, wealth, abundance, importance or respect."[76] As mentioned in a previous chapter, *Shêm* is the Hebrew word for "Name" as it relates to "Father" as the divine being of God. *Strong's Concordance* defines *Shêm* as "authority and character." *The Ancient Hebrew Lexicon of the Bible* describes Name or *Shêm* as it pertains to God the Father as

---

[75] *Strong's* #G2570; *Thayer Greek Definitions Dictionary*
[76] *Strongs* #3519: AHLB#: 2246 (c)

breath or wind – descriptions of the Spirit of God that represent and inspire His authority and character.[77]

This parable tells us that good ground is "Father ground." It is full of what He is because everything around it is conducive and open to His authority, character and inspiration. As a result of falling on this "good ground," you will produce the Kingdom assignment that He desires for you to manifest in your life. If you function in the identity and character of God by hearing and understanding the spoken words of God, you are growing in this good ground.

This is the core reason that this parable is about hearing the voice of God through prayer rather than the traditional teachings on this parable. A point that is worthy to note is that these four grounds or conditions of people's prayer lives got progressively better as the parable went on.

The first three had obstacles of distraction that hinder our prayer life. The fourth and most desirable prayer life is the one where your mind is constantly renewed with the refreshing wind of God's spoken word that will ultimately lead to knowledge of the perfect will of God for your life. This knowledge will enable you to ultimately fulfill the mandate from Jesus: "Therefore be perfect, even as your Father in Heaven is perfect" [Matt. 5:48].

> *"I beseech you therefore, brethren, by the mercies of God, that you present your bodies a living sacrifice, holy, accept-able to God, which is your reasonable service. And do not be conformed to this world, but be transformed by the renewing of your mind, that you may prove what is that good and acceptable and perfect will of God"* [Rom. 12:1-2].

The three results of the good ground are bearing fruit – "thirty, sixty and a hundred fold" – which is in sync with the good, acceptable and perfect will of God. Ultimately, the spoken word of God reveals the Kingdom assignment that is within you.

---

[77] *Strongs* #8034: AHLB#: 1473-A (N)

Once this word is deployed into the world, you hit the ultimate goal and perfect will of God for your life. [Rom. 12:1-2]

One of the greatest struggles that I have encountered in my spiritual development was that I had to unlearn some of the things that I was taught through traditional Christianity, including practices on prayer. I had put aside my preconceptions and practices and simply admit to myself that there was more to learn on this vital topic. When we think that we have found what we need in the area of learning to pray and hear the voice of God, we stop looking. Though some of these prior lessons, beliefs, and practices helped me to a certain degree; they still left my life in a mode similar to the first three "grounds" found in this parable. Previously in this chapter we explored that a heart that is "waxed gross" is a heart unable to discern God's presence or hear His voice:

> *"For this people's heart is waxed gross, and their ears are dull of hearing, and their eyes they have closed; lest at any time they should see with their eyes, and hear with their ears, and should understand with their heart, and should be converted, and I should heal them"* [Matt. 13:15 KJV].

The word "converted" in this passage, from a Greek perspective, means to "revert back to something." It comes from the two Hebrew words *shûb* and *shâma*.[78] *Shûb* is defined as "to turn back or restore." *Shâma* is defined as "to hear intelligently" and "a careful hearing of someone or something as well as responding appropriately in obedience or action."[79] It is described as an ability to perceive and discern the distinct sound and presence of God.

The foundational purpose Jesus had in teaching this parable was to express the most important restorative healing that mankind is in need of today. Jesus wants to restore us back to the

---

[78] *Strongs* #7725: AHLB#: 1462-J (V)
[79] *Strongs* #8085: AHLB#: 2851 (V)

place where we can hear the voice of God and respond to what we hear so that life no longer seems like a parable.

> *"I have spoken these things to you in parables, but the time is coming when I shall no more speak to you in parables, but I will show you plainly of the Father"* [Jn. 16:25].

A serious believer is a continual seeker at heart. His or her pursuit of the voice of God is a lifelong journey where the only thing that suffices is hearing the voice of God through His Holy Spirit of Truth. The result of this type of pursuit is paramount. It brings us to understand our God-ordained purpose and sets us on the path to fulfilling our destiny in Him.

CHAPTER SUMMARY:

- The "seed" – the spoken word of God – gives you the details as to why you were created; it reveals how you are meant to become an answer to a problem that God has predestined for you to partner with Him to solve.

- Jesus exemplified the soil of "good ground." This was the life He lived while on earth.

- True spiritual perception and understanding can only be attained as we use our inner senses of hearing and seeing.

- Iniquity renders us unable to be sensitive to the presence and voice of God.

- Many people are not looking to receive information *from* God in prayer. They use prayer as a tool or medium to tell God what they need.

- The greatest lesson that all humanity needs to learn is to *hear the voice of God.*

- To seek first the Kingdom of God and His righteousness is literally the primary purpose for prayer.

- Knowing the will of God for your life is the key to having your prayers answered.

- If you function in the identity and character of God by hearing and understanding His spoken words, you are growing in "good ground."

- A serious believer is a continual seeker at heart. The only thing that satisfies them is hearing the voice of God through His Holy Spirit of Truth.

APPLICATION:

1. Our optimum knowledge and spiritual intelligence can only be acquired through experiences with God, not through ordinary educational processes. Do you depend on your physical and mental education when making decisions, or do you look to God for spiritual intelligence and wisdom that can only come from Him?

2. A quote in this chapter states, "One of the greatest struggles that I have encountered in my spiritual development was that I had to unlearn some of the things that I was taught through traditional Christianity, including practices on prayer." Write down some things you might need to "unlearn" in order to learn what God has for you.

3. When we think we have found what we need in the area of learning to pray and hear the voice of God, we stop looking. Are you still looking? Do you believe that you still have things to learn about hearing God's voice?

CHAPTER EIGHT:

The *Logos* Book for Your Life

> "A failure to discover the book that God has authored for your life is a failure to discover the story of your life as it should be."
> – Julio Alvarado Jr.

One of the most impactful discoveries I have ever made is the revelation that God has authored a book on my life. This is a concept I was unaware of even though I had been a born-again Christian for over 20 years. Though I was taught that God knows everything about me, including the number of hairs on my head, no one ever taught me that God had written a book on my life before I was even conceived on this earth.

This revelation came to me during my personal study time and was confirmed by God Himself during one of my prayer sessions with Him. His confirmation that such a book existed led me to take a deeper look into the written scriptures to see if the Bible that I've been using for over 20 years contained information on such a book.

What I discovered literally put me in a state of shock. Over those 20 years, I've probably attended 2,000 church services, numerous religious conferences, and hundreds of Bible studies.

I've also completed a number of religious certification courses. I don't ever remember someone teaching me about or even mentioning that such a book exists.

What shocked me the most was that after I discovered that this book is a biblical concept I quickly realized that my life to that point did not line up with the contents of that book, which contained the detailed will of God for my life. I was writing my own book according to my will. This book included my assumptions of God's will for my life. The problem was that, when it comes down to it, assumptions don't cut it. I was in essence writing a book of fiction with my life. I wasn't living from a reference point of truth that originates in God. At times, my life took on the story line of a joke book. In other seasons of my life, it probably looked more like the plot of a horror story. Some parts might have read like a romance novel, and in a few places followed the line of inspirational fiction ... but it wasn't the true book of my life as God had foreseen and written before I was even born.

Written in the Book

My journey to discover that such a book existed led me to discover that even Jesus had a book on His life:

"Therefore when He comes into the world, He says, 'Sacrifice and offering You did not desire, but You have prepared a body for Me. In burnt offerings and sacrifices for sin You have had no pleasure. Then I said, Lo, I come in the volume of the Book it is written of Me to do Your will, O God'" [Heb. 10:5-7].

Traditional understanding of this scripture has been that this "volume" or "book" refers to the Old Testament. A scripture that is used to validate this belief is, "And He said to them, 'These are the words which I spoke to you while I was still with you, that all things must be fulfilled which were written in the Law of Moses and in the Prophets and in the Psalms about Me'" [Lk. 24:44].

Though there are numerous indisputable prophetic scriptures about Jesus recorded in the Old Testament that He fulfilled, the *details* of His daily assignments are not found in the Old Testament writings. The details for His daily life came from another book, which was also a form of scripture that came straight from the mouth of God. Jesus received those details from God the Father on a daily basis through prayer.

An in-depth examination into Jesus' prayer life as well as some of the words that He spoke and that were spoken about Him reveal the presence of another book that coincided with the Old Testament writings of His life. The following verses give us proof that Jesus did much more than what was documented about Him in the Old Testament scriptures:

"And truly Jesus did many other signs in the presence of His disciples, which are not written in this book" [John 20:30].

"And there are also many things, whatever Jesus did, which if they were written singly, I suppose the world itself could not contain the books having been written. Amen" [John 21:25].

Another major clue is given to us through other statements that John was inspired to write in reference to Jesus' origin:

"In the beginning was the Word, and the Word was with God, and the Word was God" [John 1:1].

The word "Word," used three times in this passage, is commonly translated from the Greek word *Logos*. According to *Strong's Concordance* this word as it relates to God is defined as: "something said" that includes "His thought, His subject of discourse, His reasoning, motive or intent, His doctrine, His work and His Divine expression."[80]

---

[80] *Strongs # G3056*

Thayer's Greek Dictionary of Biblical Words defines *Logos* as: "a word uttered by a living voice that embodies a conception or idea, the sayings of God, a narration reported in speech." This definition clues us into the fact that the books of the Bible itself are a form of *Logos* in that they convey the ideas and sayings of God. He inspired the different writers and narrated His message through them to create the 66 books of the Bible.

> *"All scripture is given by inspiration of God, and is profitable for doctrine, for reproof, for correction, for instruction in righteousness: That the man of God may be perfect, thoroughly furnished unto all good works"* [2 Tim. 3:16-17 KJV].

Though the reference in the above passage to "all scripture" is traditionally taught to mean the written Word of God – the Bible – let me introduce a deeper perspective to the meaning of "all scripture." The Hebrew root word for scripture is *kâthâb*, which means both "something written" as well as "the act of writing." We see this in God's instruction to Jeremiah. Jeremiah was instructed to write (*kâthâb*) – specific words pertaining to his life through the narration of God's speech towards him:

> *"This is the word that came to Jeremiah from the LORD: 'This is what the LORD, the God of Israel, says: "Write in a book all the words I have spoken to you."'"* [Jer. 30:1-2 NIV].

These words became scripture for Jeremiah's life! We see another example of an instruction to record what was told to them by God in the following passage:

> *"In the fourth year of Jehoiakim son of Josiah king of Judah, this word came to Jeremiah from the LORD: 'Take a scroll and write on it all the words I have spoken to you concerning Israel, Judah and all the other nations from the time I began speaking to you in the reign of Josiah till now'"* [Jer. 36:1-2 NIV].

When you take the time to listen to and record daily instructions from God as He lets you know His will for your life, this "something written" through "the act of writing" becomes scripture for your life. You end up recording a book that contains the details of your life, which were documented by God before you were ever conceived on this earth.

"Your eyes saw my unformed body; all the days ordained for me were written in your book before one of them came to be. How precious to me are your thoughts, God! How vast is the sum of them!" [Ps. 139:16-17 NIV].

The Potential of Words

The most common and closest Hebrew expression used for the Greek word *"Logos"* from John 1:1 is the word *dabar.* According to *Strong's Concordance*, a simplified definition of this word would be: "a word that is spoken concerning a matter or a thing." Also included within the details of its full meaning is a reference made to the existence of a book or chronicle. We must examine the root understanding of this profound word to understand the full scope of not only its meaning but also its connection to other key words and their application.

According to the *Ancient Hebrew Lexicon of the Bible*, *dabar* is described as, "A careful arrangement or placement of something that creates order that comes through speech."[81] In Hebrew thought, words contain the potential to create tangible substance. *Dabar* isn't just a sound or doctrine that comes from the mouth of God; the purpose of God's words is to create action or an event. When someone received *dabar* from the mouth of God, it was dynamically filled with a power that compelled the recipient to move towards producing something and acting out what was said. Fundamentally, *dabar* is not just a word but also a deed. The implication according to Hebrew thought is that

---

[81]   *Strongs* #1697: AHLB#: 2093

when someone truly receives *dabar* from the mouth of God as it relates to God's purpose for his or her life, the requirement is that it produces an inner drive, a passion to bring forth the reality of what has already seen by God!

An example of this would be Moses when he was given chronicles of instructions to build the tabernacle. God had a problem. There was no place for people to worship Him. Moses was given a *dabar* from God that produced a tabernacle [Ex. 25-27, 31:1-11].

In the days of Noah, God was about to bring a flood across the earth, yet He wanted to spare a handful of people and animals in order to start over again. Noah got a *dabar* from God. He was given chronicles of instructions to build an ark [Gen. 6:5-22].

Though biblically there are many great examples of specific God-given words that produced deeds to answer the world's problems, the greatest of them is found in the following passages:

"And the Word became flesh, and tabernacled among us. And we beheld His glory, the glory as of the only begotten of the Father, full of grace and of truth" [John 1:14].

"Then I said, Lo, I come in the volume of the Book it is written of Me to do Your will, O God" [Heb. 10:7].

When God gives you a *dabar,* He designs and purposes for you to flesh it out into your life! Then you become an answer to a world problem – just like Jesus. *Dabar* is one of seven key Hebrew words that we must explore in order to understand the full essence of what John 1:1 is saying as it refers to the word "Word."

The first and foundational word that *dabar* comes from is the Hebrew word *peh.* It is defined as "the organ of speech or the mouth."[82]

---

[82] *Strongs* #6310: AHLB#: 1373-A (N)

The second key word that comes out of *peh* is the word *Ruach*, which is where we get the English word Spirit as it relates to God. *Ruach* is defined as "the wind, breath or mind of God."[83] Together these two words produce what is more commonly referred to as the breath that comes from the mouth of God. In ancient Hebrew thought, *Ruach* is illustrated and described as the breath of God that refreshes through His exhaling a prescribed path, and the spirit of man inhaling that prescribed path. The word "pre*scribed*" implies something that is pre*written*.

The third key word that comes out of *Ruach* is the word *emet*,[84] which is where we get the English word "Truth" as it relates to God. Simply defined, Truth is "original information that originates from the mouth of God that is purposed to nurture the agreement or covenant that God has with you." When God speaks a *dabar* (spoken word) to you, it is Truth. Truth is the language of God.

What comes out from *emet* is the fourth key word, *emer*,[85] defined as "an appointed saying." It's the specific utterance for your life that comes out of the mouth of God. It has detailed specifications of the purpose and path that is appointed for you. Your *emer* defines how you are an answer to a specific world problem. *Emer* is also characterized as the Wisdom of God in that it produces a call to action.

What comes out of *emer* is the fifth key Hebrew word, *amar*,[86] which in Spanish means love. In Hebrew thought, *amar* is characterized as a promise that is declared. *Amar* is God's love language towards you; He speaks to you His promises. *Amar* has a unique root word definition: "A continuation of segments, which fill the whole." It is God's continual provision of spoken words towards you that make you complete!

---

[83] *Strongs* #7307: AHLB#: 1445-J
[84] *Strongs* #571: AHLB#: 1290
[85] *Strongs* #561: AHLB#: 1288-C (N)
[86] *Strongs* #560: AHLB#: 1288-C (V)

Amar introduces us to the sixth key word, *dabar*. Once again, this word is defined as: "A careful arrangement or placement of something that creates order that comes through speech." It is from the word *dabar* that we get to the seventh key word in order to understand the full scope of the Greek word "*Logos*" (Word) used in John 1:1 and 14.

This seventh key word is a dual-word Hebrew expression called *Sêpher Siphrâh*.[87] *Sêpher Siphrâh* is the ultimate Hebrew expression and manifestation of the Greek word *Logos*. It is associated with the written word. *Siphrâh* is the act of writing based on an account that is given. *Sêpher* is the book or document that is produced from that writing. Combined, *Sêpher Siphrâh* scripturally is described as the act of writing a book based on an account given to you by God. This was a process used in numerous biblical accounts.[88]

The equivalent of the Greek word *Logos* from an Aramaic perspective – in which many of the ancient scriptures were also transcribed, such as the Aramaic Peshittas and Targums – coincide with the Hebraic perspective in using the word *Miltha* for the word "Word" in John 1, verses 1 and 14. From an Aramaic perspective, *Miltha* is defined as "an instruction, sentence, story that is fully formed that runs from beginning to end." This describes a book. A book is composed of forms of instructive knowledge that form sentences telling a story from beginning to end.

Kingdom Life Book

Logos or *dabar* contain God's continual exhaling of scripture for your life that must be inhaled and treated as sacred content in that it must be transcribed or recorded in some way. This resource will eventually end up being the accumulation of your

---

[87] *Strongs* #5612: AHLB#: 2500 (e1), (N)
[88] See list in Appendix 3.

life's true story. The foundational purpose of this God-inspired resource will serve to provide you with your personal "Second Timothy 3:16-17 experience." It will contain:

1. God's specific and personal doctrine (teachings) for your life [See Deut. 32:1-2, Ps. 119:99-102, 1 Jn. 2:27].

2. God's specific and personal reproof and correction (firm admonishment and provision of specific courses of action that rectify any tendency to commit error) for your life [See Prov. 1:23, 3:11-12, 6:23, 10:17, 12:1, 13:18, 15:5, 31-32].

3. God's specific and personal instruction in righteousness (consistent coaching and mentoring that teaches you and introduces the potential to be upright and perfect as He is) [See Prov. 4:1, 8:33, 23:12, Ps. 23:3, 119:142, 144, Jer. 23:33, Matt. 5:48, 13:43].

Through this process, you will receive the preciseness of God's overall will for your life, including specific details of the Kingdom of God that is within you.[89] The following are three major components that Jesus mentioned when He taught on the subject of prayer:

- "Thy Kingdom come"

- "Thy will done in earth as it in Heaven"

- "Give us this day our daily bread"

When you document the words given to you from these three key components of prayer, you will end up with your very own "Kingdom Life Book" that will contain the daily details of such information. The importance of understanding the full scope of the fact that God has authored a book on your life is magnified in the following passage:

---

[89] This will be a primary focus of the next book in this series titled *The Mystery of the Kingdom of God Revealed.*

"And I saw the dead, the small and the great, stand before God. And books were opened, and another book was opened, which is the Book of Life. And the dead were judged out of those things which were written in the books, according to their works" [Revelations 20:12].

The word "books" in Revelations 20:12 comes from the Greek word *biblion*, defined as a "book, scroll or writing." The Hebrew expression that was originally used here is *Sêpher Siphrâh*, which we saw earlier is "a book or document that is based on an account given to you by God."[90] God has authored and continues to add to His own book titled "The Book of Life" [See Ex. 32:33, Phil. 4:3, Rev. 3:5, 13:8, 17:8, 20:12, 15, 21:27, 22:19]. The works that God's judgments are going to be based on are the works that the following verse expresses:

"For we are His workmanship, created in Christ Jesus to good works, which God has before ordained that we should walk in them" [Eph. 2:10].

These works that God has preordained are then meant to be "fleshed out" by us in our daily lives. The details of these works are contained in the volume of the book that God has personally authored for your life.

The awesome privilege of getting the transcriptions of your God-authored book, as you hear from God on a daily basis, must not be taken lightly. It is the most accurate information that you can receive from God Himself as it pertains to the mandate to continually renew your mind. This process is required in order to get to the stage where the perfect (mature and complete) will of God is revealed to you. This process also protects you as it will expose any contaminating worldly influence that is keeping you from fulfilling God's assignments for your life.

---

[90] *Strongs* #5612: AHLB#: 2500 (e1), (N)

*"And do not be conformed to this world, but be trans-
formed by the renewing of your mind, in order to prove by
you what is that good and pleasing and perfect will of God"*
[Rom. 12:2].

Many traditional religions teach that the Bible is the primary
resource that one should use to renew the mind. Though there is
of course great value in this practice, the Bible does not contain
the specifics for your life. This can only be found in the mouth
of God. When someone makes a concentrated effort to learn
to hear the voice of God and to record what He tells them on a
continual basis, this becomes a precise and effective resource in
renewing your mind and spirit.

I'm not suggesting that you actually put this information in
book form with chapters and headings, though this may not be a
bad idea. It could be something as simple as putting the current
date in a notebook and jot down or make bullet points of what
you sense God speaking to you about your life.

Sometimes I will document bullet points of key things that
God says to me. Other times I will write word-for-word what God
has shown me for that day. There are also times that, instead of
writing, I will audio or video record myself speaking what I hear
God saying to me. It doesn't matter how you do it or what form of
media you use to record God's words to you; what is important
is that you *do it on a continual basis*.

I have used notebooks and journals (some I've bought and
some that I designed myself) to record my journey with God. I am
currently transitioning to electronic media on my Apple laptop
using an application called Mac Journal that I can synchronize
with my iPhone, which allows me to have my recordings with me
at all times and gives me the ability to add to them throughout
my day and print them if necessary. It is with the advancement
of this type of technology and tools that I can now add audio and
video recordings of me documenting my experience with God to
further enhance "The Kingdom Book" for my life.

This resource provides me with a blueprint for my life. Coupled with the actions I take to obey the instructions that God gives me, I convert this blueprint into what I call the "Truth-Print" for my life. It literally becomes a script for a life that is based on a true story – the story that God has written. I must then act it out on a daily basis. As I do so, I become a living epistle that all humanity can read [2 Cor. 3:2]. These resources straight from heaven equip me with the tangible knowledge that furnishes me with the right works according to the perfect will of God.

"That the man of God may be perfect, thoroughly furnished unto all good works" [2 Tim. 3:16-17 KJV].

Many people record in diaries and journals those things that have *already* happened to them in life. Recording God's *pre*written book for your life approaches this from the opposite direction. You write what you hear from God so that you know what *should* happen in your life.

A deeper look into the word "perfect" reveals the magnitude of how someone benefits from the practice of recording the *Logos, Sêpher Siphrâh*, or the volume of the book on your life. From a root perspective, the word "perfect" is defined as, "Someone that is upright, whole, complete or full." A further study of this key word reveals that it also describes one who is full of marvel and wonder in that they have the capacity to perceive spiritual insight from God![91]

"I will praise You; for I am fearfully and wonderfully made; Your works are marvelous and my soul knows it very well" [Psalms 139:14].

Another Hebrew perspective of the word "perfect" explains that those who do not have this key characteristic of perfection are "not complete because they are orphaned or fatherless."[92] In other words, those who are not "perfect" are those who have

---

[91] *Strongs* #8549: AHLB#: 1496
[92] *Strongs* #8549: AHLB#: 1496-L

no Father (God) to read to them the detailed story of their life! The result will be that your soul *will not* know very well how fearfully and wonderfully God created you, thus robbing you of the knowledge that contains the marvel, wonder, completeness and uniqueness of whom you truly are!

From a traditional religious standpoint, the state of being perfect has been marred by the erroneous teachings of grace from a Greek understanding as opposed to a root Hebrew word understanding.[93] Much of traditional Christianity teaches grace as God's answer to man's imperfections instead of the portal to truth which introduces God's answers that will direct us to correct our imperfect actions.

From a secular viewpoint, the word "perfect" carries the definition of one who is flawless. Statements such as "nobody is perfect" have penetrated traditional church doctrine, thus causing people to be more sin-conscious than God-conscious. An accurate understanding and application of "be perfect" introduces the importance of God-consciousness.

The mere fact that Jesus stated, "Be perfect, even as your Father in Heaven is perfect" [Matt. 5:48] implies that we do have the potential to experience a perfect state of being according to the original meaning of perfect. From an Aramaic perspective, the word *gmar* is used for the word perfect. It is a verb that summons one to a commitment of "actions of development" that are necessary to reach this state of perfection and completion.

In the New Testament, the other word used for "Word" is *Rhema*, a Greek word defined as "an utterance or orally spoken word." As mentioned earlier, it is connected to the Hebrew words *emet, emer, amar* and *dabar*. When combined, *Rhema* is actually the appointed sayings of truth from God declaring His promises that are based on what He has already seen about you. This is meant to ignite within you a call to action that results in you experiencing the Wisdom of God, which will create order

---

[93] This is a topic that I cover extensively in the first book of this series titled *The Mystery of Iniquity Revealed*.

for every aspect of your life – causing you to be complete, whole, and yes, perfect!

From a Greek perspective, *Rhema* is the narration of spoken scripture from God that comes from your written scripture – *Logos* – given by God's only authorized narrator: The Holy Spirit of Truth. This same concept is put forth in the Hebraic perspective as well: *Dabar* is the narration of spoken scripture from God of your written scripture – *Sêpher Siphrâh*. Once again, the source is God's only authorized narrator: The Holy Spirit of Truth. This was the inspiration and process that kept Jesus so precise throughout His earthly existence and ministry.

> *"Then I said, Lo, I come in the volume of the Book it is written of Me to do Your will, O God"* [Heb. 10:7].

The word "volume" is the Greek word *kephalis*, which refers to a circular or round document that comes in the form of a roll. The Hebrew word that was originally used here is *megillâh*, defined as "a scroll" and "a second time around of a time or event."[94] Again, the word "book" in this passage is the Greek word *biblion*, which means writing. The original Hebrew word used is *Sêpher Siphrâh,* which we learned earlier is "a recording of a story" and is also described as "evidence" and "from the speaking of a record."[95]

This would be similar to someone writing an autobiography or true story of your life based off events from your life *before* they actually happened. In other words, this passage of scripture is saying that a recorded story on Jesus already existed about His life on earth *before* He came to earth. This story was based on times and events that had *already taken place in the mind of God*. The volume of the book God wrote about Him was fulfilled through His earthly life! This information was primarily revealed to Jesus as He consistently positioned Himself to be taught those things that were already *pre*scribed and written for His life.

---

[94] *Strongs* #4039: AHLB#: 1058-M (k1)
[95] *Strongs* #5612: AHLB#: 2500 (e1) (N)

"The Lord has given me a well-instructed tongue, to know the word that sustains the weary. He wakens me morning by morning, wakens my ear to listen like one being instructed" [Isa. 50:4 NIV].

Receiving the Script

In my opinion, when we fail to hear the voice of God at the beginning our day, we end up writing our own book for our lives. It will end up being a book based on fiction and not facts. This result in what I call "spiritual amnesia." Our souls will not know very well how fearfully and wonderfully God created us, nor will we have the accurate knowledge of the marvelous works that God has preordained for us to reproduce.

The things I have recorded in my personal ongoing book, which God has been continually revealing to me over the years, have served me in a number of ways. This vital information serves as my personal vision book that contains the laws for my life. It serves as a guide to make sure that my life is aligned to what God has already seen and prewritten about me. A scripture that has become a framework for my personal "Kingdom Life Book" is found in Proverbs 29:18: "Where there is no vision, the people perish: but he that keepeth the law, happy is he" [KJV].

The word "vision" used here is the Hebrew word *châzôn*, which is defined in *Strong's Concordance* as "a mental sight or revelation that is exposed through an oracle." The word "oracle" used here refers to one that is "an expert, specialist, mentor, adviser, that is of an authority status." The word "perish," used in Proverbs 29:18, is the word *pâra*. This describes someone who has "cast off restraint through avoidance or refusal because of a lack of self-control or self-discipline." The word "law" used in this verse is the Hebrew word *Torah*, commonly defined as "what keeps order." Yet in this particular verse, the word is defined as "the direction that one is to take in life through teaching that ultimately comes from the mouth of God."[96]

The word "happy" is the word commonly known as blessed.[97] According to its root definition, we are happy or blessed when we live a straight life. An in-depth view of the word "happy" or "blessed" according to ancient Hebrew thought is the result of "one who is connected to a source of life through an umbilical cord" – similar to a baby who is connected to the mother inside of the womb. In this view, it is speaking of mature persons who remain attached to their place of origin from where they receive constant nurturing and development through the constant yoking or binding of thoughts between them and their original source of creation, God [See Gen. 49:25, Eph. 1:3-4].

A deeper understanding of this key principle of someone truly happy or blessed is illustrated from the context of a marital "nuptial chamber." In a physical marriage from a Hebrew perspective, this is the place where a covenant is consecrated and mutual desire takes place. It is where conception and birthing begins. Spiritually, it is the place where two courses of life become one, a relational intercourse or union with God that takes place where one becomes pregnant with the ideas of God that relate to one's preordained purpose. It is also where nurturing takes place in order to birth those ideas into the world. This is the ultimate place of discovery that Jesus referred to when He made what was perhaps the most profound statement of His earthly existence:

> *"But seek first the kingdom of God and His righteousness; and all these things shall be added to you"* [Matt. 6:33].[98]

We see this process embedded in the instructions that came from God's mouth:

---

[96] *Strongs* #8451: AHLB#: 1227-H (i1)
[97] *Strongs* #835: AHLB#: 1480-C (N)
[98] This is a crucial topic that will be explored in the next book of this series titled *The Mystery of The Kingdom of God Revealed*

"This is the covenant that I will make with them after those days, says the Lord; I will put My Laws into their hearts, and in their minds I will write them" [Heb. 10:16]. *[See also Jer. 31:33-34]*

Scripturally, the word "oracle" in English is the Hebrew word *dabar* that we examined earlier, defined as, "A careful arrangement or placement of something that creates order that comes through speech." The Oracle of God (an expert, specialist, mentor, adviser, that is of an authority status) is The Holy Spirit of Truth.

"Howbeit when he, the Spirit of Truth, is come, he will guide you into all truth: for he shall not speak of himself; but whatsoever he shall hear, that shall he speak: and he will shew you things to come. He shall glorify me: for he shall receive of mine, and shall shew it unto you" [John 16:13-14 KJV].

When you position yourself to hear from God through the Holy Spirit of Truth, you receive His spiritual insights and thoughts, which pertain to your present and future. The prophet Habakkuk needed an answer to a problem that he was facing. When he positioned himself in a place that was absent of distractions, God gave him words that created the vision for his life pertaining to how he was to respond to the issues at hand. God had a prescribed answer for the prophet Habakkuk's situation that he was required to document according to the details that God narrated to him:

"I will stand on my watch and set myself on the tower, and will watch to see what He will say to me, and what I shall answer when I am reproved. And the Lord answered me and said, Write the vision, and make it plain on the tablets, that he who reads it may run. For the vision is still for an appointed time, but it speaks to the end, and it does not lie. Though it lingers, wait for it; because it will surely come. It will not tarry" [Hab. 2:1-3].

The Greek word "shew" in John 16:14 means "to show, rehearse, to announce in detail." According to the *Ancient Hebrew Lexicon of the Bible*, this word is rooted in the Hebrew word *châzôn*, which in this verse means "to mentally gaze at or perceive, to see or have vision for."[99] What is interesting about both the Greek and Hebrew definitions is that, when they are combined, the Holy Spirit shows us that the vision we are to mentally perceive (or gaze at) comes through words that can be converted into the scenes that have already taken place in the mind of God. To put it another way, we're basically seeing into our own futures, or the future that God wants us to create according to His perfect plan.

This vision is announced through detailed words and/or images by the Holy Spirit telling you what has already been written about you and taken place in the mind of God for your life. This is similar to an actor getting a script from the screenwriter for a part they are about to portray in a motion picture. The script will contain words that the actor must repeat as well as details of the scenes in which the episode will take place. The script equips the actor with foreknowledge and visualization. The actor is given a glimpse of the future before it comes to pass. In a sense, it is knowledge converted into vision. Further proof of this is found in a profound statement that was made about Jesus. John stated, "In him was life; and the life was the light of men" [John 1:4].

In Hebrew thought, *light* as it relates to God is a metaphoric reference to illuminated knowledge, which is known as truth that comes from His mouth. *Darkness* is a metaphoric reference to ignorance or lack of illuminated truth. Illuminated knowledge from God comes with vision. The *Ancient Hebrew Lexicon of the Bible* also defines vision as, "To have the ability to see beyond what is seen, as light piercing through darkness."[100] The ability to see beyond what our natural eyes see can only come through the knowledge that God gives according to what He has already seen.

---

[99] *Strongs* #2377: AHLB#: 1168-A (j)
[100] *Strongs* #2372: AHLB#: 1168-H (V)

This vision will expose and remove any system or manifestation that has perverted the original intentions of God. To put it in another way, when God gives someone a vision, it is always to bring improvement or correction to something that is out of His divine order.

The vision for your life is found in the illuminated knowledge of the truth of what is already written about you! The light or full story of illuminated truth that was in Jesus came in the context of a *Logos* or *Sêpher Siphrâh*. Jesus was a living epistle, a volume of a book of truth walking on two feet. He was a walking true story of illuminated knowledge, living what was already written about Him. He became the example of the life all humanity should live by, based on the story that should be illuminated to each person.

We are also ordained to be living epistles, truth walking on two feet. Truth is the purest form of light or knowledge. It has the power to expose and eliminate any form of darkness or lack of knowledge in our lives. It is the only substance that accurately exposes and removes inaccuracy within us.

Jesus was the illuminated example of accurate living, which comes through a calling from God. At times I wondered why Jesus made the conditional statement, "Many are called but few are chosen" in the parables of "The laborers" and "The marriage feast" [Matt. 20:1-16, 22:1-14]. A root-word study of the word "called" revealed the answer. From the Greek perspective, this word is *klētos*, simply defined as "one who is invited or appointed." From an original Hebraic perspective, the word used is *miqrâ*, described as "a meeting" that is called where "a scroll is read."[101] This is exactly what God desires to do when someone encounters God in pure and unhindered prayer. This was the type of prayer meeting that Jesus had with the Father every morning:

---

[101] *Strongs* #4744: AHLB#: 1434-E (h)

"The Lord GOD has given Me The tongue of the learned, That I should know how to speak a word in season to him who is weary. He awakens Me morning by morning, He awakens My ear To hear as the learned. The Lord GOD has opened My ear; And I was not rebellious, Nor did I turn away" [Isa. 50:4-4].

In both of these parables, the lesson conveyed is that these individuals did not have what I call "Speech Recognition." Because they failed to recognize who was calling them, they failed to attend to what was prescribed (written) for them! This key lesson of "Speech Recognition" based on what is prewritten about you is contained in these key verses:

"Let each one abide in the same calling in which he was called" [1 Cor. 7:20].

"Therefore, brothers, rather be diligent to make your calling and election sure, for if you do these things, you shall never fall" [2 Pet. 1:10].

Though many people approach prayer from a standpoint of *speaking to God*, a vital form of prayer focuses completely on you *hearing from God*. King David was inspired to write about this meeting where knowledge, understanding, and experience come from the mouth of God to man when he penned these words:

"I have more understanding than all my teachers: for thy testimonies are my meditation" [Ps. 119:99 KJV].

The King James Version of the Bible correctly uses the word "meditation" instead of "prayer" or "statutes" that is used in other translations. Meditation is a form of prayer. Meditation is the disciplined practice of sweeping away or removing your own thoughts in order to have the thoughts of God placed within the chambers of your mind [Jer. 29:11-13, Isa. 55:6-11]. This can only be done from a hearing perspective and not from the traditional speaking perspective.[102]

---

[102] The topic of meditation will be covered further in a subsequent chapter.

The word "testimonies" used in Psalms 119:99 is the Hebrew word *edûth*.[103] It describes the knowledge that comes out of a witness as an "event or person's testimony recounting another event or person." It is also defined as "an appointed place, time and event that is repeated over and over again."

In ancient Hebrew thought, this event is portrayed as one who "sees a specific door." Once this door is opened, key knowledge is revealed. This door is called the "door of the eye" since it is knowledge of what has been seen or witnessed before that comes from the mouth of God.[104]

"For the Lord gives wisdom; from His mouth come knowledge and understanding" [Prov. 2:6].

This type of knowledge is personified in the following passage:

"Through wisdom a house is built, and by understanding it is established; and by knowledge the rooms shall be filled with all precious and pleasant riches. A wise man is strong; yes, a man of knowledge increases strength" [Prov. 24:3-5].

The word "house" used in this passage is a direct reference to the temple of the human body [1 Cor. 3:16-19]. It is where you experience the true joy of the Lord if you position yourself to receive His original knowledge for your life. God also provides you with understanding, which should motivate you to build a life that manifests the prewritten, preordained and pre-purposed works of God! This is the process that led to the fulfillment of the joy of the Lord that Jesus experienced.

---

[103] *Strongs* #5715: AHLB#: 1349-A (N), L
[104] *Strongs* #1847: AHLB#: 1085

"Therefore since we also are surrounded with so great a cloud of witnesses, let us lay aside every weight and the sin which so easily besets us, and let us run with patience the race that is set before us, looking to Jesus the Author and Finisher of our faith, who for the joy that was set before Him endured the cross, despising the shame, and sat down at the right of the throne of God" [Heb. 12:1-2].

The term "Author and Finisher" is a figure of speech that defines someone who is an originator and perfecter of something – which in this case is faith. Jesus' faith came from the mouth of God, who not only authored His faith but also gave forth a continual provision of information that brought perfect completion to His life. The volume of the book that God wrote about Jesus was read to Him during His times of Morning Prayer. The actions that He produced as a result of His times of prayer brought forth a powerful outcome. Jesus lived a precise life based on the book His Father wrote of His life.

With such implications and the vital importance of such a book, wouldn't it make sense to accurately steward the words of God by recording them so that the constant deposit of God's words can cause you to live a life of power, perfection, and precision? Keeping a record of these words will also enable you to review them to ensure that all God has shown you will come to pass in your life.

What will this book do for you? How can recording the thoughts and words of God for your life make a significant difference?

- It becomes your personal curriculum, your personalized life handbook.

- God Himself becomes your personal mentor, life coach and teacher!

- Your life goals will be clarified without the contamination or substance of selfish ambitions.

- God's thoughts become your thoughts, enabling you to convert His ways into your ways.

- When you convert His words into pictures and script for your life, you obtain a vision for your life.

- Hearing from Heaven gives you spiritual intelligence that exceeds your human intellect.

- The assumptions you have about your life are replaced with certainties.

- You begin to act out a script for your life that is based on a true story – *His*-story.

- You become refreshed with the accuracy of God-prescribed direction.

- Your preordained purpose is renewed and revealed to you day by day.

- You record the mysteries of the Kingdom of God within you and then produce the goals to bring them to pass.

- You archive the chronicles of the book of His-story for your life that becomes the His-present and His-future for your life.

- Your perspective takes on a future-conscious mindset based on the destiny that God reveals ahead of time.

- You record the ideas that God impregnates you with and receive instructions on how to birth them into the world.

CHAPTER SUMMARY:

- When you take the time to listen to and record daily instructions from God, this "something written" through "the act of writing" becomes scripture for your life.

- When someone truly receives *Dabar* (Logos, or "Word") from the mouth of God as it relates to His purposes, this produces a passion to bring forth the reality of what has already seen by God!

- When God gives you a *Dabar*, He purposes for you to flesh it out into your life! Then you become an answer to a world problem – just like Jesus.

- *Amar* is God's love language towards you where He speaks His promise towards you. God's continual provisions of spoken words towards you make you complete!

- God's judgments at the End of Days are going to be based on works that God has preordained for us, and whether we have lived our predestined life purpose.

- From a Greek perspective, *Rhema* is the narration of spoken scripture from God that comes from your written scripture – *Logos* – given by God's only authorized narrator: The Holy Spirit of Truth. This same concept is put forth in the Hebraic perspective as well: *Dabar* is the narration of spoken scripture from God of your written scripture – *Sêpher Siphrâh*.

- True life and the vision for your life are found in the illuminated knowledge of the truth of what is already written about you!

- The "temple" of your body is where you experience the true joy of the Lord if you position yourself to receive His original knowledge and understanding for your life. This process will lead to the joy of the Lord.

APPLICATION:

1. The awesome privilege of getting the transcriptions of your God-authored book, as you hear from God on a daily basis, must not be taken lightly. Think and pray about how you can begin to hear from God and record His thoughts and words for your life. Determine a time and place to do it today.

2. Some options for recording God's word to you are: notebooks, word documents, electronic media applications, audio recordings, and video recordings. Although you do not have to stick to the same one, it would be good to start somewhere. Consider what method of recording God's instructions will work best for you at this time.

3. A quote from the above chapter states, "With such implications and the vital importance of such a book on your life, wouldn't it make sense to accurately steward the words of God by recording them so that the constant deposit of God's words can cause you to live a life of power, perfection, and precision?" Pray and ask the Lord to help you be a wise and faithful "steward" of His Words.

CHAPTER NINE:

PaRDeS - Understanding *Script*ure from Jesus' Perspective

"The primary purpose of the Written Word of God is to introduce you to the Spoken Word of God."

— Julio Alvarado Jr.

To have an accurate understanding of Jesus' teaching on prayer, we must consider some important details. First we must look at the education that Jesus and many of His followers would have been exposed to according to the traditional Jewish educational system. This education would have begun as early as the age of six.

The Jewish educational system originated as early as 1300 BC, and it is still practiced today.[105] The entry point of this educational system was called *Bet Sefer*, which meant "The House of The Book." The only text used at this level was the first five books of the Bible (Genesis, Exodus, Leviticus, Numbers, and Deuteronomy), known as The Torah. This stage of education

---

[105] Information found at: **http://en.wikipedia.org/wiki/History_of_education_in_ancient_Israel_and_Judah**

began with the instructor smearing honey on the student's writing slate, followed by uncovering the ancient scrolls of the Torah. The rabbi would then have the students lick the honey from their slates and tell them that The Torah is sweeter than the honeycomb [Psalms 19:10, 119:103]. Can you imagine the impact this would have on a young child? Whenever that child tasted honey he was always reminded of the Torah!

This stage of education introduced children to concepts they were encouraged to develop, such as courtesy, honesty, integrity, truthfulness, inner beauty, courage, kindness, patience, self-discipline, a feeling of wholeness, and a sense of responsibility. Children also became familiar with prayers and rituals and were given the opportunity to participate in cultural worship services. The *Bet Sefer* phase of education ended when the student was ten years old, with the primary focus and result being the memorization of The Torah. Yes, students had the first five books of the Bible memorized by the age of ten.

The second level of education was called *Bet Midrash*, defined as "The House of Learning." During this time, students would continue to enhance their memorization skills primarily through the books of Psalms and the Prophets as well as other key portions of the Old Testament. It wasn't uncommon in that day for a good student to have the entire Old Testament memorized by the age of fourteen, which is when this level of education ended. During this four-year period, the student would begin to learn what was called *the art of listening and asking questions.* This was illustrated in the account of Jesus' earthly parents finding Him in the Temple at the age of 12. Mark 2:46 says, "They found Him in the temple, sitting in the midst of the teachers, both *listening to them and asking them questions.* And all who heard Him were astonished at His understanding and answers."

The third level of education was only for the best students, *Bet Talmud*, defined primarily as "The House of Study/Seeking" but also as "The House of Interpretation." This level of education started at the age of 15 and lasted until the age of 30. This phase would be similar to one pursuing a higher education by seeking admittance to the best school possible. In the Rabbinical Talmud process, the student pursued a respected Rabbi by asking him if he could become one of his "disciples." The Rabbi would ask the student many questions to find out if he qualified to be one of his students. The reason for this was that each Rabbi wanted to pass on his unique thinking, philosophy, and interpretation of Scripture to his students. This was called *taking on the yoke of the Rabbi*. The Rabbi would want to know, when questioning this potential disciple, "Is this young man able to become a Rabbi himself and to teach and spread my yoke?"

This is the context understood by listeners when Jesus made the following statement: "Take My yoke on you and learn of Me, for I am meek and lowly in heart, and you shall find rest to your souls. For My yoke is easy, and My burden is light" [Matt. 11:29-30 MKJV]. According to the *Ancient Hebrew Lexicon*, the word "yoke" is symbolized as strength. It is defined as, "the stronger authority teaching another authority to work together through the eye of experience and knowledge."[106] Again, in Hebrew and other cultures, when oxen were trained to plow a field, they always yoked an experienced ox with an inexperienced one so that the knowledge of the older ox would influence the inexperienced ox. This is illustrated in the following verse:

"I will instruct you and teach you in the way you should go;
I will guide you with My eye" [Psalms 32:8 NKJV].

At this point you may be asking, "What does any of this have to do with prayer?" It has *everything* to do with prayer. *Jesus' teaching on prayer was a part of His yoke.* This is why it is so crucial that we understand the framework of The Lord's Prayer that Jesus taught.

We must also consider the cultural language that Jesus' spoke when teaching on prayer, which was primarily Hebrew. The

---

[106] *Strongs* AHLB #1012

Hebrew language and mindset is very different from the Greek language and mindset – which many believers today have been exposed to when it comes to teachings on prayer. Greek-based teaching leads to a limited and single-level of understanding and interpretation of scripture.

In the ancient Jewish education system, Jesus and many in his audience would have been exposed to a system of learning known as PRDS.[107] This is an acronym for the Hebrew and Aramaic word "Pardes." The Pardes system is a four-level learning system that was used to interpret scripture. These levels of interpretation are a systematic approach to biblical interpretation that is still being used in rabbinical Judaism today.

The purpose of this type of training was to lead the student through a progression and ultimately a mastery of these four levels of interpretation, resulting in a deeper revelation of the scriptures; the primary result of this was a more intimate understanding of and relationship with God. To fully understand Jesus' intent and purpose in His lessons on prayer, we must take a look at these four levels of scriptural interpretation.

The Apostle Paul would have also been familiar with this level of teaching through his rabbinical training. He encouraged the process in the following passage by using four distinct words that describe the Pardes system of interpretation and revelation:

> *"That Christ may dwell in your hearts by faith; that you, being rooted and grounded in love, may be able to comprehend with all saints what is the **breadth** (width) and **length** and **depth** and **height**, and to know the love of Christ which passes knowledge, that you might be filled with all the fullness of God"* [Eph. 3:17-19 MKJV].

The word "comprehend" from verse 18 means "to seize, possess, apprehend, attain, come upon, find, obtain and perceive." It's to search out what is beneath the surface of the scriptures.

---

[107] Information found at: **http://www.ancient-hebrew.org/emagazine/044.pdf**

God's Word in some ways can be likened to an iceberg: only a small portion is visible to the natural eye, but a deeper search reveals the hidden fullness of the complete iceberg.

Pardes is the Hebrew word used in the Bible for a forest, orchard, or garden; it is referred to as a Paradise. It corresponds with the Greek word *paradeisos,* which also means a garden, Eden, or paradise. Each letter in the acronym represents a new dimension of Biblical understanding of the scriptures; exploring all four dimensions leads to a direct, face-to-face (presence-to-presence) communion with God Himself as was experienced in the first paradise, the Garden of Eden!

The apostle Paul encouraged all people to encounter God by searching for our own paradise or "Eden" experience through a breadth, length, depth, and height understanding of the Written Scripture and Spoken Scripture.[108] This understanding will guide us into a pure relationship with God. He was encouraging us to journey into our very own Pardes with God! The journey into Pardes represents a journey into deeper levels of intimacy with God our Father. It represents a journey into the relationship that humanity once had in the Garden of Eden, hence the word Pardes – Paradise.

Here are a few of those who experienced this level of relationship with God:

1. Adam, Enoch and Noah walked with God (Gen. 3:8; 5:22,24; 6:9)

2. Abraham was a friend of God (Isa. 41:8; Jam. 2:23)

3. Moses knew God face to face (Num. 12:6-8; Ex. 33:11)

It is not uncommon to see Pardes spelled as "PaRDeS" since in the original Hebrew language, vowels were not used and were only later added to aide in pronunciation and understanding. PRDS represents the first letters of the Hebrew words *Peshat, Remez, Darash* and *Sod,* each word representing a different level

---

[108] More on "Spoken Scripture" will be explored in a subsequent chapter.

of revelation of the scriptures. This revelation is a journey into a relationship. In fact, it is a *return* to the relationship that God originally intended for all humans to have with Him.

Originally, these four levels were primarily used to study and understand written scripture, which is considered a form of the voice of God. This form of teaching came through a teacher instructing his student in how to interpret scripture. This was human knowledge and understanding being transferred from one human to another, resulting in their human intellect and understanding being increased.

Jesus functioned in this capacity as a teacher in human form. Yet He hinted towards the coming of another teacher who would be available to all after His earthly departure [See John 16:13, 1 John 2:27]. This Teacher – the Spirit of Truth – would also transfer knowledge, understanding and interpretation, but from a place of *spiritual* intelligence versus *human* intelligence.

In exploring the PaRDeS system, we will look at:

1. The Hebrew definition of each level.

2. How each level is used to interpret written scripture from a Rabbinic perspective.

3. How Jesus taught at each of the four levels.

4. How the purpose of each level applies to the foundational framework of "The Lord's Prayer" that Jesus taught [See Matt. 6:5-13, Lk. 11:1-4].

Biblical Interpretation Level One: *Peshat*

Definition: The plain or simple width of a meaning.

Rabbinic perspective:

This level seeks to illuminate the simplest meaning of a text. It is viewing the scripture using the customary meanings of the words by looking at literary style, historical and cultural setting, and context. It is often considered the most straight-forward method for reading and understanding biblical text. This level of understanding is known as simply the corner-stone of interpretation. It is similar to what modern Christian hermeneutics calls "Grammatical Historical Exegesis," also known as "The Literal Principle." This method concerns itself mostly with the literary and grammatical context of Scripture.[109] This was one of the methods that Jesus used to interpret Scripture to the audience of His time and culture.

Practitioners of exegesis sometimes call the understanding of anything beyond the literal text "eisegesis," since it carries the possibility of interpreting a portion of text in such a way that it introduces one's own presuppositions, agendas, and/ or biases onto the text.[110] This is an unfortunate error, since there are in fact "levels" of interpretation that must be taken into consideration.

This level of understanding and interpreting scripture is the entry point whereby new believers are encouraged to understand the Word of God. At this level we study the literal history of the scriptures. We learn about the Bible "heroes." We learn about importance of memorization. The purpose of this level is to "mold, shape, form, or fabricate" – which is the

---

[109] Information found at: **http://en.wikipedia.org/wiki/Historical**-grammatical_ method

[110] Information found at: **http://en.wikipedia.org/wiki/Eisegesis**

definition of *platos*, the Greek word for breadth (width) from Ephesians 3:18. *Peshat* is the beginning of our understanding in Christ. It's where we start coming to Christ as a "little child." It is a very important level. Although it is the simplest, it's probably also one of the most perilous in that it molds, shapes, and forms our belief system.

Unfortunately, many people never go beyond this level of understanding. Many churches teach at this level of teaching without providing the proper training to further a believer's knowledge, understanding and revelation of Scripture. Though we start out in *Peshat*, we are not meant to stay there very long. We are to come to Jesus Christ as a little child [Mark 10:15], but we certainly are not to remain children in that sense of spirituality. We are encouraged to move towards maturity. Paul referred to this stage in his first letter to the church in Corinth:

> *"When I was a child, I spoke as a child, I understood as a child, I thought as a child: but when I became a man, I put away childish things. For now we see through a glass, dimly; but then face to face: now I know in part; but then shall I know even as also I am known"* [1 Cor. 13:11-12 NKJV].

Paul's statement in verse 12 is a reference to someone not having a clear understanding of themselves and life – which includes a mature knowledge of the scriptures – until they mature into a relationship with God where He Himself gives them that understanding and interpretation directly from His mouth.

JESUS' TEACHING AT THIS LEVEL:

We see Jesus using the *Peshat* (plain or literal) level of teaching during His ministry. He expressed literal interpretation of the scriptures mainly when addressing the Pharisees or other religious leaders. These were the straightforward one-liners that did not need to be defined. It is worth noting that Jesus rarely used this level to teach the crowds who followed Him.

The Lord's Prayer at the Peshat level of understanding:

At this level, the application of this prayer is to simply repeat it word for word.

In this level of understanding, we come to know simple meaning – the Breadth of God's Word. However, we are encouraged to move on to the next level of meaning and understanding of scripture.

Biblical Interpretation Level Two: *Remez*

Definition: A parable or allegory that hints or refers to a deeper insight of a meaning.

In the Hebraic way of study, this is known as a "wink" in the text; there is something more happening here than meets the eye. It hints of a deeper meaning beyond the literal words. It is described as the implied meaning of a hidden truth. The purpose of this level is to make larger, to expand or make bigger, to make strong (all referring to maturing in the understanding of scripture) which is the definition of *mēkos*, the Greek word for "length" in Ephesians 3:18.

Rabbinic perspective:

The word "parable" in the New Testament is a symbol or narrative that is used as a comparison. The purpose for teaching in parables, or symbols, was to get the people to think and to ask questions. It is the first step into the journey beneath what is plain or literal. Parables are our first lessons in symbolism. They teach us to make comparisons, which exercise the mind to think, the result of which should be asking questions.

Parables are taking something spiritual and framing it in a story. A student of God's Word is meant to think about the literal concept and then convert it to its spiritual counterpart. This comparison thinking then opens up the mind to allegory, which is the next step on this level of understanding. An allegory is a little different from a parable. Where a parable takes what is spiritual and makes it literal, an allegory (an analogy) takes what is literal and makes it spiritual.

Jesus' teaching at this level:

"And He spoke many things to them in parables" [Matt. 13:3]. Jesus used *Remez* when He taught through parables. He would make statements like "The Kingdom of God/Heaven is like..." and then give an allegorical situation that had a hidden meaning. Sometimes He would give the interpretation of parable; other times He left it to the person to search for the understanding. The disciples asked Jesus why He taught through parables:

> *"And the disciples said to Him, Why do You speak to them in parables? He answered and said to them, Because it is given to you to know the mysteries of the kingdom of Heaven, but it is not given to them"* [Matt. 13:10-11].

In the previous passage Jesus clues us into why the mysteries of Heaven were given to His disciples and not to others. The mystery could only be revealed through the voice of God Himself.

The *Remez* level of teaching is what Jesus used to begin teaching the masses The Beatitudes from Matthew Chapters five through seven. Jesus' teaching during the Sermon on the Mount hinted towards a deeper meaning than the literal words that He used.

The Lord's Prayer at the *Remez* level of understanding:

At this level, students begin to expand their application of this prayer beyond just quoting it. At this level they may begin to dissect the prayer into segments that they apply in their prayers. Examples of this would be:

- "Our Father who art in Heaven" ... here they may begin praising God for being their spiritual Father.

- "Hallowed be thy Name" ... at this point they may worship the Name of God and or Jesus.

- "Thy Kingdom come; thy will be done" ... here they may begin to focus their prayer on acknowledging that the will of God supersedes their own will.

Once we have matured and expanded our mind (in Remez) to understand the principles of parables and allegories and are able to discern what is literal and what is spiritual, we are mature enough to expand our understanding of the scriptures. After comprehending breadth (width) and length in our faith, we are encouraged to move further, into depth. The purpose of this next level is to "seek and search out the deep and profound mysteries," which is the definition of *bathos*, the Greek word for "depth" in Ephesians 3:18.

Biblical Interpretation Level Three: *Darash*

Definition: To inquire, search, explore or seek for the depth of meaning.

A believer at this level begins to inquire into the interpretive meaning of the text, seeking a deeper and broader explanation of the "story behind the story" or the "meaning beneath the meaning" of a text.

Rabbinic perspective:

This is a level of understanding of the scriptures that many people never attain due to a lack proper training. This level of understanding ventures into realms that are not literal, parable, or allegoric ... it goes even deeper. It's peering into the very core and nature of the individual words of the Bible by going back into the original languages and other texts for the purpose of discovering and understanding intended idioms and ideas.

I have discovered that attempting to study the Bible through my English or Spanish understanding limits my full comprehension. Though value can be found in the numerous translations of the Bible, relying on them alone limits my understanding of the original ideas and concepts God intended for them.

Do you remember the gossip or telephone game? You might have played it as a child. You would whisper a short sentence into someone's ear and they would turn and whisper it to the person seated on their other side. By the time the message had passed through a dozen people it was so different from the original message that all the players would find it amusing. Unfortunately, when it comes to scripture, an occurrence similar to the "telephone game" is not a laughing matter. When our understanding of the Bible is based on what has been passed down from person to person or translation to translation, chances are that the original understanding has either been distorted or lost completely.

It is for this reason that I began to study Ancient Hebrew and Aramaic – not so that I can learn to speak them but so that I can understand the original biblical manuscripts that were written in these languages. It is not enough to read the Bible literally (first level) or to even limit our understanding at a parable or allegoric degree (second level). We are challenged to search out the fullest intent of the divine Word of God.

Many Christians are afraid to look at texts other than the Bible because they have been taught it is wrong and that no other text is inspired. This was my experience. In a church that I once attended, I was instructed not to read materials that were not denominationally authorized because they likely contradicted that denomination's beliefs.

I have come to learn that God has inspired many texts *if what you are looking for God within them*. We should not be afraid of reading or studying other texts. We are supposed to have developed enough in *Peshat* (Breadth) and *Remez* (Length) to where we have the knowledge, understanding and wisdom to look at any text and perceive what is or isn't inspired by God. That is the benefit and freedom that comes with developing discernment and the leading of the Holy Spirit of Truth. Many do not attain this level because the study is very intense and they do not have the desire, focus, or determination to do it. They would rather "keep it simple," which is perfectly okay if that satisfies them. However, for those that are searching for deeper truths that will eventually lead and synchronize them to the mind, heart, and mouth of God, keeping it simple is just not an option.

Many may ask, "Why would anyone want to look so deeply into the scriptures?" Only a *Darash* level seeker could answer the question – Why? Because we have to. It's a love and passion! It's like the question, "Why would anyone want to climb a mountain or go into outer space?" The answer always comes back, "Because it's there!" For pioneers – even "spiritual pioneers" – it's a good enough reason. It's in their nature to explore. The question that we have to ask ourselves is, "What type of exploration is worth the time, energy and resources that we put into it?"

Many people know that there is more to them and more to God than what they are currently experiencing. They have a hunger that remains unsatisfied. This leads them to seek beyond traditional means of seeking. God has promised in the Bible, "You shall seek me and find me, when you search for me with all your heart" [Jer. 29:13]. This seeking will eventually lead back to a "Genesis 1:26"[111] experience where someone can finally begin to take on the image, likeness and functioning of God. This is what God originally intended for every human to experience. A *Darash* level of learning opens up the portal for this experience.

This level of study requires us to discover, develop and utilize our inner eyes and ears – the senses of the spirit – so that we may connect with the sight and hearing that the Holy Spirit of Truth is designed by God to provide [See John 16:13]. These two spiritual senses are required to accurately connect with God. *Darash* is also the level where *"the transfer of teachers"* begins. You literally go from a place of being taught by other human beings to an experience of being taught by God Himself though His Holy Spirit of Truth – The Ultimate Master Teacher.

> *"But the anointing which you received from Him abides in you, and you do not need anyone to teach you. But as His anointing teaches you concerning all things, and is true and no lie, and as He has taught you, abide in Him"* [1 John 2:27 MKJV].

---

[111] "Then God said, 'Let us make mankind in our image, in our likeness'" (Gen. 1:26a NIV).

I'm not implying that after achieving this level you will never again need a human to teach you. One form of God communicating with and instructing us is through other human beings. Yet we must be aware that our greatest teacher will always be God Himself.

One of the most powerful and influential statements that Jesus made about Himself and the Holy Spirit as it pertains to teachers is the following: "And they shall all be taught of God" [Jn. 6:45]. Jesus demonstrated this transfer of teachers. His followers were learning from a God-sent "Man" (Himself) [John 14:10, 20], but eventually would be taught through the inspiration of a God-sent Spirit [See John 6:45, 16:13]. Unfortunately, this is a level of teaching that many today are unfamiliar with. I used to be one of them.

Jesus' teaching at this level:

The greatest example of Jesus teaching at a *Darash* level is found in His parable of The Soils [Matt. 13:1-23, Mark 4:12, Luke 8:4-15]. It was in this parable that He made the deep statement: "To you it is given to know the mystery of the Kingdom of God." Within this parable He also asked a conditional and qualifying statement: "Do you not know this parable? And how then will you know all parables?" Jesus hinged all understanding of other parables on the clear understanding of this particular one! As we learned in the previous chapter, a deeper look into this parable reveals that it was about prayer.

It is worthy to note that this third level – the *Darash* or "seek" level – is the entry point towards pursuing God at the highest level possible. In my opinion, the word "seek" is one of the most important words in scripture. This word is so important to me that I have its complete definition written in my primary Bible according to multiple Hebrew and Aramaic descriptions. I find myself constantly referring to it to see if my life is currently calibrated and synchronized according to its multifaceted and intricate definitions.

Following is my personal *99-word* definition of this dynamic
and life-changing word, which I have transcribed in my Bible:

Seek = Darash: *To pursue, to study, to explore, to
understand, to inquire, to desire to know, to learn, to
have intelligence of, to consider-ponder-meditate, to
have passion for, to be diligent, to be diligently dedicated,
to perceive and identify, to have an awareness, to gush
or swell over, to search out, to beg, to make inquisition
through questioning, to plead-petition-request, to
appeal, to lobby, to preoccupy yourself with something,
to tread or to frequent, to follow, to pry into, to attain-
find and acquire, to demand counsel, to pray, to rise up,
to enquire early, to bring in the eyes of God!*

I have personally discovered that by working to identify
my life according to this definition, it has introduced a God-
consciousness that has initiated me into the deepest level of
understanding: the *Sod* level. It has transformed my life in
ways that were foreign and unimaginable to me before. I am
learning to live by two key principles pertaining to God and
prayer.

1. My "seek level" will determine my "find level."

2. My "hunger level" will determine my "feed level."

If I seek God with all of my heart, I literally come upon a
Kingdom-of-God Consciousness that has completely tran-
scended my former traditional religious belief system.
When I am truly hungry for God-consciousness, I am fed a
manner of nourishing that I never even knew existed. It is
a realm that cannot be found anywhere on this earth. This
has been the greatest discovery of my life. This discovery
is not an experience that is exclusive to me; it is available
to all human beings. It is available for you! I feel blessed to
know that a stream of my life purpose and goal is to teach

others to discover the same nourishment directly from God for themselves.[112]

> *"Seek the Lord while He may be found; call on Him while He is near"* [Isa. 55:6].

The Lord's Prayer at the *Darash* level of understanding:

This is the application of prayer where the ones praying begin to seek detailed information *from God* as to how the complete framework of The Lord's Prayer pertains specifically to their lives.

This now leads us to the final level of interpretation and understanding of scripture. Thus far, we've comprehended the *Peshat*-Breadth, the *Remez*-Length, and the *Darash*-Depth. Now it's time to move on to the Height, the *Sod* level...

Biblical Interpretation Level Four: *Sod*

Definition: The height of the inner secret, origin of the meaning, secret counsel, the potential.

This level reveals the spiritual truths that are hidden in the text – truths that can only be inspired, revealed and interpreted for you directly from the mouth of God. The result would represent the paradise or "The Eden" experience of one who is truly "Walking in the Spirit." The purpose of this level is to "cross over, lift up, elevate to the sky," which is the definition of *hupos* – the Greek word for "height" in Ephesians 3:18.

---

[112] Subscribe to my website to stay updated on the events and resources that I'm developing in order to teach what I have learned to others: **www.julioalvaradojr. com**

Rabbinic perspective:

As mentioned earlier, traditional rabbinic teaching of the four levels of PaRDeS were mainly used to understand and interpret written scripture. Most rabbis taught the yoke of a rabbi who had come before them. On rare occasions, a rabbi would come along who excelled at such a high level that he would teach a new yoke. He would have developed a new way of interpreting the Torah, one that surpassed other rabbis. This was rare and extraordinary. A rabbi of this stature was classified as a master of all teachers who had what was called *Shmikah*. This meant he was "one who had authority to interpret scripture."

A rabbi who taught with *Shmikah* would say things like, "You have heard it said ..., but I tell you ..." He was basically saying, "You have heard people interpret that verse this way, but I tell you that this is what God really means in that verse." A study of Jesus' yoke and ministry illustrated this unique and authoritative mastery of teaching [See Matt. 5:21, 27, 33, 38, 43].

To the rabbis, the mindset and purpose of the PaRDeS was to acquire knowledge and intimacy with God based off the Torah or Written Word of God. When Jesus arrived on the scene, He introduced the PaRDeS from a Kingdom perspective that the religious leaders of that day were unfamiliar with – hence their struggle with adapting and accepting His knowledge and style of teaching.

The Kingdom perspective of the PaRDeS introduced a level of intimacy with God where the *Spoken Word* from His mouth was made available. Now "the mysteries of the Kingdom" – also known as "the secrets of God" – were available to anyone who believed on His Name and had the desire to search deeply enough to find them.

Jesus' teaching at the Sod level:

This is a level of understanding that very few people experience. Why? Because God will only expose the mystery of Himself to those He can trust ... those who walk the closest to Him. The ultimate example was demonstrated by Jesus Christ himself. Jesus chose Peter, James, and John from among His disciples, and took them to The Mount (symbol of Sod – Height) where they witnessed His transfiguration accompanied by The Voice and affirmation from God the Father. The disciples did not understand what they experiencing. They did not realize that they were witnessing Jesus Christ internalizing or transfiguring "The Light of the World" and the *Sod* level of the Kingdom that was within Him [See Matt. 17:1-13, Mark 9:2-13, Luke 9:27-36].

Once scripture has been internalized, as with Jesus' example on the Mount of Transfiguration, the interpretation and understanding of the scripture – both written and spoken – takes on the same nature and character as that intimate, personal relationship that Jesus had with God. When the scriptures become internalized, God is able to meet us face-to-face right where we are in Christ. When this type of identity has been both realized and enjoined, there is one last facet of understanding within *Sod*. It is an experience beyond understanding because of the magnitude of the internalization. This experience introduces an "As I hear my Father speak I speak" and an "As I see my Father do I so likewise experience" way of living [John 8:28, 12:49-50, 5:19]!

One then has the potential to journey from an interpretive understanding of the written Word to an understanding of the Spoken Word (which is also Scripture) directly from The Interpreter (The Holy Spirit). One goes from an understanding of the Kingdom of God as the written scriptures originally introduce it to an understanding of the Kingdom of God *within* them. This understanding gives detailed knowledge and instructions that, once applied, become the Wisdom of God for your life. It's the affirmation and revelation from the heart of God of who you are in Christ. It is also the revelation of detailed information contained within The Book on Your Life that is delivered to you from God Himself via the Holy Spirit of Truth.[113] This is the ultimate face-to-face (presence-to-presence) experience that Paul declared in First Corinthians:

> *"For now we see in a mirror dimly, but then face to face. Now I know in part, but then I shall fully know even as I also am fully known"* [1 Cor. 13:12 MKJV].

In the PaRDeS system, when a level of mastery is pursued in both a Written Scripture perspective and a Spoken Word perspective, it will create a different hunger and seek level. Each level comes with a sense of responsibility that will lead to a sacred and reverential place of "The Fear of the Lord."

The *Sod* level is also paralleled with the Wisdom of God! It gives you access to the secrets of truth, knowledge, understanding and application for *your* life. It also gives you access to that same knowledge and application of all *God* is for your life. These things can only be found in His mouth. You gain access to the direct counsel of God – the same things Jesus had access to. This is a level of hearing described as "quick understanding."

> *"And shall make him of quick understanding in the fear of the LORD"* [Isa. 11:3 KJV].

> *"Have you heard the secret counsel of God? And do you limit wisdom to yourself?"* [Job 15:8]

The Lord's Prayer at the *Sod* level of understanding:

This was a level of prayer that not even the traditional rabbis with *Shmikah* were aware of. Their prayers were mainly composed of quoting scripture. This would have been part

---

[113] In my next book, *The Mystery of The Kingdom of God Revealed*, I delve deeply into this little known reality.

of the yoke of their teaching. Jesus was now introducing a different level of prayer.

The Pardes is both process and fulfillment! By opening lines of communication with the Spoken Word of God, one is already on the way to Paradise while yet on earth! This method of spiritual growth and understanding is probably the fullest, most comprehensive, and balanced penetration of the Kingdom of God within you.

The *Sod* level reconnects you to your personal Eden or paradise with God. You actually hear the mysteries of the Kingdom of God. They are not literal. They are not parable. They are not "out there." You don't have to try to find the knowledge from other sources. They are here, inside each and every one of us!

Paul was very careful to not boast about himself. Though it may read as though Paul was writing about someone else, this is what Paul experienced and referenced when he was inspired to write the following words. He was speaking about himself and his Sod level experience:

"Indeed, it is not profitable for me to boast. For I will come to visions and revelations of the Lord. I know a man in Christ fourteen years before (whether in the body, I do not know; or outside of the body, I do not know; God knows) such a one was caught up to the third Heaven. And I know such a man (whether in the body, or outside of the body, I do not know; God knows), that he was caught up into Paradise and heard unspeakable words, which it is not allowed for a man to utter" [2 Cor. 12:1-4].

A *Sod* level experience gives you access to the voice of God walking with you directly in your environment. It gives you access to The Tree of Life once again, which is not just a future event but one that should be a present experience in our lives today:

"He who has an ear, let him hear what the Spirit says to the churches. To him who overcomes I will give to eat of the Tree of Life, which is in the midst of the paradise of God" [Rev. 2:7].

The question that we must ask ourselves is: "Do we have an intimacy with God and an ear to hear at this level?"

CHAPTER SUMMARY:

Following is a point summary of the *Pardes* system, a four-level learning system used to interpret scripture, purposed to result in a deeper revelation of the scriptures and a more intimate understanding of and relationship with God:

"Peshat"

- The plain or simple width of a meaning.

- Viewing scripture by looking at literary style, historical and cultural setting, and context.

- The purpose of this level is to "mold, shape, form, or fabricate."

- The beginning of our understanding in Christ.

- Many people never go beyond this level of understanding.

"Remez"

- A parable or allegory that hints or refers to a deeper length of meaning.

- A "wink" in the text; there is something more happening than meets the eye.

- It hints of a deeper meaning beyond the literal words.

- The purpose of this level is to make larger, to expand or make bigger, to make strong.

"Darash"

- To inquire, search, explore or seek for the depth of meaning.

- To inquire into the interpretive meaning of the text, seeking a deeper and broader explanation of the "story behind the story" or the "meaning beneath the meaning."

- This level of understanding ventures into realms that are not literal, parable, or allegoric ... it goes deeper.

- It's peering into the core and nature of the individual words of the Bible by going into the original languages and other texts to understand idioms and ideas.

"Sod"

- The height of inner secrets; discovering the origin of a meaning and secret counsel.

- The fullest potential of understanding.

- This level reveals the spiritual truths that are hidden in the text – truths that can only be inspired, revealed and interpreted for you directly from the mouth of God.

- This is a level of understanding that very few people experience.

- God will only expose the mystery of Himself to those He can trust ... those who walk the closest to Him.

APPLICATION:

1. Our "seek level" will determine our "find level." What is your seek level? Are you eager to discover more and deeper truths from the mouth of God?

2. Our "hunger level" will determine our "feed level." Meditate on this scripture: "As the deer pants for streams of water, so my soul pants for you, my God" (Ps. 46:1). Do you feel that you hunger after God at this level? If not, think about what steps you can take to head in this direction.

3. Ask yourself: "Do I have an intimacy with God and an ear to hear at the highest and deepest level?" It will probably be a process and will take time and focus, but make it your goal and it will transform your life.

PART THREE:

PRAYER PRACTICES

CHAPTER TEN:

Prayer and Fasting

---

*"What the eyes are for the outer world, fasts
are for the inner."*
                              – Mahatma Gandhi

Some readers might initially be inclined to skip over this
chapter due to its subject matter, as fasting does not seem to
be a popular theme in traditional Christianity at large these
days; yet I believe it is one of the most important chapters of
this book. Fasting holds unique potential as it relates to prayer
and connecting to God. Personally, the discipline of fasting has
become my greatest asset in learning how to hear the voice of
God. It has enabled me to acquire a "God consciousness" that I
was not familiar with in my past.[114]

Throughout my earlier years of Christianity, I rarely practiced
fasting. When I did attempt to fast, I quickly became overwhelmed
with hunger pangs, headaches, weakness, irritability, mental
cloudiness, dizziness, and other symptoms. In terms of time,

---

[114] Note: You should always consult with a physician before attempting any short- or
long-term fasting if you have a health condition that might be negatively affected
by fasting.

instead of a "fast" for me it became a "slow." It seemed as though time just slowed down because of the physical discomforts I was experiencing.

Physically, the sudden change to not eating can result in the body going through a detoxification process, which can include symptoms such as changes in sleep and dream patterns, body aches, feeling cold, dehydration, constipation or diarrhea, abnormal body odor, and bad breath due to the release of toxins in the body. At first glance, these seem more like "cons" than "pros" to fasting.

However, the physiological discipline of fasting from various foods has numerous benefits. The many physical health benefits of fasting far outweigh any drawbacks. It gives our digestive system a rest. It detoxifies vital organs. It boosts the immune system, promotes weight loss, and helps to break physical addictions. Once you get beyond the physical adjustments and withdrawals associated with fasting, the numerous mental and spiritual benefits start to become apparent. You begin to experience bursts of energy and a heightened mental alertness, clarity and focus.

Many books have been written on the topic of biblical fasting that give examples of different types of fasting such as "the Daniel fast," "the widow's fast," "the disciples' fast," "the partial fast," and "the absolute fast." The history of fasting goes back thousands of years. Many religions – including Christianity, Judaism, and Eastern religions – used (and still use) fasting as a tool for physical and spiritual purification and communion with God. Physicians and holistic practitioners have used it and currently prescribe it as a healing process to cure mental and physical sicknesses and disorders. Fasting affects not only our physical being, but our mental, emotional, and spiritual self as well.

Initially, my reasons for fasting were mainly to break various mental strongholds that I had been struggling with, or in an attempt to become "more spiritual," or to experience a personal revival in order to get closer to God. I remember saying to myself and at times even making vows to God that I would fast for one day, three days, or seven days without eating any food. The majority of these attempts always ended in failure. I would succumb to the physical discomforts of fasting and break the fast by eating well before my intended goal.

Later I tried to build myself up to go on a long-term fast by only eating certain foods or drinking certain liquids and then eventually going without food completely for three to seven days. Many of these attempts also ended in failure. Once I tried to cut all foods from my diet, I ended up giving in to the feelings of physical discomfort and eating.

My initial reason to fast was to couple the action with prayer in order to make spiritual progress, yet there were times when I would complete one or two days without eating and I would be too mentally defocused and tired to pray. It was these times that I found myself more on a hunger strike than a spiritual fast. One of the main lessons that I learned during those 16 years of attempts here and there was that I was not a disciplined person; I was addicted to food and unhealthy liquid choices such as soda and coffee. Though I believe that God honored my attempts, I did not understand the true purpose of fasting or the preparation process I needed to first go through before entering a time of fasting. Though my motives were genuine, I lacked the knowledge, discipline and focus that a true lifestyle of prayer and fasting required.

The word "fast" according to the Bible is the Hebrew word *tsôm,* which is simply defined as an abstinence from food.[115] My primary focus in this chapter is to look into the fasting that Jesus referred to and that He Himself practiced, which was to abstain from all sources of food (only liquids were consumed). This type of fast was the one most commonly practiced in the Bible. It introduced Jesus to another source of appetite: a diet of spiritual nourishment. My personal experience with fasting has

---

[115] *Strongs* #6685: AHLB#: 1404-J (N)

taught me that fasting completely from all solid foods and only consuming liquids (primarily water and some natural juices) has been the most rewarding.

Biblically, all fasts fell under one of three types:

- The Normal Fast: No solid food is eaten but liquids are consumed [Matt. 4:1-2, Lk. 4:2].

- The Absolute Fast: Abstaining from both food and liquids [Acts 9:9]. [Note: Due to the modern toxins and pollutants found in many food sources, it is advisable to at least consume water to flush the body of these harmful chemicals.]

- The Partial Fast: Diet is restricted from certain types of food; or meals that are normally consumed during certain times of the day are skipped rather than total abstinence from food [Dan. 1:15; 10:2-3].

What is traditionally known as the "Daniel fast" was a result of Daniel and his friends refusing to eat food that was unlawful for them as Jews to consume [See Dan. 1:8-14, 10:3]. Some call this a partial fast. Though this is a change in one's diet – which does have some benefits in temporarily eliminating some type of foods – it is not a fast in the truest sense of the word, which is to abstain from *all* food. Daniel did practice a fast in which he abstained from all solid foods [Dan. 9:3], yet the "Daniel fast" often spoken of is the partial fast from the first chapter of Daniel rather than the complete fast from Daniel Chapter nine. The Daniel fast has probably become the most "popular" Christian fast as it accommodates a sense of a spiritual accomplishment without the greater physical discomforts of abstaining from all forms of foods.

Since deciding in January of 2009 to make fasting a normal part of my life, I have lost over 20 pounds. Sin-wise I have also lost a lot of weight due to the practice of fasting coupled with strategic prayer.

"Let us lay aside every weight, and the sin which so easily ensnares us" [Heb. 12:1].

I started out in my journey to make fasting a lifestyle by making a covenant with God where I planned to fast at least one day a week for an entire year. That year I recorded 51 days of fasting. I fell short by one day of my goal. In looking back at the year, I experienced exponential spiritual growth that I attribute to fasting. The following year, I set out with the same goal of fasting one day a week and ended up fasting for a total of 112 days. This number came about through fasting for a combination of between one to 15 days throughout the year, with each session having a specific purpose. I kept a journal of each experience.

For the last two years, fasting has become a non-negotiable element in my life. Through its practice I have experienced numerous benefits in my physical body, my soul, and my spirit. Fasting has given me a heightened awareness of who I really am and who I am supposed to be. It has also brought me to a better understanding of whom and what God is meant to be in my life. It has given me a unique consciousness of both God and my own life that I was not experiencing before I decided to make it a part of my lifestyle.

Today in the Western Hemisphere, many chronic health problems result from bad eating habits. In the United States it is now estimated that over one-third of the population is obese. In the world today, some people are over-nourished; others are malnourished. Some are actually both. People are accustomed to eating for the taste and the feeling of fullness rather than eating the small portions that are actually needed for proper nourishment. The amount of food that the typical American consumes in one sitting is more than the body needs and can effectively digest. Unfortunately, the American diet is primarily comprised of chemically altered, high-fat, toxic foods that clog the eliminative systems, causing ineffective digestion. Poor eating practices and dietary choices affect our health, energy levels and spirituality more than we realize.

One day I was having a conversation with a co-worker named Terence. We were discussing spiritual maturity and discipline. He made a statement that was revelatory to me. He said, "Julio, the more spiritual one becomes, the less food you should have to eat." I have since come to believe that one does not *become* more spiritual as life goes on but rather *discovers* more of their spirituality as life goes on. Still, what he said made sense to me. When someone matures in their spirituality, natural disciplines should take effect in every facet of their life, including their diet. More importantly, there is such a thing as a "spiritual diet." Our spirits need spiritual nourishment that can only come from God.

We are accustomed to either feeding ourselves spiritually or we allow other humans to "feed" us and we consider it spiritual feeding. Though this type of feeding may contain value, it often caters more towards an acquisition of knowledge that adds to our human intellect. Only Spirit can feed a spirit. When the Spirit of God is feeding your spirit, you end up acquiring true spiritual intelligence, which will always supersede human intellect.

Knowledge from this world cannot effectively feed your spirit; it might feed your mind or bring some sustenance, but that is not enough. Fasting has the potential to activate a lifestyle and level of prayer that can only be experienced through this discipline. The vast majority of Christians who neglect fasting will fail to experience this same level of prayer and connection to Christ.

In one biblical account, Jesus reveals a secret as to what made Him so effective in His earthly ministry. In this account, a father had a son who was demon possessed. This boy suffered from epileptic seizures and would cast himself in fires and water while in the midst of a fit [See Matt. 17:14-21, Mk. 9:14-29, Lk. 9:37-42]. The father of the boy stated that Jesus' disciples had not been able to cast the demon out of the boy.

Right before and after Jesus cast the evil spirit from the boy, He made some interesting and pointed statements as to why the disciples could not cast the demon out. These reasons all had to do with faith. First, He called them faithless. This did not imply that they did not believe enough in order to help the boy, since they made an honest attempt to help him. What the word faithless meant here is that their belief did not come from the place where faith should originate. In other words, they had self-imposed faith instead of God-revealed faith.

After this, the disciples asked Jesus why they could not cast the evil spirit from the boy. Jesus' response to them came in the form of an analogy of faith being like a mustard seed. In another parable, Jesus stated that the mustard seed of faith has to be fully grown or matured in order to effectively function in its God-ordained purpose [Matt. 13:32]. Jesus summed up the lesson by saying, "This kind can come out by nothing, but by prayer and fasting" [Mark 9:29 KJV].

In order to understand the depth of Jesus' teaching on faith likened to a mustard seed, we must first understand what true faith is and where true faith comes from:

> *"So then faith comes by hearing, and hearing by the word of God"* [Rom. 10:17 NKJV].

"Word" in this passage is the word *Rhēma* in Greek. It means "an utterance or a narration that comes through speech."[116] In Hebrew, the root word is *emer*, which means "something said." *Emer* comes from the word *emet*, which is the Hebrew word for "truth." If you position yourself to listen to the voice of God – which is truth – you will discover what you are to have faith in and for. Faith is believing what God told you or showed you is His will for you. This faith should compel you to produce the works necessary in order to bring His plan to pass.

The word "kind" that Jesus used is the Greek word *genos*, which is where the English word genes comes from – the foundational word for generations. From a Greek perspective, it is defined as "a kin, a descendant of the same species or offspring born from

---

[116] *Strongs* #4487

the same country." The Hebrew word originally used here is *mîyn*, which is described as "strength that is continued through the blood." It is also described as "the passing of strength and skill to the next generation through the nourishment of truth."[117]

What Jesus was saying here is that unless you function like the offspring of your heavenly Father, you will not be able to exercise the strength and skill that only comes through a level of nourishing truth. This level – unattainable by other means – is a natural result of a lifestyle of prayer and fasting.

People primarily fast from a *re*active standpoint – because something is wrong or out of order in their life. Jesus fasted from a *pro*active standpoint – to maintain order in His life. When Jesus said, "Pray that you enter not into temptation for the spirit is willing but the flesh is weak" [Matt. 26:41], we must remember that He was in a mode of fasting when He was tempted by the Devil. This is how His spirit was strengthened to where He did not give in to the temptations that He faced. [See Matt. 4:1-11, 26:41, Mk. 14:38, Lk. 22:40, 46]

When we fail to fast, we tend to rely heavily on traditional religious activity and experiences as well as the Written Word of the Bible for feeding. Fasting introduces us to heavenly knowledge from a Spoken Word perspective that becomes a form of personalized scripture that directs us towards specific "Kingdom life" activities and experiences.

Jesus always approached God in a "fasted" state – in the mornings when He would go to a quiet place to learn from God. (The word breakfast denotes the time where we break the fast of not eating or drinking throughout the night.) These prayer sessions introduced Him to verbal instructions that came directly from God and contained daily details for His life. These details became scripture for His life. They were not found in the Bible, yet they led Jesus to fulfill what the Written Word (the Bible) prophesied about Him [See Isa. 50:4-5, Heb. 10:7].

---

[117] *Strongs* #4327: AHLB#: 1290-C (J), (N)

Fasting is a multidimensional and multi-beneficial experience. I have found that fasting provides me the opportunity to release myself from the earthly ties that would otherwise keep me from experiencing a sacred and deep connection with God. Fasting has introduced me to the priority of the first commandment, which is to love God with all of my heart, soul, and mind. I am learning that this commandment has to be mastered before I can love myself and others accurately [Mk. 12:30]. Fasting has been the primary conduit for me to fulfill Jesus' mandate to "Seek first the Kingdom of God and His righteousness" [Matt. 6:33]. It has transformed my prayer life into a richer, deeper experience where the voice and presence of God are much clearer and easily perceived.

Strategic fasting coupled with prayer has been the primary catalyst in approaching God with humility, which is a requirement in seeking the face or presence of God. King David made a profound statement in the book of Psalms when he stated, "I humbled my soul with fasting and prayer" [Ps. 35:13]. The word humbled that is used here is the Hebrew word *anâh*, which is defined as "an affliction that is necessary in order to watch over something of importance." It further describes what is watched over as "the temple or dwelling place of a god."[118]

The purpose of fasting was viewed as a "self-affliction" that was accomplished through abstaining from food in order to watch over one's soul, to ensure that it was kept naked of anything that would negatively affect it. The discipline of fasting was necessary in order to humble oneself and to ensure that no form of pride or carnality would come between the individual and God:

---

[118] *Strongs* #6051: AHLB#: 1359-A(N), J(A)

"If My people who are called by My name will humble themselves, and pray and seek My face, and turn from their wicked ways, then I will hear from heaven, and will forgive their sin and heal their land. Now My eyes will be open and My ears attentive to prayer made in this place" [2 Chr. 7:14, 15].

One of the major benefits of strategic prayer and fasting is discovering and developing our spiritual senses – the inner eyes and ears of the spirit. These were the inner senses that navigated Jesus' life, which maximized and fulfilled the Kingdom of God that was within Him.

Fasting will take you to a place where you will not get knowledge *about* God but knowledge *from* God Himself. If practiced consistently and strategically, it will introduce you to a different appetite that is simply out of this world. It provides you with a visualization of your current spiritual condition. Through strategically and consistently practicing it, fasting will provide you with accurate guidance that ultimately leads you to a true Kingdom mindset. The counsel of the Holy Spirit will lead you to the righteousness of God free from any outer trappings that may negatively influence you.

In order to understand the primary purpose of fasting as it relates to spiritual growth and development, we must look at two key words from Jesus' experience in the wilderness before His public ministry began:

"Then Jesus was led up by the Spirit into the wilderness to be tempted by the devil. And when He had fasted forty days and forty nights, afterward He was hungry" [Matt. 4:1-2].

The first key word is "wilderness." From a Greek perspective it is the word *erēmos*. It is described as "an uninhabited outer environment where solitude takes place such as a desert or forest." From a Hebrew perspective it is the word *midbar*, described as "an outer environment that affects an inner environment." It is defined as "an inner sanctuary or a place where speech creates order through what is heard."[119] The primary root word of *midbar* is *dabar*, which is defined as "an arrangement of words that comes through speech that creates order."[120]

The second key word is "fasted," which comes from the Greek word *nēsteuō*, defined simply as "an abstinence from food." From the ancient Hebrew perspective the word "fasted" is both the words *tsôm* and *qârâ*. The word *tsôm* is once again defined as "an abstinence from food." The word *qârâ* describes what should eventually happen during the process of one fasting from food when coupled with prayer. This eventual outcome describes what is spoken *to* you *from God* rather than what you speak to God. *Qârâ* is described as "an event or meeting where one experiences an encounter." In the case of fasting, the encounter is between you and the Spirit of God. It also describes what takes place at this encounter, as *selected individuals who are sensitive to the distinctive call on their lives who position themselves in order to have a scroll read to them at this meeting.*[121]

This gives more meaning to Jesus' statement that "many are called but few are chosen" [Matt. 20:16, 22:14]. Every human being is called by God, but few submit to the lifestyle of prayer and fasting that is purposed to show them the exact details of their calling. You will only be exposed to God's call on your life by consistently opening your soul to the unhindered voice of God. It is through this process that you gain access to the "scroll" of what has already been prescribed, prewritten and pre-purposed for your life. Many confuse and limit the calling of God with a ministry position. A ministry is just a function of one's calling; it is not the actual calling itself. The calling of God is *miqrâ* in Hebrew, which is described as "a rehearsal where a reading takes place."[122] What is read to you is the script for your life,

---

[119] *Strongs* #4057: AHLB#: 2093 (h)
[120] *Strongs* #1697: AHLB#: 2093 (N)
[121] *Strongs* #7121: AHLB#: 1434-E
[122] *Strongs* #4744: AHLB#: 1434-E (h)

based on what God has written about you, which He has called you to act out or perform in your life.

The wilderness is a place of unhindered inner growth. Jesus fasted by being led from a higher influence when the Spirit of God directed Him to fast for 40 days. As a human being He also fasted from His lower inner human spirit nature in order to remain connected to the higher "Spirit of God" influence.

Fasting coupled with prayer from a hearing perspective is what gave Jesus the ability to test all things and only attach Himself to those things that were good and assigned for His life in order to experience the God of peace. This is when the God of peace feeds you. This experience is what preserved and kept Jesus whole, complete and sanctified, set apart from any worldly influence or evil. This is what enabled Him to remain holy, pure and balanced in His spirit, soul and body.

> *"Test all things; hold fast what is good. Abstain from every form of evil. Now may the God of peace Himself sanctify you completely; and may your whole spirit, soul, and body be preserved blameless at the coming of our Lord Jesus Christ"* [1 Thess. 5:21-23].

It was through a lifestyle of fasting and prayer that no worldly system or influence was allowed to govern His life. The system that did govern and influence His life was the government of the Kingdom of God within Him. Through fasting, Jesus was introduced to an appetite that was not from this world but was the environment of The Kingdom of Heaven.

Fasting is one of the most neglected disciplines and admonitions, yet it is where *the fullness* of the counsel of God's spirit takes place. It is where we can lower the volume of physical pursuits in order to focus on spiritual pursuits that lead to us living according to the perfect will of God. It was what gave Jesus what the scripture calls "quick understanding" [Isa. 11:3]. One who has quick understanding is one who breathes the breath – or in Hebrew terminology, the *Rûach* – of God's words.

Even though fasting is not a commandment, it is a spiritual mandate. God expects us to fast: "*When* you fast" [Mat 6:16] ... not "if you fast." Fasting is an act of humility and obedience to God. I have come to learn that fasting doesn't move God; it moves me towards God.

During a fast, you may experience a roller coaster of spiritual struggles and victories, discomforts and failures. In the morning you may feel like you are on top of the world, but by evening you may be wrestling both physically and emotionally. You may be constantly tempted to raid the refrigerator and you will undoubtedly be counting how many days are left in your fast. This is especially true if you are new at fasting. To counteract temptations, I find that what you focus on is what becomes larger to you. I try to focus not on the fact that I am not eating physically, but that I am going to be fed spiritually. This spiritual benefit far outweighs any benefit that physical food gives me.

Fasting can bring indescribable blessings to a Christian's life and spiritual walk with God, but it is not always easy. During such a time of discipline, self-sacrifice, and reflection, do not be surprised if you experience mental and physical discomforts. One of the greatest difficulties you will likely face is the challenge of refraining from eating. The root of much of the evil today is found in the inability to discipline and control oneself. The fact that so many people today are overweight or even obese gives credence to the fact that few have the discipline to stop eating when they have had enough; they overeat or indulge in more than the body needs, resulting in unnecessary weight gain. If nothing else, fasting is a vital lesson in self-control, yet it has so many more benefits than just that one.

Chapter 58 of the book of Isaiah is a sort of "instruction guide" on the purposes and the benefits of fasting. These Scriptures address many of the problems that are found in the individual, the church and in the world today. The chapter begins with a message from God, describing some of the abuses that were often practiced during a fast. Starting in verse six of this chapter, He states four primary purposes and benefits of fasting:

> *"Is this not the fast that I have chosen:*
> *To loose the bonds of wickedness,*
> *To undo the heavy burdens,*
> *To let the oppressed go free,*
> *And that you break every yoke?"* [Isa. 58:6]

Regardless of what the condition is – whether it is a harmful addiction or some type of mental or spiritual struggle – it will most likely fall under one or more of these four conditions: bonds of wickedness, heavy burdens, oppression, or an ungodly yoke.

"To Loose the Bonds of Wickedness"

According to ancient Hebrew thought, wickedness is described as "someone who has departed from the correct path."[123] The correct path will always be the path of life that God has prescribed for you. It is vitally important to learn to hear the voice of God so that you can know God's will for every day of your life. As extreme as this may sound, anyone who is not operating within God's will for their lives is scripturally classified as "dysfunctional, wicked or evil."[124]

"To Undo the Heavy Burdens"

These heavy burdens are defined as "a group of things that can include people." They are those things we have allowed to invade our lives, things that we were originally not designed

---

[123] *Strongs* #7562: AHLB#: 2799 (N)
[124] "Wicked" – *Strongs* #7563: AHLB#: 2799 (N), "Evil" – *Strongs* #7451: AHLB#: 1460-A (N)

or ordained to carry or be connected to.[125] Examples could be our workload, our financial situation, or certain relationships that we maintain. These things can cause us to be poor in spirit, resources, or understanding.

For me, these "heavy burdens" included ministries that God did not intend for me to be involved in, or ministries that I was involved in for too long because I was not sensitive to the seasons that God had ordained for my life. I was also burdened by the weight of sin from my past. I was constantly tormenting myself with them because I was unwittingly not accepting the forgiveness of God and refused to forgive myself.

"To Let the Oppressed Go Free"

A person oppressed is described as "someone who is crushed to pieces" due to some type of struggle that has been placed upon them.[126] Someone else might have placed this struggle or weight on the person or it could be self-inflicted. In any case, the end result is heavy oppression.

Oppression often comes as result of someone treating you badly by abusing authority or power in order to put an unjust burden on you. This can cause depression, which results in sadness, discouragement, despair and hopelessness – feelings that always devalue the true worth of a person. These conditions can lead to bitterness, resentment, an inability to forgive and even unbelief.

I have experienced oppression from spiritual leaders who lacked understanding regarding true, God-ordained authority. Such authority will never use manipulative practices in an attempt to demand submission. I have found that when spiritual leaders act this way, they are either insecure, have a self-imposed view of spiritual authority, or they have been trained

---

[125] *Strongs* #92: AHLB#: 1050-J (n1)
[126] *Strongs* #7533: AHLB#: 1455-B (V)

from a humanistic religious or denominational perspective. True spiritual authority comes from being trained by God Himself.

Oppression is a sign that complete freedom is not being experienced – physically, mentally, spiritually, or any combination of the three. Knowledge and application of the truth that comes from the mouth of God is the highest and most effective source of freedom. It is one of the primary benefits that we experience when we decide to abide in the words that God has for our lives. When we listen to the words from His mouth, we are qualified as a student of God, and the subject matter is always truth – knowledge that is predestined and prescribed for our life, designed and purposed to give us freedom in every aspect of life.

"That You Break Every Yoke"

Even as a believer, I have to admit that I went through seasons where I felt suffocated under the weights and stresses of life. I longed to be free. Ultimately, fasting has the ability to remove any negative yoke from your life that has become a form of bondage because you are not designed to be attached to it. Scripture tells us, "Stand fast therefore in the liberty by which Christ has made us free, and do not be entangled again with a yoke of bondage" [Gal. 5:1].

The access to unhindered truth that produces liberty started with Jesus' crucifixion. The ongoing provision of liberty comes through the words that The Holy Spirit of Truth provides. Such freedom keeps us from being entangled by any yokes. This reality is exemplified in Jesus words, "And you shall know the truth, and the truth shall make you free" [Jn. 8:32].

True freedom actually introduces you to another yoke. It is a yoke that doesn't produce bondage but is a yoke that you are designed to be attached to. Scripturally, there is only one yoke authorized and prescribed for your life. In the following portion of scripture Jesus describes this kind of yoke:

"Take My yoke upon you and learn from Me, for I am gentle and lowly in heart, and you will find rest for your souls. For My yoke is easy and My burden is light" [Matt. 11:29-30].

The word *yoke* that Jesus uses in this particular passage has a dual meaning. First, it is synonymous with the word "fast." It is the Hebrew word *motot* and the Aramaic word *tevâth*, which are both simply defined as "fast or fasting."[127] This verse can be easily read as "take my kind of fasting upon you and learn from me or where I get my learning from."

The second meaning of this word comes from an ancient Hebrew perspective where the word "yoke" is described as "to work together through the eye of experience and knowledge."[128] As mentioned in a previous chapter, in Hebraic and other cultures, when they would train oxen to plow a field, they always yoked an experienced ox with an inexperienced one so that the knowledge of the older ox would influence the inexperienced ox. In other words, when we yoke ourselves to God, He will lead us with His sight, knowledge and experience.

This is where the concept of "the light of God" comes from. Light, from an ancient Hebrew perspective, is "knowledge that illuminates." When Jesus said, "My yoke is easy and My burden is light," Jesus was implying that this kind of illuminated knowledge comes through fasting. Through fasting we receive the knowledge of the burden that we are designed and purposed to carry. Jesus illustrated this concept in the following scripture:

In the meantime His disciples urged Him, saying, "Rabbi, eat." But He said to them, "I have food to eat of which you do not know." Therefore the disciples said to one another, "Has anyone brought Him anything to eat?" Jesus said to them, "My food is to do the will of Him who sent Me, and to finish His work" [Jn. 4:31-34].

---

[127] *Strongs* H2908
[128] *Strongs* #5923: AHLB#: 1357

In other words, "I am yoked to the will of my father and this is what nourishes me." Jesus was describing His burden – His yoke –, which was to do the will of God. He continually received knowledge of His Father's will through a consistent lifestyle of fasting that was coupled with prayer primarily from a hearing standpoint. This is the yoke that makes life simple because you come to understand God's burden for your life – the burden that He has placed within you that must be discovered and developed. You receive details of this burden through knowledge that will illuminate your path.

Iniquity is the root cause of the failure to receive what the Bible describes as "the simplicity that is in Christ" [2 Cor. 11:3]. This simplicity is the ability to hear the unhindered voice of God. Satan uses iniquity to rob believers in crafty ways that are for the most part unbeknownst to them. The word "simplicity" originates from the Hebrew words *tom* and *yosher*. Combined, these words describe what is necessary to make someone "mature, whole, full, complete, perfect and upright."[129]

The burden of God is not a negative burden but a positive one. It simplifies your life rather than makes it more complex. The burden of God for your life is the reason why He created you. It contains God's will for your life that defines you as an answer to a problem in this world. His burden is, in a way, solved through your life when you live according to His script.

Bringing the Good News

Although verses Isaiah 58:7-12 could be applied to fulfilling some type of physical need, it is important to understand that they are also metaphoric expressions that should be applied spiritually. These six verses have two key subjects. The first is to rid yourself of any yoke that hinders you from experiencing God-likeness – your original state of being – which is necessary

---

[129] *Strongs* #8537: AHLB#: 1496-J (N); *Strongs* #3476: AHLB#: 1480-L (g)

so that you are able to clearly hear from God. When you are out from under the burden of any hindering yokes, you are freed to experience the second subject matter of these five key verses: to discover and fulfill your preordained responsibility (yoke) toward others:

> *"Is it not to share your bread with the hungry, and that you bring to your house the poor who are cast out; when you see the naked, that you cover him, and not hide yourself from your own flesh?"* [Isa. 58:7]

Although this verse can of course be applied from a natural standpoint in providing food, shelter and clothing to someone who is in need, the term "and not hide yourself from your own flesh" carries a deeper spiritual meaning. As mentioned in chapter four, the word flesh is *basar*, which is commonly defined as "the skin and muscle or the whole of the person." In the *Ancient Hebrew Lexicon of the Bible, basar* is also defined as "someone who brings good news," which is the definition for the word "gospel." This concept is derived from the ancient Hebrew perspective of someone who functions as a messenger who brings good news from another environment [See Rom. 10:15, Eph.6:15].

From a spiritual perspective, to "not hide yourself from your own flesh" means that we should not keep the Gospel a secret. We are meant to share the good news with others. Fasting at this level introduces you to your specific Gospel (good news), which is the preordained purpose that you are to flesh out into the world.

A deeper look into the key words "hide yourself" describes what is hidden as "ancient information that is in the past or future, as a time hidden from the present."[130] It further describes someone who is without such information as "one who is foolish in that they are without the wisdom of God."[131] In the next verse,

---

[130] *Strongs* #5956: AHLB#: 2544
[131] *Strongs* #3808: AHLB#: 1254-J (N)

God promises what we will receive when we are faithful to live according to His instructions in the previous scripture:

"Then your light shall break forth like the morning, your healing shall spring forth speedily, and your righteousness shall go before you; the glory of the LORD shall gather you" [Isa. 58:8].

From an ancient Hebrew perspective, light is a reference to illuminated knowledge. Healing is a reference to original restoration. Righteousness is a reference to the uprightness of God. The glory of the Lord is the full weight or measure of God. The spiritual application of this verse is that God's foreknowledge about you is exposed to you in the mornings. It introduces spiritual healing, restoration, and exposure to your original perfect state of being – which is you created in the likeness and image of God. This enables you to be upright or righteous like God. The full weight or essence of God enlightens you as to the full weight or essence of who you are.

Jesus experienced this in the mornings when He positioned Himself to pray from a hearing perspective. It is what gave Him the power to become a healer of many while He was on earth and ultimately to bring spiritual healing to the nations [See Isa. 50:4-5, 61:1-3].

This illuminated knowledge for your life has the potential to produce healing in your spirit, soul or body. It introduces you to God's definition of righteousness for your life. The full weight and essence of who God is will guard and preserve your life so that you may fulfill your purpose. Living in this manner gets God's attention. It causes you to function like Jesus did – as a light unto the world, a life that brings illuminated knowledge that becomes an answer to someone else's problems.

"Then you shall call, and the LORD will answer; you shall cry, and He will say, 'Here I am.' If you take away the yoke from your midst, the pointing of the finger, and speaking wickedness, if you extend your soul to the hungry and satisfy the afflicted soul, then your light shall dawn in the darkness, and your darkness shall be as the noonday" [Isa. 58:9-10].

What is interesting about these two verses is that there are four key "removal requirements" that precede the primary benefit of the Lord presenting Himself in a "Here I Am" position in your life. The first is "to remove any yoke from within you," which we explored in verse six. Any yoke other that than the yoke of God for your life will always leave you susceptible to a distorted life.

"The pointing of the finger" is an ancient Hebrew term that is rich in depth. It signifies that something or someone – which can include yourself – is being allowed to negatively instruct or direct your life. The pointing of the finger is also a term that is ascribed to God which is known as the *yârâh yârâ*. It describes God as a teacher or instructor that points the correct way of life.[132]

"Speaking wickedness" is a term that means "to speak vanity."[133] Vanity is the Hebrew word *aven*, which is also the word for iniquity. In other words, in this scripture, to speak wickedness is to speak iniquity. To speak iniquity is to pervert the *dabar* of God, which is the word of God – also known as the truth.

The word "soul" in the phrase "to extend your soul to the hungry and satisfy the afflicted soul" is the Hebrew word *nephesh*. It is defined as "the mind and heart of a person" which is where the whole or the will of the person resides. A fact that

---

[132] *Strongs* #3384: AHLB#: 1227-H
[133] "Speaking" – *Strongs* #1696: AHLB#: 2093 (V); "Vanity-Iniquity" – *Strongs* #205: AHLB#: 1014-J (N)

is unknown to many is that God also has a soul [Isa. 41:1]. When God breathed into Adam, he became a living soul [Gen.2:7]. When God created Adam, he received what I call "Soul-to-soul resuscitation." As it relates to God, His *nepesh* is "what refreshes the whole of the person."[134] God is a Spirit that contains a soul that is always purposed to refresh human beings. The Spirit of God contains the breath of God. When He breathes knowledge into you, you receive a part of His soul, which contains His mind, heart and will for your life. So "to extend our soul to those that are afflicted" is to extend the knowledge that God has breathed into you that is an answer to the affliction that the other person is experiencing. In essence it is soul-to-soul resuscitation or refreshing. This is important to understand because it sets the tone for the rest of the benefits of fasting.

> *"The LORD will guide you continually, and satisfy your soul in drought, and strengthen your bones; you shall be like a watered garden, and like a spring of water, whose waters do not fail"* [Isa. 58:11].

We have already explored how God satisfies your soul. Let's now explore the depth of the metaphoric expression in how "the Lord strengthens your bones." Biologically, blood cells are produced within the marrow of the bones.

As mentioned in chapter three, the Golgi Apparatus, also known as the Golgi Complex, are protein cells found next to the nucleus that holds the DNA. The Golgi Apparatus is designed to collect and store behaviors, histories and memories that are transferred to the next generation. When you properly appropriate the blood of Jesus into your life, you get the Golgi Apparatus of God. In other words, you get the complex "traffic" of truth information – the genes, character, behaviors, histories, and the very memories – of God Himself. God-consciousness will be traveling through your body and spirit, affecting your

---

[134] *Strongs* #5315: AHLB#: 2424

thoughts and spirit in a wonderful way. This is the secret of what made Jesus so "Father-conscious."[135]

The three metaphoric expressions that relate to water in verse 11 are symbolic of the spoken word of God that cleanses and nourishes [See also Deut. 32: 1-3, Isa. 55:10-11, Ps. 119:9, Eph. 5:26].

"Those from among you shall build the old waste places; you shall raise up the foundations of many generations; and you shall be called the Repairer of the Breach, The Restorer of Streets to Dwell In" [Isa. 58:12].

To "build old waste places" and "to raise up the foundations of many generations" are both metaphoric expressions that signify the rebuilding process of bringing people back to their original mindset and foundation, where all of humanity originally came from before the foundations of the world. This place is in the mind of God. When we allow ourselves to be used by God in this capacity, we are classifies as a "Repairer of the Breach and a Restorer of Streets to Dwell in." We become, in a sense, a bridge for those that are disconnected from God; we help put them on the correct roadway for their lives.

The power of strategic and properly motivated fasting cannot be underestimated and should not be overlooked. In my opinion, it is the necessary discipline that aids in the process of removing all that is not like God within the human being. It introduces us to all that is like God within our body, soul and spirit. Physically we need natural food that comes from this world to sustain our bodies. Yet our souls and spirits need spiritual nourishment to sustain us. This level of sustenance can only come from another world, from the Kingdom of Heaven, which is where the mind of God does this feeding from.

---

[135] This topic is explored further in my first book in this series, titled *The Mystery of Iniquity Revealed.*

Helpful Tips for Fasting from Personal Experience

I have personally used fasting to remove addictions from my life. Through personal experience, I have come to firmly believe that the fastest way to kill an addiction is to starve it.

When I am fasting, I avoid temptation by not going to places or events where food is being served.

I try to stay away from all forms of media such as T.V. and radio broadcasts, even if it is spiritual programming. I want to be sensitive to the voice of God and not the voice of man.

I do not accept invitations to social events especially if there is some type of entertainment involved.

I exercise moderately by walking or jogging on a treadmill (an exercise bike could also work) and use a vision board while exercising that has images of projects that I am working on and goals that I want to achieve.

I practice meditation throughout my day for the purpose of improving my inner ability to be still and concentrate solely on hearing the voice of God in order to experience "teachable moments" from God.

I drink water throughout the day to stay hydrated. I also drink natural, unsweetened juice and mentally imagine that as a meal.

I do not keep "junk food" in the house and ask my wife not to prepare foods that will serve as a greater temptation than I can bear.

CHAPTER SUMMARY:

- Fasting gives you a heightened awareness of who you really are and who you are supposed to be. It helps you better understand who and what God is meant to be in your life.

- When people mature in their spirituality, natural disciplines should take effect in every facet of their life, including their diet.

- Our spirits need food that can only come from God. Knowledge from this world cannot effectively feed the spirit.

- Fasting has the potential to activate a lifestyle and level of prayer that can only be experienced through this discipline.

- Unless you function like the offspring of your heavenly Father, you will not be able to exercise the strength and skill that only comes through a level of nourishing truth, which is a natural result of a lifestyle of prayer and fasting.

- Fasting releases us from earthly ties that would otherwise keep us from experiencing a deep connection with God.

- The spiritual benefit of fasting far outweighs any benefit that physical food gives us.

- Through fasting we receive the knowledge of the burden that we are designed and purposed to carry.

APPLICATION:

1. "Many confuse and limit the calling of God with a ministry position. A ministry is just a function of one's calling; it is not the actual calling itself." Pray about whether you have confused "ministry" with "calling" and if so, seek the Lord as to what your true calling is.

2. Harmful addictions, mental struggles and spiritual battles often fall under one or more of these four conditions: bonds of wickedness, heavy burdens, oppression, or an ungodly yoke. Review these sections and take notes on whether you are experiencing the negative effects of any of these conditions. Do you believe that complete freedom is available to you? Perhaps the missing component is fasting and prayer.

3. The power of strategic and properly motivated fasting cannot be underestimated and should not be overlooked. Physically we need natural food, yet our spirits need spiritual nourishment to sustain us. Pray and ask the Lord whether you should begin fasting, using one of the following methods: The Normal Fast [Matt. 4:1-2, Lk. 4:2]; The Absolute Fast [Acts 9:9]; The Partial Fast [Dan. 1:15; 10:2-3]. Read the related scriptures and determine what type of fast would be best for you to take on, and how to go about it.

CHAPTER ELEVEN:

Kingdom Meditation

"One who fails to meditate fails to prepare the meeting room for the mediation between themselves and God."
– Julio Alvarado Jr.

Meditation can probably be classified as the most important practice relating to prayer; yet, similar to fasting, it is probably the least understood and practiced discipline. The word "meditation" in Hebrew has two primary definitions. The most common one is defined from the Hebrew word *hâgâh* and it means "to cud, to imagine, to ponder or muse in being in continual contemplation over a matter." The following verse reveals the application of this definition:

"This book of the Law shall not depart out of your mouth, but you shall meditate on it by day and by night, so that you may be careful to do according to all that is written in it. For then you shall make your way prosperous, and then you shall act wisely" [Josh. 1:8].

Joshua was instructed to meditate day and night on what today are the first five books of the Bible, known as the Torah or the Law of Moses. From this particular passage we can see that meditation was not just limited to the mind in thinking but also had something to do with the mouth. The words were not to depart out of Joshua's mouth. This implies a reading of the Scriptures as well as a verbal and vocal interaction with God in His word. A key to this verse is found in the following words: "so that you may be careful to do according to all that is written in it," which resulted in one's way being made "prosperous."

Joshua experienced the presence of God through hearing the voice (the spoken word) of God through his physical ears [Josh. 1:1-9]. With his physical eyes also, Joshua experienced the Torah (the written word) on which he was commanded to meditate day and night. The Spirit of God, who spoke to him from an external position, led Joshua. Today our lives become "prosperous" when we are led by the Spirit of God; it is referred to as being spirit-filled – which is being led by the voice of God's Spirit in our minds.

Traditionally in religious environments, the teaching of meditation is taught from a "Joshua 1:8" perspective. The person is instructed to simply pick a portion of scripture and to think and quote the passage repeatedly in order to internalize the scripture. Though this practice may help the student to memorize the verse and to extract valuable principles from it, this is only one form of meditation. This form of biblical meditation is object oriented. It begins with reflective reading and rereading of a passage of scripture and is followed by reflection on what has been read and committed to memory. While there are benefits to this practice, it's certainly not the full scope of meditation.

The lesser known and other primary word for meditation in Hebrew is *siyach*. One example of this word for is what is conveyed in the verse, "I will meditate in thy precepts, and have respect unto thy ways" [Ps. 119:15 KJV]. According to the *Ancient Hebrew Lexicon of the Bible,* the word *meditate* in this key verse is *siyach,* which is defined as, "A sweeping away in thought."[136] A deeper look into this definition exposes that rubbish is swept away in this thought process. Rubbish is another word for "trash, garbage, refuse or waste." In other words, meditation is the

---

[136] *Strongs* #7878: AHLB#: 1330-M (V), J(N)

sweeping away or removal of any thoughts classified as waste. God has to refuse these thoughts because they don't come from a reference point of truth. This form of meditation in its purest form is the practice and discipline of clearing our mind in order to get the thoughts and mind of God!

A helpful scripture in examining this fact is, "For My thoughts are not your thoughts, nor your ways My ways, says The Lord. For as the heavens are higher than the earth, so are My ways higher than your ways, and My thoughts than your thoughts" [Isa. 55:8-9]. God makes it clear that there is a vast difference between our thoughts and ways and His thoughts about us – which are the ones that really matter. The verse prior to this key scripture clues us into why there can be such a difference of thoughts and ways between our own and God's:

"Let the wicked forsake his way, and the unrighteous man his thoughts; and let him return to The Lord, and He will have mercy on him; and to our God, for He will abundantly pardon" [Isa. 55:7].

The word "wicked" in this verse is accurately defined as "one who has departed from the correct path or way."[137] Wickedness according to this translation is not practicing Satanism or committing murder or some other heinous crime. Although we generally consider these greater crimes to be evil or wicked, the reality is that being wicked is simply "one is who is not following the specific will of God for his or her life." Sobering, but true.

This tragedy leads to the main reason why someone may be guilty of unrighteousness. The word unrighteousness here is the Hebrew word *âven*, which is the primary root word for the true biblical understanding of "iniquity." This is the same word that Jesus used in the tragic account found in Matthew 7:21-23 where many thought that their actions reserved a place for them in heaven, but their lives were actually classified as unrighteous because they didn't line up with the will of God:

---

[137] *Strongs* #7563: AHLB#: 2799 (N)

"Not everyone that saith unto me, Lord, Lord, shall enter into the kingdom of heaven; but he that doeth the will of my Father which is in heaven. Many will say to me in that day, Lord, Lord, have we not prophesied in thy name? and in thy name have cast out devils? and in thy name done many wonderful works? And then will I profess unto them, I never knew you: depart from me, ye that work iniquity."

My first book in this series, titled The *Mystery of Iniquity Revealed*, focuses thoroughly on the tragic spiritual cancer of iniquity, how it is destroying people inside and out of the church, and the remedy for it. To summarize unrighteousness at its core, it is vanity. It is worthlessness that results from the absence or perversion of the power of truth designed by God to reproduce or create His purposes.[138]

The word "thoughts" found in Isaiah 55:7-9 is the unique and yet very powerful Hebrew phrase, *"machăshâbâh machăshebeth."* According to the *Ancient Hebrew Lexicon of the Bible*, it is defined as "design or purpose and imaginations." What God is saying in these key passages is that He knows the design and purposes for your life. It makes perfect sense because He who created us has already imagined and predestined our lives! Whenever we decide to design our lives and create our purposes according to our own imagination, we are guilty of biblical wickedness and unrighteousness.

To put it another way, we are supposed to take the thoughts of God for our lives and convert them into the ways or purposes of God. If we do this accurately, our actions and lives will always be in line with what God has already imagined.[139] This is success, prospering, and living life at its highest level possible.

When you position yourself to meditate in this way – where your mind is cleared of self – it opens the door for the conveyance

---

[138] *Strongs* #205: AHLB#: 1014-J (N)

[139] In my next book in this series titled *The Mystery of the Kingdom of God Revealed* I explain in detail this little known truth and phenomenon.

of God's thoughts. They become His Words towards you that are filled with the potential of purpose for your life. This truth is illustrated in this oft-quoted verse:

"For I know the thoughts which I think towards you, says the Lord; thoughts of peace and not of evil, to give you a future and a hope" [Jer. 29:11 NKJV].

Meditation at this level requires consistency, practice, and discipline combined with a removal of all personal thoughts and a complete absence of words coming from your mouth. This becomes what the Bible refers to as *stillness* in the scripture, "Be still and know that I am God" [Ps. 46:10]. A posture of disciplined stillness is required in order to experience God intimately as He shares with you His heart and secrets about you.

Whether it is Buddhism, the Bahai Faith, Christianity, Hinduism, Islam, Jainism, Judaism, New Age, Zen, Vipassana, Sikhism, Transcendental Meditation or any other belief that practices meditation – the primary purpose of meditation is for the individual to train and discipline the mind to induce a mode of consciousness that will bring some type of benefit.

I am not a proponent of any form of secular or religious meditative beliefs, practices or techniques that promote mysticism or a belief structure that minimizes, limits, perverts or excludes the Almighty God of The Bible. In all my years attending traditional churches, I was told to stay away from meditation since any form of meditation that was not taught in a church setting was considered satanic. Very few – if any – churches promoted, much less taught, about meditation because it is often regarded taboo due to its use by eastern religions. My extensive studies and life experiences have brought me to the conclusion that traditional Western Christianity defines other beliefs and practices as erroneous, mystical or following a secular philosophy, yet Christians often fail to view that in many cases their own practices have a degree of these three same components. In other words, any practices we as Christians continue that are not in line with the true teachings of Christ and the original teachings of the Bible are also "erroneous" and following a secular or culturally accepted philosophy.

Many people are initially surprised, as I was, to discover that meditation played a role in biblical teachings. One of the greatest mysteries of the Bible involves the prophets and other writers of the Bible using meditation to attune their minds to a higher state of consciousness in order to gain the information that they were given by God to write.

For a person that has never had any contact with meditation, the subject is a shrouded mystery. Our perception of God is often clouded. We often think of God as being "out there" far away from the world. But it is important to realize that God is also "in there" in the deepest part of our souls. Meditation is a crucial practice if we want to truly discover God.

The primary purpose of meditation is to have controlled thinking. One of the primary goals of meditation is to gain control of the subconscious part of the mind. Sometimes different parts of the mind seem to be acting independently. The conflict between two parts of the mind can sometimes be so strong that the person feels like they are two separate individuals. During such inner conflict, it seems that one part of the mind wants to do one thing while the other part wants to do something else. This is often the struggle between the carnal or physical part of our mind "warring" against the heavenly or spiritual part of our mind. Meditation helps us to better discern this and have the spiritual discipline to make the right choices in this struggle.

One of the most powerful uses of meditation is to gain an awareness of the spiritual. It can be used to attune the mind to certain truths. Although we may be surrounded by a sea of spirituality, we are usually not aware of it. One of most elusive truths is a deeper awareness, understanding, and knowledge of the self.

In my studies of meditation, I noticed certain commonalities about people who practiced it. They were, for the most part, very disciplined people and they had a high level of peace about themselves and their respective circumstances. Many of them testify that before learning to practice meditation, their lives were in chaos in one way or another. Meditation helped introduce peace into their minds and order for every facet of their lives.

Through my studies of meditation practiced by people from various organizations and religions, I have come to learn that God originally inspired some practices that have been adopted by certain groups. Over time, however, they have been perverted in some way.

Particularly on the subject of meditation, I have found it necessary to take a look into other beliefs and practices besides those of Christianity's – which I'm already familiar with – since I believe that some of these have insight into the original meditation process intended to strengthen the whole person of a God-fearing believer. From my studies on meditation beliefs and practices from different groups, one thing that intrigued me was the commonality of esteeming and respecting the art of discipline for all facets of their lives. I have found that in many cases those who practice the Christian faith fall short in the area of discipline. I had a hard time reconciling myself to this; it didn't make sense to me since our God is a God of discipline and order. I was inspired to take a deeper look into other meditation beliefs to see what made them different in the two key areas of self-discipline and God-consciousness.

Ten Meditation Attributes

One belief that caught my attention was the practice of Kabbalism. The word *Kabbalah* is defined as "received teaching." It is a complex method, discipline and school of thought. Original Kabbalism focuses specifically on receiving concealed teachings from the Torah. The original goal of Kabbalah was to reveal what was known as "the mystery or secret doctrine." This drew my attention to two key statements that Jesus made:

"And answering, He said to them, 'Because it has been given to you to know the mysteries of the kingdom of Heaven, but it has not been given to those'" [Matt. 13:11].

"And He said, 'To you it is given to know the mysteries of the kingdom of God. But to others I speak in parables, so that seeing they might not see and hearing they might not understand'" [Luke 8:10].

Kabbalah was originally conceived in Judaism and was developed entirely within the realm of Jewish thought. There are many written works that still exist today on the ancient practice of Jewish meditation. Unfortunately many of them remain in manuscript form and are locked away in libraries and museums. Today practitioners of Kabbalah often use classical Jewish resources to explain and demonstrate their complex teachings. These teachings are held by certain followers of Judaism to define the inner meaning of the Hebrew Bible, traditional rabbinic literature, the significance of Jewish religious observances, and the overall complexity of the Torah.[140]

Over the years, other works bearing the name Kabbalah have arisen under the umbrellas of New Age, Christianity and Syncretism – which is a belief that blends different traditions, religious beliefs and schools of thought. Groups of occultists and others who dabble in magic and witchcraft arose from the original practice of Kabbalism, which causes much misunderstanding about the original Kabbalah belief and practices.

What became of special interest to me about the original Kabbalah belief structure were key attributes used as meditation focuses. They are parts of what Kabbalists call "The Tree of Life."

---

[140] Information found at: **http://en.wikipedia.org/wiki/Kabbalah**

This tree of life progresses through different levels of meditation to bring individuals to a place where they:

1. Establish priorities for accurate living according to a preordained purpose

2. Translate spiritual concepts that produce actions which are synchronized with God

3. Perceive carrying their personal cross as a privilege rather than a burden

4. Experience true peace by keeping their activities in line with the will of God

5. Receive "quick understanding" in their thought life, which yields peace and freedom

6. Focus on the love and compassion of God through the *spirit* of the law

7. Transform their heart and mind through predetermined knowledge that creates a bond between man's intellect and God's intelligence

8. Grasp understanding that awakens within them the joy of the Lord

9. Receive a revelation or flash of vision to then apply in God's perfect timing and manner

10. Integrate divine revelation and maturity, resulting in "perfect faith" and creating divinely inspired actions

The idea is not to adopt Kabbalism in order to effectively meditate, but to understand that, according to various religious practices, meditation enables an individual to access a higher level of thought and understanding of God's plan and will for one's life.

Biblical Meditation

From a biblical perspective, meditation is intended to help practitioners disconnect their attention from any sensory impressions from the outer world in order to perceive a God consciousness through the Kingdom within them. In Hebrew thought, to meditate upon the Scriptures is to quietly repeat them in a soft murmuring sound while utterly abandoning outside distractions. The original goal and result of meditation was to attune the inner self with God in order to hear another soft sound, the still small voice of God.

Students were taught how to discipline their mind in order to be sensitive to internal instruction by the Spirit of God, leading students to internalize a specific portion of scripture in order for God to use it as a means to communicate something specific to the person. Meditating on the written word (*hagah*) prepared students for the spoken word *(siyach)*. Meditating on the book of the law was purposed to establish additional specific thoughts that were transferred from the mind of God to the mind of the student. The next step for the student would be to create works and thereby prosper by fulfilling the will of God.

Jesus followed this same process. In other words, Jesus was taught to meditate on written script in order to get spoken script. This spoken script became the "the book of the law" for His life. Jesus meditated on a volume of a book that was written about Him which was the personal Kingdom book on His life [Heb. 10:5-7]. As a result, it pointed Him in the direction He was to walk each day. One of the secrets about Jesus' prayer life that few people are aware of is that He positioned Himself to pray by first preparing His mind in meditation. The purpose of His meditative mindset was so that He could hear the thoughts of God towards Him, which were revealed by the Spirit of God that resided within Him.

This is the secret that gave Jesus a precise awareness of all the events that He encountered before they ever happened. In

Jesus' prayer sessions, He was doing a lot more hearing than speaking. We all have access to this same level of prayer yet few people experience it because so few understand the importance of meditation to prepare the heart to hear the voice of God in prayer. Jesus came to introduce to us a whole new level of knowledge and understanding the Kingdom of Heaven and the Kingdom of God.

Mature, Kingdom-minded persons want to hear from God for every aspect of their lives. A well-developed meditative routine brings this lifestyle to fruition. Embedded within the following scripture through a root word study is the revelation of an experience that needs to become the primary pursuit for all of humanity. The result of such a pursuit is an inward discovery where the true meaning and purpose for life are revealed, and we receive ongoing guidance in how to bring God's plan to fruition.

*"It is the glory of God to conceal a **thing**: but the honour of kings is to **search out** a matter. The heaven for height, and the earth for depth, and the heart of kings is **unsearchable"** [Prov. 25:2-3].*

The word "thing" in the above verse is the Hebrew word dabar, defined as "an arrangement of word placement that creates order."141 The phrase "search out" is described as "a place of depth that has to be penetrated that unless a search begins it remains as a place that is unexamined."142 The word "unsearchable" is defined as "to search for a place of unknown origin." This verse is telling us that our lives will never be clearly understood unless we initiate a "seek process" to discover our place of origin, and God's perfect direction for our lives!

---

141 Strongs #1697: AHLB#: 2093 (N)
142 Strongs #2713: AHLB#: 2198 (V), (K)

Jesus' Meditation Training

As mentioned in chapter nine, the ancient rabbinical education consisted of three levels of training – *Bet Sefer* (The House of the Book), *Bet Midrash* (The House of Learning), and *Bet Talmud* ("The House of Study/Seeking" but also as "The House of Interpretation.").[143] The discipline of meditation was taught in all three of these stages in order for a student to learn how to be God-conscious. It was not uncommon for students to practice meditation for up to one hour before reciting their prayers.

Upon graduating from His rabbinical process, Jesus entered another level where His prior training in meditation performed a vital role in His wilderness experience.

"Then Jesus was led up by the Spirit into the to be tempted by the devil. And when He had fasted forty days and forty nights, afterward He was hungry" [Matt. 4:1-2].

Why would Jesus be led into an environment such as a wilderness to be tempted by the devil instead of a more common place like His home or a place of worship? The answer is found in understanding the root perspective and purpose of the word "wilderness." Such a word conjures up in our minds a place inhabited primarily by animal, plant, reptile and insect kingdoms. A deeper look into the word "wilderness" reveals that it has a dual meaning that describes an outer and inner environment. From the Greek perspective, the word "wilderness" is the word *erēmos*, defined and described as "an uninhabited outer environment where solitude takes place such as a desert or forest."

From a Hebrew perspective it is the word *midbar*, described as "an outer environment that affects an *inner* environment." It is defined as "an inner sanctuary or a place where speech

---

[143] These levels of education are further explained in chapter nine, "Pardes – Understanding Scripture from Jesus' Perspective."

creates order through what is heard."[144] The primary root word of *midbar* is *dabar*, which is defined as "an arrangement of words that comes through speech that creates order."[145]

The wilderness is a place of unhindered inner growth. It is in this inner wilderness that another type of Kingdom (the Kingdom of God) is discovered and developed, unhindered and according to its original design.

Jesus often left His disciples and the crowds to distance Himself. He entered the wilderness areas of Palestine to engage in long periods of spiritual meditation wherein He communicated with God. The highest form of spiritual truth and wisdom are not found in the words or environments that come from an external source such as a human being or organization. They are found in the "wilderness" environment of inner silence, a place that is the prerequisite for God to speak in an unhindered manner.

Each morning and at crucial moments in His life, Jesus would find a solitary place in order to reorient Himself by opening His inner ear to discover His daily direction. What Jesus was seeking to acquire was insight that *could not* be communicated through an ordinary educational process. As a human, Jesus created a dialogue with God as secrets were revealed about His life. The mysteries of His life were revealed to Him through a focused meditative mindset.

Many Bible prophets were often secluded in mountains or caves. Their seclusion detached them from outward influences, which prepared their minds through meditation to experience an ongoing connection with God. John the Baptist was one of these prophets. His meditative training in the wilderness enabled him to receive revelations to prepare him as the forerunner of Jesus. Such knowledge could not have come through his traditional Jewish rabbinical education.

---

[144] *Strongs* #4057: AHLB#: 2093 (h)
[145] *Strongs* #1697: AHLB#: 2093 (N)

One of the greatest mysteries of Bible involves how the prophets and other writers of the Bible used meditation to attune their minds to a higher state of consciousness in order to gain the information that they were inspired by God to write. Isaac and King David were practitioners of *siyach* meditation, which was the meditative practice that was used to clear their thoughts in order to get the thoughts of God [See Gen. 24:63, Ps. 119:15, 23, 48, 78, 148].

King David is famously known as a man who was after God's own heart. There is no better way to pursue and capture God's heart than by positioning oneself to hear the thoughts that come from God. Ancient Jewish practitioners of meditation believed that it was only through meditation that a person truly became attached to the Creator of the Universe. It was the only way that the true inner-self was revealed to them by God.

There is also ample evidence that during the periods of time when the Bible was written, meditation was practiced by many of the Israelite people. Meditative practices were widespread throughout Jewish and early church history. References to meditation are found in major Jewish texts in every period from the biblical to the pre-modern era. One reason this has not been universally recognized is that the vocabulary of meditation has been lost to a large degree, especially during the last century.

Apostle Paul's Meditative Experience

The Apostle Paul wrote about the ability to acquire an inner Kingdom level of knowledge:

"That the God of our Lord Jesus Christ, the Father of glory, **may give to you the spirit of wisdom and revelation in the knowledge of Him, the eyes of your understanding being enlightened;** *that you may know what is the hope of His calling, what are the riches of the glory of His inheritance in the saints"* [Eph. 1:17-18].

"That their hearts might be comforted, being knit together in love, and to all riches of the full assurance of the understanding, **to the full knowledge of the mystery of God, and of the Father, and of Christ; in whom are hidden all the treasures of wisdom and knowledge"** [Col. 2:2-3].

Paul was not talking about receiving knowledge through our physical eyes and ears. At the time that he was inspired to write these key passages of scripture, Paul had become reacquainted with the skill of meditation that was taught to him through his early rabbinical education. Paul is talking about knowledge that is received spiritually through the inner eyes and ears of the mind – by which God conveys His thoughts and imagery that ultimately produce purposed knowledge and vision.

Before our unique purpose and vision can be accurately revealed and manifested as an outward expression, the Kingdom of God that resides within us must be discovered and developed. We accomplish this through taking on a stillness of the mind that produces a God-consciousness, which then disburses this, level of knowledge. A meditative mindset is required in order to still our inner being so that we may receive this level of information delivered through only one Source and Teacher – God Himself.

Just as a consistent lifestyle of eating healthy foods and drinking water nourish us through our bloodstream, so authentic, God-connecting meditation nourishes a Kingdom stream of hearing and learning from God. It is impossible to be an undistracted and focused disciple or student of God without the practice and discipline of meditation. Meditation is the mental discipline necessary to remove the barrier between your mind and God's mind. A meditative mindset positions you to enter the realm of the Kingdom of Heaven within the mind of God.

What if the practice of meditation was no longer seen as taboo in church? What if it was no longer seen as a threat to Christianity? What if meditation classes were taught in conjunction with classes on prayer? What if meditation was taught in such a way that the importance of its practice was viewed as the prerequisite in order to prepare the mind to hear the voice of God? It would be safe to assume that the life experience of believers would be more focused and keyed into life as *it should be* instead of experimenting with their lives according to external influences or self-centered desires. True meditation attaches our wills to God's as we hear and learn from Him. Through this process, we discover our potential and abilities according to God's predestined purpose.

Every one of us has an inner-learning environment that comes from Heaven, which is the meeting ground that God has built into us from before the foundation of the world. This is the place we are meant to reach through prayer. When God says, "Give ear, O ye heavens, and I will speak; and hear, O earth" [Deut. 32:1], He is telling us to listen with our spirits that are housed within our bodies. This level of receiving the precise and personal direction from God can only be accomplished through the discipline of meditation.

Jesus Taught Meditation Principles

Among Christians there is a wide variety of opinions concerning meditation. Some see it as beneficial and practice it occasionally. Some practice only written word meditation. Some practice it daily. Others see meditation as "the work of the devil" and avoid it like the plague. Only too few practice it to hear and learn from God. What would Jesus say about the practice of meditation? What would Jesus do? Did Jesus meditate?

Jesus would have been no stranger to meditation. Meditation is mentioned several times in the Old Testament and, as mentioned before, it was a discipline that was taught as part of the ancient Jewish and Rabbinical education. Jesus would have never taught something that He wasn't doing, especially anything related to prayer. Since He knew how to effectively hear and learn from God, He would naturally have taught from His experience and with His techniques.

In Gospel accounts, Jesus rose from sleep before His disciples so He could go to a quiet place. If Jesus believed in not repeating vain prayers and in keeping spoken prayers short, what would He have been doing for hours on end? In retreating to these places for long hours of solitude, Jesus was engaged in what we would call "meditation" today. He was spending time listening to God. In short, Jesus meditated. Jesus stilled His mind in order to enter a state of complete God-consciousness. When Jesus positioned Himself to hear from God, He was hearing with the ears of the spirit. This can only be effectively accomplished through meditation.

When the disciples approached Jesus and asked Him to teach them to pray as John (the Baptist) taught his disciples, He undoubtedly would have taught them how to meditate [Luke 11:1-3]. It was one of the prerequisites to prayer mentioned in Matthew's account of Jesus' teaching on prayer [Matt. 6:6-8]. Jesus modeled this activity before His disciples and throughout His public ministry for over three and a half years. This would have been approximately 1,277 consecutive days of showing His disciples how He would start His day by preparing His mind through meditation in order to hear and learn from God.

Jesus taught the same doctrine that John taught - the doctrine of the Kingdom of God. This teaching was purposed to lead the student to eventually be counseled and taught by God Himself. John the Baptist's doctrine came from the same source: God. They both acquired these doctrines by stilling their minds in order to be taught by God through meditative practices.

God has "hidden" Himself in a place that all of humanity has access to. We access this secret place through meditation.

Simple Technique

To many people, the term "meditation" brings forth the image of sitting with their legs crossed in a "lotus" position, their eyes closed in serene concentration, perhaps chanting some words.

Though there are numerous purposes for meditation, our primary purpose to meditate should not be to find inner peace, but rather to experience God's presence and to clearly hear His voice, which brings true peace and so much more. The original purpose of meditation was to experience a deep level of God-consciousness. I have found that the most effective way to learn proper meditation is by simply asking God to teach me to meditate. The simplest way meditation works for me is by quieting all parts of my mind in order to remove thoughts that would interfere with my ability to concentrate on the immediate experience.

I plan a *time and place* daily where I position myself to meditate. I focus on the present moment, viewing that specific time as *sacred time* where I meet with God. I don't bring my agenda. I don't think about my "to-do list" or what happened in the past or anything related to my future. As a result, I receive God's agenda and His "to do list" for my life that creates my future through the works that I produce according to His instructions.

Meditation prepares your mind to hear from God. Meditation will set you free from other people's ambitions and agendas, things that are not God's purposes for your life. Meditation brings a personal awareness of God's plan for you. It requires no special equipment and is not complicated to learn. Though the best environment to meditate is in a quiet place, it can be practiced anywhere, at any given moment, and it is not time consuming.

Practice makes permanent. I have found that consistency is the key. We must remember that in ancient times, meditation was taught to children as early as five years old. As such, it easily became a permanent practice in their lifestyle. Learning to meditate at a later age can be challenging, but it is definitely doable. Not only that, but it can be the most rewarding activity of your day.

Best of all, meditation has NO negative side effects. Bottom line, there is nothing but positive to be gained from it! With such a huge list of benefits, the question that we should asking is, "Why am I not meditating yet?" or "Why isn't meditation being taught at the house of worship that I attend?"

The Breath of God

The ultimate goal of true spiritual meditation is for the human soul to mirror the divine nature of God. In other words, with this type of meditation, God is breathing into you His mind and heart. His intention in doing so is to produce the original shape, makeup and purpose of the soul that should then influence our spirit and flesh accordingly. The desired end result is for the relationship between the human soul and the divinity of God to have no differentiation but a completely similar nature.

Physical Benefits

Medical practitioners and scientists who study human biology are discovering the impressive physical benefits of meditation. It is an effective practice that has multiple benefits including relaxation, decreased or eliminated anxiety, discipline of the mind, controlling one's thought life, controlling one's streams of thought, boosting the immune system, removal of depression and anger, strengthening the power of attention, leading a balance life, changing gene activity or expression, greater focus ability, less chaotic or uncontrollable thoughts, whole brain thinking, and better sleep patterns.

Spiritual meditation has the potential to introduce these same physical benefits, as well as spiritual insights and benefits that many are not even aware of. These benefits introduce you to "The Real You" and "The Real God" that simplify your true predestined self. You experience God through a forum of truth that contains a continual flow of details.

"Blessed be the Lord, Who daily loads us with benefits, The God of our salvation! Selah" [Ps. 68:19 KJV].

The part of the human brain that responds the most to meditation is the Corpus Callosum. This is the area in the brain that sets the tone for how the rest of the brain will function. When we choose to experience the thoughts of God for our lives, we are literally choosing life as it should be according to His predestined purpose.

Meditation introduces the mediation of the Spirit of God towards the spirit of man. It is, in essence, the silent forerunner that introduces the Spirit of the Lord into our lives. It is therefore the prerequisite that causes our vocabulary to cease, which introduces the vocabulary of God. It creates an environment where truth is manifested in the posture of silence rather than through speech.

Meditation is a natural extension of prayer time with God. Meditation is crucial in the development of our inner ears and inner eyes – the senses of the spirit. The proper understanding and application of meditation creates the atmosphere of the secret place that Jesus referred to [Matt. 6:6, Lk. 8:10] where the mysteries (secrets) of the Kingdom for your life are revealed to you.

Meditation was foundational for spiritual transformation in ancient times. The practice of meditation disappeared when the church became institutionalized in the centuries following Jesus' teachings. Meditation is clearly specified in scripture, yet due to the mysticism that has been added to its practice – combined with the limited understanding of the original meanings of key words that specify meditation from a Godly perspective – the art of meditation has been lost in the church today.

My personal experience with meditation has introduced to my life a level of hearing the voice of God that I was not previously experiencing. It has literally caused me to hear the voice of God at a frequency free from distracting static or lack of focus. What I found interesting was that much of the defocusing during my times of prayer had to do with areas that pertained to what I had to do that day. I was not giving God the time and place to tell me how to prepare for or live my day according to His plan. We might not see one little day as important, but the way we approach each day eventually translates into the way we live our whole lives.

I believe that meditation was a large part of Jesus' prayer life. He was listening more than He was talking. This is why He had access to the quick understanding mentioned about Him in Isaiah 11:3: "And shall make him of quick understanding in the fear of the Lord: and he shall not judge after the sight of his eyes, neither reprove after the hearing of his ears." I also believe that this was one of the main reasons that Jesus rarely prayed in groups. He chose instead to go to a place absent of any form of distraction, especially other humans.

When I began to think about this, I asked God, "What was Jesus doing when He would pray on earth?" God's initial response to me was to take a deeper look into the practice of meditation. Once I did this, I began to gain insight and understand why Jesus' prayer life was so disciplined, consistent and effective. Through the lost art of meditation, He spent hours listening and little time talking. Christianity has reversed this process in praying for hours and listening very little or not at all.

God prayed (communed) more towards Jesus than He prayed (communed) towards God. This is the original meaning and purpose of prayer as it relates to meditation. Jesus was being inspired with the continual breath of God through His meditative process. He then exhaled back towards God the works that He was daily being inspired to do. This is worshipping the Father in Spirit and in truth in its purest form [See John 4:23-24].

Due to the insights that I have gained in studying meditation from different beliefs I prefer to call my personal meditation time "Kingdom Meditation." These discoveries have changed my thinking patterns and have created a portal to a level of prayer where I can now accurately hear the voice of God and pray according to the thoughts that He thinks towards me. These have introduced me to the plans that God has predestined for my life. This life-changing revelation has freed me to posture my heart to be a primed environment for hearing God's voice. Now I can truly seek and search for God by emptying my whole heart so that I can be refreshed with His breath. I am blessed to find and experience His presence every time![146]

---

[146] The practice of meditation from an original biblical perspective will be further explored in my next book in this series titled *The Mystery of the Kingdom of God Revealed.*

CHAPTER SUMMARY:

- Meditation helps us sweep away or remove any thoughts classified as waste, enabling us to receive the thoughts and mind of God!

- We are supposed to take the thoughts of God for our lives and convert them into the purposes of God for our lives.

- One of the most powerful uses of meditation is to gain awareness of the spiritual.

- Meditation provides the necessary discipline and portal to receive the unhindered breath of God that contains heavenly knowledge.

- Meditation assists the believer in shifting from human consciousness to God consciousness. The ultimate goal of true spiritual meditation is for the human soul to mirror the divine nature of God.

- Meditation has multiple benefits including relaxation, decreased anxiety, discipline of the mind, controlling one's thought life, boosting the immune system, removing depression and anger, strengthening the power of attention, leading a balance life, changing gene expression, greater focus, and better sleep patterns.

APPLICATION:

1. Meditation is meant to be a natural extension of our prayer time. Think about how you can schedule your times of prayer to include meditation.

2. God prayed (communed) more towards Jesus than Jesus prayed (communed) towards God. This is the original meaning and purpose of prayer as it relates to meditation. When you start to meditate, ensure that listening to God and receiving His thoughts toward you is a primary focus of your times of meditation.

3. If you are not familiar with meditation for the purpose of hearing and learning from God, find someone who can teach and guide you in order to achieve this level of consistent connectivity to God through its practice.

4. You may also subscribe to my website to view current and future video teachings and tutorials on meditation from a biblical perspective and application. **www.julioalvaradojr.com**

CHAPTER TWELVE

Practical Prayer Pointers

"The greatest manifestations of abuse are caused by ignorance of what God originally said."

– Julio Alvarado Jr.

Praying in Jesus' Name

Many of our prayers end with, "In Jesus name, amen." Let's take a deeper look to see if our understanding about this traditional prayer ending needs to be adjusted. What does it mean to pray "in the name of Jesus?" Many people today, including me, have used the name of Jesus like a rubber stamp after prayer. We use the following scripture to validate this practice:

"And everything, whatever you do in word or deed, do all in the name of the Lord Jesus, giving thanks to God and the Father by Him" [Col. 3:17].

I was taught to take this scripture literally according to how it is read in the English language. We must remember, however, that the Bible was written through a Hebraic culture of thinking and understanding. If it were so, then according to the passage, we should do everything – including going to the bathroom and brushing our teeth – in Jesus' name. I'm sure you get my point that this is not the correct intention for the verse. We in modern Christianity have misapplied these passages.

As covered in a previous chapter, the modern Hebrew word for "Name" as it relates to God is *Shêm*. *Strong's Concordance* defines *Shêm* as "authority and character." The *Ancient Hebrew Lexicon of the Bible* describes "Name" as it pertains to God as His breath or wind.[147] From these definitions, one praying in "the name" is one who allows him or herself to be inspired by the breath or wind of God, which will cause them to be positioned in the authority, character and position of the God, the one who inspired them. In other words, they have positioned themselves to become a "Father Impersonator."

By this definition, we can see that invoking the name of Jesus is more than a verbal application to a prayer or task. In prayer there is no magic in applying the name of Jesus verbally. There is, however, the supernatural access that comes as a result of *praying in the righteous position of a child of God.*

In several passages from the Gospel of John, Jesus instructs us to pray in His name. For example: "I will do whatever you ask in my name, so that the Father may be glorified in the Son. If in my name you ask me for anything, I will do it" [John 14:13-14] [See also John 15:16; 16:23-24, 26]. This command has led many to end their prayers with something like "in Jesus' name" or "through Christ our Lord" before they say "Amen." I have often ended my prayers with "in Jesus' name." But when Jesus told us to pray in His name, He wasn't talking about the words with which we end our prayers. Perhaps the clearest proof of this comes in "The Lord's Prayer." In this model prayer lesson, Jesus did not end it with "in my name" or anything of the sort.

If praying in Jesus' name is not saying "in Jesus' name" at the end of the prayer, what is it? We get closer to answering this

---

[147] *Strongs* #8034: AHLB#: 1473-A (N)

question as we look at passages in which Jesus uses the phrase "in my name."

"Whoever welcomes one such child in my name welcomes me" [Matt. 18:5].

"Again, truly I tell you, if two of you agree on earth about anything you ask, it will be done for you by my Father in heaven. For where two or three are gathered in my name, I am there among them" [Matt. 18:19-20].

Neither of these passages has to do with saying the words "in Jesus' name." Rather, they're about doing something under Jesus' authority or as His representative.

In Matthew 18:5, "in my name" means something like, "Whoever welcomes one such child under my authority and representing me, welcomes me." The verse from Matthew chapter 18 is especially telling because verse 19 speaks of prayer, and verse 20 speaks of gathering in Jesus' name, but not using His name as some sort of ending to a prayer. In other words, one who truly prays in Jesus' name is one who prays in the same identity of what Jesus was: an offspring of God not just in title and belief, but in how He functioned as a son. Jesus operated in complete obedience to what He saw and heard from the Father.

If we are to pray "in Jesus' name," this means our prayers should reflect Jesus' own values and purposes, which originated from the will of God for His life. Praying "in Jesus' Name" is praying along the lines of the will of God. When Jesus prayed, the will of God was accomplished. Jesus prayed for things that He already knew He had access to because He was pre-informed of the Father's will for His life. This is what constantly positioned Him to walk in the power and confidence of God and work miracles without hesitation. As we follow this same pattern, we will be filled with that same confidence and miracle-working power.

"And this is the confidence that we have toward Him, that if we ask anything according to His will, He hears us. And if we know that He hears us, whatever we ask, we know that we have the petitions that we desired of Him" [1 Jn. 5:14].

Our prayers should be saturated with the kingdom agenda that is within us. In order to pray "in Jesus' name," our minds and hearts should mature to a place where they are constantly being shaped by what we hear. This once again stresses the importance of learning to hear the voice of God so that we remove from our prayers anything that doesn't line up with His will.

Interestingly, from the Aramaic perspective, the word "name" is *sema*, as is the word for "hear." They are considered synonymous. As it relates to God, one who functions in the Name is one who has the ability to hear an inner sound that comes from an inner atmosphere. The inner sound is the voice of God and the inner atmosphere is the environment of the Kingdom of God that resides within the human being.

If we bring the original understanding of praying in the name of Jesus into the numerous passages of scripture where Jesus healed or performed a miracle, we see that He never verbally applied a name. Rather, He was functioning in the name of God:

"Jesus answered them, I told you and you did not believe. The works that I do in My Father's name, they bear witness of Me" [Jn. 10:25].

No one can claim the status of praying in Jesus' name without having an official child-of-God status.

"But as many as received him, to them gave he power to become the sons of God, even to them that believe on his name" [Jn. 21:12].

One who truly believes in God must learn to hear from God. Once you receive God through Jesus Christ our Lord, you should eventually begin to get the words from His mouth, which gives you the power to truly believe in His identity. This enables you to position yourself to be just like Him in authority and character.

Believing or praying in His Name is more than a mental belief or application. It is a mentality and life structure built from God's words spoken to you, words that you must apply to your life. As you do so, you will in essence be fulfilling the words of Colossians 3:17:

> *"And everything, whatever you do in word or deed, do all in the name of the Lord Jesus, giving thanks to God and the Father by Him."*

Praying in Tongues

Praying in tongues is one of the most controversial topics of the Bible. The purpose of praying or speaking in tongues is to experience a level of prayer and hearing from God that transcends our natural understanding and practice of prayer.

Three primary beliefs have been put forth regarding the practice of speaking or praying in tongues throughout history. The first belief is that it was a practice only for the infancy stages of the New Testament Church, found in the book of Acts. The second belief is that its practice is still for today and that it is the evidence or manifestation of someone who has received the gift of the Holy Spirit. The third belief is that those who practice it are being influenced by the devil. The number of people of this third category has grown less. Some religions that have preached and taught against its practice have now accepted tongues as part of their doctrine and have begun to practice it as a part of their spiritual lifestyles.

The word "tongue" (or tongues) from a biblical perspective is simply the word "language" (or languages). From a Greek perspective, it is the word *glōssa*, which is defined as "a language that is not acquired." From a Hebrew perspective, it is *lâshôn*

226 The Mystery of Prayer Revealed

leshônâh, which is defined as "the language that comes from the movement of the organ of the tongue."[148]

Though the Old Testament has numerous prophetic statements concerning tongues, the book of Acts in the New Testament is where we can actually read about how the gift of tongues began. The Apostle Paul was the primary instructor inspired by the Holy Spirit to document information and instruction concerning tongues. Jesus also spoke about tongues, saying that it would be one of the signs that would be a part of the believers' life.

Jesus qualified how the tongues would be administered: by saying "in my name" [Mk. 16:17]. This is one of the keys that unlock the significance of speaking or praying in tongues. When we place ourselves in the position, authority, character and identity as an offspring of God, we have the ability to not just speak or pray in tongues, but to also get the interpretation of what was spoken or prayed.

This brings up the issue of whether or not Jesus spoke in tongues. It is once again important to understand that Jesus would not have taught something that He was not doing. After all, Jesus was functioning in the pure essence of the spirit of God – "the name" that He encouraged others to function in.

It is a common belief that Jesus spoke both Aramaic and Hebrew but that He primarily spoke in Hebrew, which is the language that He used in His communications with His disciples and with the Apostle Paul [See Acts 26:14]. On the cross, Jesus made a statement that was preserved in its original Aramaic language: "Eli, Eli, lama sabachthani." This would have been foreign to the Roman or Greek-speaking people that were crucifying Him. Mark (the inspired writer of the book of Mark) and those that translated the Bible from its original language were inspired to not only preserve Jesus' original Aramaic statement, but also to provide the interpretation of what He said:

---

[148] *Strongs* #3956: AHLB#: 2325 (c)

"My God, my God, why have you forsaken me?" This is a simple biblical illustration of what "tongues" is. It is a spoken language unfamiliar to the hearer; an interpretation is then given in the language the hearer is familiar with.

Though we may not have more scriptural proof that Jesus prayed in tongues, the "Jesus said it, so that settles it" argument may not suffice some people. Yet as mentioned numerous times throughout this book, God will only show you what you are looking for. Spiritually speaking, your "seek level" will determine your "find level," and your "hunger level" will determine how you receive knowledge and experiences from God.

Personally I do pray and speak in tongues and have done so since becoming born again on October 22nd of 1989. My born-again experience happened in a United Pentecostal Church. That day I was water baptized in a full-immersion ceremony and was instructed that once I came up out of the water, I would speak in new tongues which would be the evidence that I had received the gift of the Holy Spirit. That day I remember feeling a sense of an inner cleansing which I had never experienced before. I also remember speaking words that made no sense to me. Inwardly, I knew something happened to me that was different from anything that I had experienced before.

A few days after that experience, I tried to repeat speaking in tongues and to me it sounded like some type of Klingon or foreign language that once again made no sense to me. I eventually became a member of this church and began to learn more about speaking in tongues from their denominational beliefs.

Throughout the years, my belief and practice of tongues has evolved. I have gone through seasons where I had doubts about its practice and power. I have also gone through seasons where I would use tongues as a "filler" in prayer or to sound spiritual when practicing it in group settings. I have gone through seasons where I felt as though what I was doing was somewhat rehearsed or forced; in a way, it gave me a false sense of spiritual power.

The Bible has much to say about speaking in tongues. The practice of speaking in tongues in group settings is mentioned in First Corinthians 12:1-11, a passage about spiritual gifts. First Corinthians 14:26-28 tells the order in which these gifts are supposed to happen.

I often used to wonder why it was necessary to speak in tongues. Why didn't God just speak in a plain language so that the hearers could understand? After all, isn't there also the spiritual gift of knowledge? To me, its practice often created confusion and doubt, especially when it wasn't practiced in the biblical order or when the "interpreter" would get stuck or quote scripture or say things that that had no depth or just didn't seem to be how God would speak.

I have asked God, "Do I have to speak in tongues?"

His answer to me was, "Do you believe that the spirit that I have placed within you has the capability to pray in a language that you are not familiar with?"

My answer to this question was, "Yes."

Then God said to me, "Do you believe that my Spirit can also interpret what your spirit prayed?"

My answer once again was, "Yes."

God's answers to my original question caused me to pursue a deeper level of understanding and personal application of not just praying in tongues but also positioning myself inwardly to get the interpretation of what I just prayed. When someone speaks in tongues, they are speaking a language they aren't familiar with. In a group setting, the interpretation comes from someone to whom God gives the meaning of what was just spoken [See 1 Cor. 14:21-28].

The purpose of speaking in tongues is two-fold. Paul clearly stated that one of the purposes of speaking in tongues and the interpretation of tongues in a corporate or group setting was that it was a sign for the unbelievers' benefit in that the secrets of their heart would be revealed. This would often result in the individual worshiping God and testifying that God is truly in that place where the event happened. The second purpose of speaking in tongues is to edify and build up the believer, with the believer being so completely in tune with the Spirit that they are the interpreter.

Both purposes of speaking in tongues are so that knowledge contained within the mind of God – scripturally known as mysteries or secrets – can be revealed [1 Cor. 14:2]. These secrets or mysteries will always fall under one or more of the following bolded categories that Paul expresses in the following passage:

*"But now, brothers, if I come to you speaking in tongues, what will I profit you, except I speak to you either in **revelation**, or in **knowledge**, or in **prophecy**, or in **teaching**?"* [1 Cor. 14:6].

This brings to light the fact that though just speaking in tongues does benefit the believers – in that their spirit is exercising another level of prayer – it is the *interpretation of the tongues* that maximizes the experience. What is revealed to you is a deeper level of God's thoughts that goes beyond the normal praying experience.

The Apostle Paul was also inspired to write about his personal experience with speaking or praying in tongues. Paul said that when he spoke in tongues it was his spirit praying but his understanding was unfruitful. In other words, he didn't understand what he was praying.

"So then he speaking in a tongue, let him pray that he may interpret. For if I pray in a tongue, my spirit prays, but my mind is unfruitful" [1 Cor. 14:13-14].

The ability to interpret tongues is one of the purest and deepest forms of encouragement that falls under the category of prophecy. Paul encourages all believers to not just pray or speak in tongues but also to prophesy. Most people use the gift or the ability to prophesy in directing it towards others, but it can also be applied at a personal level. When I get the interpretation of what my spirit prayed in tongues, I am encouraged and thus prophesy to myself by the interpretation that is given to me.

"So then, brothers, seek to prophesy, and do not forbid to speak in languages" [1 Cor. 14:39].

The key to understanding how we can become fruitful by praying in tongues is found in a root-word study of the following scripture:

"Likewise the Spirit also helps our infirmities. For we do not know what we should pray for as we ought, but the Spirit Himself makes intercession for us with groanings which cannot be uttered. And He searching the hearts knows what is the mind of the Spirit, because He makes intercession for the saints according to the will of God" [Rom. 8:26-27].

If we have learned to clearly hear the voice of God, why would the Spirit need to help us in informing us what we should be praying for? The answer to this valid question has introduced a level of freedom into my personal life. It has fulfilled and continues to fulfill the life-changing words of Jesus when He stated, "You shall know the truth and the truth shall make you free."

The word "helps" in verse 26 from a Greek perspective is the word *sunantilambanomai*, which is defined as "to take hold of something that is currently opposite in order to bring together or to co-operate." From the Hebrew perspective, the word "helps" is *kûn*, which is defined as "to set something firmly in place with words."[149]

From a Hebrew perspective, there are two key words that describe the "groaning" from Romans 8:26. First it is the word *nehâmâh*, which is defined as an event of "speaking from a semi-

---

[149] *Strongs* #3559: AHLB#: 1244-J (V)

conscious state declaring the words of God."[150] In other words, I'm conscious that it is happening but I'm not conscious of what I am saying. The consciousness comes when I get the thoughts of God from what I just said.

Second, it is the term *hêrôn hêrâyôn*, which is defined as a "conception that causes a pregnancy" and further describes this conception as "thoughts that cause mental pregnancy."[151] To put it another way, the Holy Spirit within you is trying to impregnate you with the deeper thoughts of God by interceding for you in order to get the information to you.

The word "infirmities," from a Greek perspective, is the word *astheneia.* It is described as "a weakness in the mind that will cause a want of vigor or strength."[152] If we don't know what to accurately pray for, we create the potential to pray vain prayers that fall under the category of iniquity, creating "weakness." Unfortunately, iniquity is the primary source of spiritual impotence and spiritual abortions.

The topic of iniquity is covered extensively in my first book in this series. In summary, iniquity from a Hebrew root-word perspective is "power that God has instilled in us that is being used for vain or other improper purposes." Praying in tongues is a part of this power, but without getting the interpretation of what was said, the power is limited. God's original desire and purpose for praying in tongues is to get the understanding of what was spoken or prayed.

The thoughts that come from God through the interpretative process provide a deeper level of encouragement from God. This encouragement will always give us vigor, strength or power and will never fail to come from the reference point of truth. The purpose of this level of encouragement from God is to give a deeper-than-normal revelation, knowledge, prophecy or teaching from God Himself [1 Cor. 14:6]. These deep insights

---

[150] *Strongs* #5100: AHLB#: 1312-D
[151] *Strongs* #2032: AHLB#: 1112-A-(Lc)
[152] *Strong's* and *Thayer's* Greek definitions (G769)

eliminate the weaknesses or ignorance that comes from lacking knowledge of the deep things of God.

From a Hebrew perspective, the word "infirmities" in Romans 8:26 is the word *shâphêl,* which is defined as "to be low in position or stature."[153] God the Father and His Holy Spirit of Truth gives us the potential to experience a "perfect and mature" or higher position and stature before Him.

"Till we all come in the unity of the faith, and of the knowledge of the Son of God, unto a perfect man, unto the measure of the stature of the fullness of Christ" [Eph. 4:13].

Spiritually speaking, we remain low in our proper position as an offspring (son or daughter) of God and our stature will remain underdeveloped if we fail to pray in tongues or to, more importantly, hear the interpretation of what our spirits just prayed. I have personally found that the interpretation that I get from God puts me back on track "to know what to pray as I ought" [Rom. 8:26]. What I hear from God removes the ignorance or lack of knowledge that keeps me from experiencing the status of "a perfect man, unto the measure of the stature of the fullness of Christ" [Eph. 4:13].

From Acts Chapter two we see that tongues was a supernatural gift and ability used to deliver the Gospel in a language that the speaker was not familiar with, yet the hearer was familiar with it. Today, the gift of tongues can operate in the same way; the only difference is that you are both the speaker and the hearer. You – the speaker – are not familiar with the language that you are praying or speaking, yet you – the hearer – also receive the interpretation of what you just spoke or prayed. The purpose of speaking in tongues, as in any spiritual practice, is to grow in a deeper understanding of God and His will for one's life.

---

[153] *Strongs* #8213: AHLB#: 2866 (V)

CHAPTER SUMMARY:

- There is no magic in applying the name of Jesus in our prayers. There is, however, supernatural access that comes when we pray in the righteous position of a child of God.

- Jesus was an offspring of God not just in title and belief, but also in complete obedience to what He saw and heard from the Father. We are meant to follow His example.

- Praying "in Jesus' Name" is praying along the lines of the known will of God.

- Praying or speaking in tongues enables us to experience a level of prayer and hearing from God that transcends our natural understanding.

- The purpose of speaking in tongues is two-fold: it is a sign for the unbeliever's benefit; it is also for the purpose of edifying and building up the believer. Both purposes of speaking in tongues are so that knowledge contained within the mind of God can be revealed to us.

- The ability to interpret tongues is one of the purest and deepest forms of encouragement that falls under the category of prophecy. Paul encourages all believers to not just pray or speak in tongues but also to prophesy.

APPLICATION:

1. Take time to think about your previous practice on praying "in the Name of Jesus." Write it down, and then write down your thoughts on this new aspect of praying in Jesus' name. How is your perspective different now? Do you feel that this understanding will make a difference in both the way you pray and the way you "do" life?

2. Praying in the Name of Jesus is a life structure you build as you apply God's words to your life. Determine to take on the practice of praying in the true Name of Jesus, which is not just a way to *pray*, but a way to *live*.

3. If you believe that you haven't received the gift of the Holy Spirit since you became a believer, ask God for it in prayer and trust Him to endow you with a fresh and heightened awareness of His presence within you.

4. You might have never spoken in tongues, or perhaps it is already a part of your lifestyle and something you practice frequently. Regardless of which end of the spectrum you fall under, determine that you will take steps, during your times of prayer, to begin praying in tongues and listening to the voice of God to receive the interpretation as well.

CHAPTER THIRTEEN:

Voices of the Mind

> *"Human beings were naturally born without knowing their original source of memory. Their sole purpose has to be to remind themselves of that source, which can only be found within the mind of God. This then becomes their soul's primary purpose."*
> – Julio Alvarado Jr.

The Bible contains numerous accounts of people hearing the audible voice of God. The Spirit or presence of God was experienced externally through some type of physical manifestation. These experiences led people to internalize what they heard and experienced. External experiences with God also often came through the medium of another human, usually a prophet.

Though God can of course choose how He wants to communicate with people, the primary method He uses to communicate with people today is through the sense of the inner ears. Some people call it the "still, small voice of the heart." The reason it is possible to hear from God in this way is because now we have access to the presence of God internally through His Holy Spirit, which was not available in Old Testament times prior to Jesus' resurrection.

Before we explore the thoughts of God and learn to hear His voice, it is imperative that we are aware of some of the other inner voices or thoughts that will contradict the voice of God or hinder us from hearing Him clearly. There are also inner voices that will agree with the thoughts of God. There are primarily four "inner voices" that come in the form of thoughts that affect our conscience. In order to learn to hear the voice of God – which primarily comes to us in thoughts – we must take a look at the other voices and discern the difference between them. These four are:

1. The voice of your reasoning

2. The voice of your flesh

3. The voice of the devil

4. The voice of God

Let's examine each one from a scriptural perspective in order to understand and differentiate between them, beginning by defining the conscience. From a biological standpoint, your conscience is the psychology of your mind. Your thought life furnishes your mind and determines what actions you carry out. Naturally, psychology is the study of the soul. Your conscience is a part of your soul; it is the place of your thought life where you recognize the difference between right and wrong. It's also the place where you establish moral and spiritual values based on the knowledge that you receive. I call it "the control center of your life."

From a Greek perspective, the word conscience is *suneidēsis*, which is simply defined as "co-perception." It comes from the Greek word *suneidōis:* "to see completely and to be informed of."[154] In other words, the information that you receive will determine the state of your conscious mind, which will determine your view of things. Information from the mouth of God will give you His view, thus giving you God-consciousness. Information

---

[154] *Strong's* # G4893, G4894

from any other source will give you that view and consciousness instead.

From an ancient Hebrew perspective, the word conscience is rooted in the word *madda^*, defined as "knowledge and intelligence." Interestingly, it is described as "the door of the eye." Further definitions tell us that "the eye is the window into man's very being," meaning that conscience is "experience that is gained through visual observation" and "an intimate relationship with an idea or an experience."[155] These definitions remind me of statements that Jesus made of Himself when He had an intimate relationship with the ideas and experiences of God: "As I see my Father do I do likewise," and "as I see my Father work I work." Jesus was experiencing a door in His mind where the thoughts and visual images of what God was saying and showing to Him influenced all that He did.

Besides hearing the voice or thoughts of God, Jesus' conscience had experiences with three other thought processes or voices that we need to explore. These were the voice or thoughts of His *reasoning*, the voice or thoughts of His *flesh* and the voice or thoughts of the *devil* – which were all thoughts He heard within the conscience of His soul. These three voices or thought processes always competed with the thoughts or voice of God for His life.

From a Biblical perspective, your conscience can be described primarily in five different categories:

1. A weak conscience

2. A seared conscience

3. A defiled conscience

4. An evil conscience

5. A good conscience

---

[155] *Strongs* #4093: AHLB#: 1085-A(a)

Let me encourage you to take some time to read the context where these conditions of the conscience are mentioned in the Bible in order to get a better scriptural background of each condition.

A weak conscience [1 Cor. 8:7] is described as someone who makes anything an idol, including food, by making these things more important than God. From an ancient Hebrew perspective, the word "weak" is *châlâh*.[156] It describes "something that is made common, profane and unholy because it is meant to be set apart for a specific function." The conscience of man was designed by God to think the thoughts of God. Whenever we allow our minds to be influenced by any other thought process than that, it puts our minds in a weakened state, keeping it from functioning in God's original design. The thoughts of God strengthen the mind and remove any other idol – including any form of addiction.

This type of thought life – a weak conscience – falls under the category of the voice of the flesh. The voice of the flesh is a pleasure-seeking thought life that caters to an undisciplined lifestyle in someone's thoughts, behaviors, and actions. This type of thought life is rooted in three primary mindsets that are recorded in the following passage of scripture:

> *"Do not love the world, nor the things in the world. If anyone loves the world, the love of the Father is not in him, because all that is in the world, the lust of the flesh, and the lust of the eyes, and the pride of life, is not of the Father, but is of the world"* [1 Jn. 2:15-16].

We can adopt a mindset that remedies these three conditions:

> *"I say, then, Walk in the Spirit and you shall not fulfill the lusts of the flesh. For the flesh lusts against the Spirit, and the Spirit against the flesh. And these are contrary to one another; lest whatever you may will, these things you do"* [Gal. 5:16-17].

---

[156] *Strongs* #2470: AHLB#: 1173-B(v)

To walk in the Spirit is to hear and obey the voice of the Spirit of God coupled with whatever actions are necessary to fulfill what is spoken to you. I have found that it is impossible to walk in the Spirit if I'm not consistently hearing the voice of God for my life. If someone is being led by the voice of the flesh – resulting in a weak, seared, defiled, or evil conscience – they will most likely engage in some form of the following works of the flesh:

"Now the works of the flesh are clearly revealed, which are: adultery, fornication, uncleanness, lustfulness, idolatry, sorcery, hatreds, fightings, jealousies, angers, rivalries, divisions, heresies, envyings, murders, drunkennesses, revelings, and things like these; of which I tell you before, as I also said before, that they who do such things shall not inherit the kingdom of God" [Gal. 5:19-21].

"For men will be self-lovers, money-lovers, boasters, proud, blasphemers, disobedient to parents, unthankful, unholy, without natural affection, unyielding, false accusers, without self-control, savage, despisers of good, traitors, reckless, puffed up, lovers of pleasure rather than lovers of God, having a form of godliness, but denying the power of it; even turn away from these" [2 Tim. 3:2-5].

A seared conscience [1 Tim. 4:2] is described as someone who has strayed from the faith or from belief in God. They have allowed him or herself to be seduced by what the Bible calls "doctrines of devils," any type of teaching that contradicts or perverts the original word of God. These perversions always come through the covert tactic of iniquity – originated by Satan himself.

The word "seared" from a Greek perspective is the word *kautēriazō*.[157] It is defined as "something that is branded or made insensitive." Searing renders something incapable of feeling. It renders the conscience unresponsive or numb to the stimuli

---

[157] *Strongs* G2743

of the voice of God. Someone who has a seared conscience has allowed the voice of the devil – which often masquerades as the voice of God – to influence their thought life.

The "hot iron" in First Timothy Chapter four that so effectively sears the conscience is a competing authority that falsely positions itself as an authority of God. What a physical "hot iron" does to flesh, the "hot iron" of foreign, ungodly thoughts does to the conscience. Accepting any other authority as equal to or greater than the authority of God effectively sears and brands the conscience, numbing it to the one true authority: the spoken word of God.

A defiled conscience [Titus 1:15] is described as one who has allowed him or herself to be swayed by the traditions and doctrines (teachings) of men that deviate from the truth of God's Word.

> *"Beware lest any man mislead you through philosophy and vain deceit, after the teaching of men, after the principles of the world, and not after Christ"* [Col. 2:8].

The word defiled is defined as "something that is tainted, polluted or contaminated."[158] A defiled conscience affects the voice or thoughts of your reasoning. Unfortunately, this type of mindset is a worldwide epidemic. We find evidence in the current existence of so many religions and beliefs that have a form of godliness but continue to deny the power of the foundational truth of God's voice.

> *"Having a form of godliness, but denying the power thereof: from such turn away"* [2 Tim. 3:5 KJV].

The "power" that this verse is speaking of is what the Bible refers to as "truth." God is truth and the only source of pure truth is His Word [See Deut. 32:1-4 KJV].

---

[158] *Thayer's Greek Definitions* G3392

"To the pure all things are pure. But to those who are defiled and unbelieving nothing is pure, but even their mind and conscience is defiled. They profess that they know God, but in their works they deny Him, being abominable and disobedient and reprobate to every good work" [Tit. 1:15-16].

God has given us the ability to reason. We have that ability so that we may rationally consider all options that are presented to us. Some of these options come in choices: blessings or curses, advantages or disadvantages, profits or losses. You can always tell when you are listening to the voice of your reasoning because you will use your natural mind to weigh the things you see and hear. You will deliberate and think things through, and afterwards, make your decision.

Though God has given us the natural ability to reason, we also have access to spiritual advice that will lead us to make the right decision every time. Sometimes the things that God leads us to do will go against our natural or carnal thoughts, but as we follow Him, we will discover that He knew best. He is the only one who sees every step of our lives before we take them, and knows where our feet should fall. It is good to look at the "pros and cons" of a situation, but we must never fail to make a decision without first seeking the wisdom and guidance that only comes from God.

"Come now, and let us reason together, says the Lord" [Isa 1:18a].

An evil conscience [Heb. 10:22] describes one whose "body is not washed with pure water." This term "washed with pure water' is not referring to natural water; it is a metaphoric expression to the spoken Word of God [See Ps.119:9, Eph. 5:26]. It is this word that cleanses your body spiritually, which results in your entire body being clean in the eyes of the Lord. This eventually produces the good conscience that is necessary for us to have a God-conscience.

The word "evil" describes something that is "rendered diseased and dysfunctional due to it being corrupted from its original purity."[159] An evil conscience is the opposite of a good conscience. It is a conscience that is affected by the root cause of all that is wrong and evil: iniquity. An evil conscience encourages a person to do wrong. Isaiah 5:20 states, "Woe unto them that call evil good, and good evil; that put darkness for light, and light for darkness; that put bitter for sweet, and sweet for bitter." This is an excellent description of a person with an evil conscience. They are desensitized to what is right. Someone who is suffering from an evil conscience constantly struggles with thoughts of fear, doubt, confusion, torment, and justification of sinful thoughts and behaviors.

The voice of the devil is the primary influence behind an evil conscience. There are many people today, including Christians, who are desensitized to the thoughts that come from Satan. Though many would associate the word "evil" with having its origin in Satan, a deeper understanding of the word evil also points to something that is not functioning in its original state according to the will of God. In other words, we can't blame all evil on the devil. As long as any of us are not functioning in the capacity and wholeness of whom we are predestined to be, we will always be prone to think and do evil. Ignorance of our original identity and our potential to function in the image and likeness of God is a primary culprit of an evil conscience.

From an Aramaic perspective, the word for "evil" is *bisa*. It is defined as someone that is unripe, unready, out of rhythm, or not fit for his or her intended purpose.[160] This perspective speaks hope in that an evil conscience can be transformed into a good conscience by getting in rhythm with the voice of God. Simply getting in rhythm with the voice of God frees us of all

---

[159] *Strongs* G4190

[160] Payne, Smith R., and Smith J. Payne. *A Compendious Syriac Dictionary: Founded upon the Thesaurus Syriacus of R. Payne Smith*. Winona Lake, IN: Eisenbrauns, 1998. Print.

that is wrong and introduces maturity towards all that is right according to God.

In most cases a weak, seared, defiled or evil conscience is going to be influenced by the voice of your flesh, the voice of your reasoning, and the voice of the devil. These consciences will always lead you in the opposite direction of hearing the voice of God and gaining a good conscience. Sincere Christians who consistently miss God's voice either don't know about the different consciences or voices, or they have not learned how to discern which voice is speaking.

A good conscience [1Tim. 1:5] should always be the desired goal for our thought life. A good conscience is necessary in order to have healthy God-consciousness. I suffered from having a seared, weak, defiled and evil conscience during much of my life, even as a Christian believer. Learning to hear from God on a consistent basis has helped me to have a "God conscience" and to discern when the voice of my flesh, my voice of reasoning, or the voice of the devil are attempting to influence me in any way.

The word "good," from an ancient Hebrew perspective, is *shâlêm*. It is defined as "something that is perfect, complete, or in a state of wholeness."[161] This describes what God is at all times. This is also a description of inner peace. The inner environment of your thought life and consciousness must be in this state in order for you to hear the thoughts of God for your life unhindered. One of the greatest portions of scripture that I use in order to train my mind to think Godly thoughts is the following:

> *"Finally, my brothers, whatever things are true, whatever things are honest, whatever things are right, whatever things are pure, whatever things are lovely, whatever things are of good report; if there is any virtue and if there is any praise, think on these things. Do those things which you have also learned and received and heard and seen in me. And the God of peace shall be with you"* [Phil. 4:8-9].

---

[161] *Strongs* #8003: AHLB#: 2845 (N)

Any type of consciousness besides a "good" one needs healing, restructuring, or complete elimination. We obtain this by educating ourselves in how to acquire a Godly thought life and following through on those things we know we should do.

Proof of someone that has a good conscience – one influenced by a God-consciousness – is someone who is hearing thoughts of righteousness, correction and reproof [2 Tim. 3:16]. These thoughts will: guide you into truth [Jn. 16:13], convict you of sin [Rom. 6:1-23], increase your faith [Rom. 10:17], and remove iniquity from your life. They will make the crooked places in your life straight [2 Sam. 22:24, Ps. 18:23, Lk. 3:5, 2 Cor. 7:1].

What Does the Voice of God Sound Like?

I recently had opportunities to teach on the topic of prayer to a group of people that had been believers for many years. Some of them had even been raised in the Church. Two questions kept coming up in these sessions: "How do you hear the voice of God?" and "How do you tell the difference between your thoughts and God's thoughts?" In my opinion, these are two of the most important questions that every human being needs answered in order to "do life" accurately.

A scriptural study of the Bible reveals that the voice of God today comes primarily in the form of thoughts. When trying to hear the voice of God, many people believe that they should be hearing some of type of deep, distinct voice – similar to the sound that Charlton Heston, who played Moses in the epic movie *The Ten Commandments*, heard from the burning bush. Then there are people who agree that God speaks through thoughts, yet they struggle with trying to figure out which thoughts are their thoughts and which ones are God's.

Throughout over 24 years of being a born-again believer, I have used many methods and tools to help and guide me in my prayer time. I have used prayer wheels, which break up an hour of prayer time in segments such as: thanking God, asking for things, asking for forgiveness, singing to God, praying for other people, quoting scripture, meditating on scripture, and praying in tongues. I've also prayed using lists and backing up each request on my prayer list with scripture.

I've read numerous books on prayer and have used their recommended strategies, which included portions where I would plead the blood of Jesus over my life and circumstances and dispatch angels to work on my behalf. In my church experiences, I have heard sermons and entire series on the topic of prayer. I have also purchased courses on prayer and have attended discipleship courses on prayer. Many of these experiences were taught from the reference point of that particular denomination's beliefs on prayer, or from the perspective of a person considered an expert on the topic of prayer.

Though all of these experiences taught me various things that improved my prayer life and relationship with God for a time, I later came to a shocking conclusion. None of these resources actually taught me, from a biblical perspective, how to hear the voice of God. They *mentioned* hearing God's voice but they didn't actually teach *how* to do it. These resources focused primarily on what you should be *saying* or *doing* in prayer rather than *how to hear* and *what you should be hearing* while in prayer. In the following scriptures, we will discover key words that unlock an understanding of prayer that has somehow gotten lost or distorted throughout Christianity.

"For My thoughts are not your thoughts, nor are your ways My ways," says the LORD. "For as the heavens are higher than the earth, so are My ways higher than your ways, and My thoughts than your thoughts" [Isa. 55:8-9].

Chapter 55 of Isaiah is actually an invitation to hear God speak. Through the metaphoric expressions found in this key chapter we discover not just an invitation to hear from Him, but also a foundational principle – the problem why people don't hear from Him. This foundational problem is summed up in one line: "For My thoughts are not your thoughts, nor are your ways My ways." The *thoughts* of God are to be converted into the *ways* of God. It is impossible for us to make this happen unless we are able to discern and hear God's thoughts inwardly in our minds. The word "thoughts" in this remarkable quote from God is the unique Hebrew expression of *machăshâbâh machăshebeth*. Key words that define this foundational expression are: "imagination, intention, advice, plan and purpose." In the English language, *machăshâbâh machăshebeth* are the words "design" and "invention." From an ancient Hebrew perspective, the thoughts of God are described and defined as the process of designing a pattern or plan for an action of a device.[162] This "device" is you.

What we see in these definitions is that God desires to transfer to your mind thoughts that He has already imagined and intended for your life. These thoughts are designed to give you advice according to God's plan for your life; they will enable you to fulfill the purpose for which He created you. Everything that God has ever created is one of His inventions created according to His design. You may have never considered yourself as an invention, but this is exactly what you are. You are a unique product and invention that God has created for His purposes. Whatever God creates, He is also responsible to provide for, according to His plans and advice on how to use it. This includes your life.

> *"For we are His workmanship, created in Christ Jesus to good works, which God has before ordained that we should walk in them"* [Eph. 2:10].

Since discovering that I am God's invention – workmanship based on His design – I have learned to pray more effectively. I seek to hear from Him the things that He has uniquely for me – His plans and instructions as to how to create, develop and

---

[162] *Strongs* #4284: AHLB#: 2213 (a1)

deploy His will for my life. This mindset in approaching prayer has caused me to discipline myself to hear more from Him as to how I can bless Him rather than bringing a list of things that I want to be blessed with.

The word "ways" in Isaiah 55:8-9, when God speaks of His ways not being our ways, is the Hebrew word *derek*. It is defined as "the course or path of life and mode of action."[163] God has intended and imagined for your life the course that He desires for you; these same thoughts contain advice as to what actions you need to take in order to bring this specific path to pass.

These thoughts from God contain in-depth information from the book that is already written about your life. God gives you these thoughts as you seek Him to know His thoughts toward you. The primary purpose of prayer is not to ask for things, but to receive the thoughts that are already prescribed and predestined for your life.

"Your eyes saw my unformed body; all the days ordained for me were written in your book before one of them came to be. How precious to me are your thoughts, God! How vast is the sum of them!" [Ps. 139:16-17]

God's thoughts contain the story of my life and yours. God's thoughts contain my future and your future. More proof of this is found in the following scripture. I memorized and quoted this passage often in my past yet I have to admit that until recently I didn't understand the depth of its meaning:

"For I know the thoughts that I think toward you, says the LORD, thoughts of peace and not of evil, to give you a future and a hope. Then you will call upon Me and go and pray to Me, and I will listen to you. And you will seek Me and find Me, when you search for Me with all your heart" [Jer. 29:11-13].

---

[163] *Strongs* #1870: AHLB#: 2112 (N)

Notice that God thinks His thoughts *towards you*. Also, they are not thoughts of evil – which is anything that is functioning out of the will of God. And notice what these thoughts contain: your future, in which you can put hope and assurance! A shocking discovery and revelation can be found in the above scripture. The only way that we can truly seek and find God at an intimate level – which requires us to search for God with all of our heart – is if *we are getting His thoughts for our life.*

We must first receive the thoughts of God to then call upon Him and accurately pray to Him. This type of hearing and praying is vital in fulfilling the life-changing mandate of, "You will seek Me and find Me, when you search for Me with all your heart." I have personally found it impossible to seek God with my whole heart if I don't know what His heart for my life is. In other words, I can't pray accurately unless I get the thoughts of God for my life first!

In John 8:28 Jesus said, "I do nothing of Myself; but as My Father taught Me, I speak these things." His quote was not just limited to what He spoke in public. The word "nothing" in this passage reveals the secret that caused Him to pray more effectively: Jesus was always walking in the will God because of what He was hearing from the Father. To put it another way, God taught Him how to pray! This revelation has lead me ask God to teach me to pray.

This has led me to daily ask in my morning "hear time" from God, "God, what are your thoughts about me today? What have you written about me today?" The practice of meditation has helped me to cleanse my mind of my thoughts during these sessions in order to get God's thoughts for my daily life. Once I ask these questions, I discipline my mind to hear His answers.

Since learning to approach prayer in this way, my life has radically changed. God has told me that one of the primary reasons that He created me was to be a teacher to the nations. This discovery has caused me to be desperate to learn from Him personally how to teach and what I should be teaching. This book and the others that I am assigned by God to write are products of my hearing from God; I am writing about the topics that He has inspired me with. These books are my small contribution to humanity. They are inspired by God and designed to bring a more in-depth understanding – through Greek, Hebrew and Aramaic root word perspectives from which the original scriptures are derived – of key topics such as iniquity, prayer, and the Kingdom of God.

Prior to learning to hear God at this level, I never would have even thought I would be a teacher, speaker or write a book at the age of 48. I am a high school dropout. I acquired a G.E.D. (General Education Diploma) later in life. I have had no formal training in teaching or speaking. I have few writing skills, poor grammar, limited vocabulary, and a desperate need of a spell check and a thesaurus. But none of that really matters. God doesn't call the equipped; He equips those He has called ... and He calls those who are willing to follow. One of the best talents is simply being willing and available.

The more I position myself to hear God, the more I am discovering what He has already written and prescribed for my life. It is as though I am discovering a person that I never knew even though I was living in his (my) body. I am also learning to discover a God of whom traditional Christianity failed to inform me. Fundamentally, I am being taught and learning about God from God Himself. What a difference! This is God's will for every human being. God uses humans such as Pastors, Teachers, Apostles, Evangelists and Prophets to take us to a certain point in learning spirituality, but His ultimate goal is to teach you all that you need to know Himself. This *"transfer of teachers"* is a level of learning that not enough people get to because they unfortunately remain dependent on other humans to teach and spiritually advise them.

This discovery and learning comes with a responsibility. I now know the reason God created me. The major stream of my purpose is to produce material and teachings that transcend traditional Christianity. I have been given a three-fold focus. I am to help people root iniquity out of their lives, teach them how to hear the voice of God, and help them discover, develop and experience the greatest learning environment that they have access to on this earth, that may be either dormant or undeveloped within their inner-being which Jesus referred to as "The Kingdom of God." I work to help people understand and deploy the Kingdom within them. Many of the thoughts that God thinks towards you are related to these key issues.

The most important things in my life are the thoughts of God toward me. I have come to learn that the greatest lesson in life that each child of God needs to master is the art of learning to hear the voice of God. Your competence in this area will determine whether you will live your life as an "experiment" or live a life of purpose revealed to you from the mind of God. True life and success is determined by living out the purpose for which you were created. An authentic, truly successful person is one who hears the voice of God and prospers in the fulfillment or preordained purpose for which they were created.

Your own thought life can interfere with the thoughts of God for your life. Your thought life can also affect your prayer life. But when you reign in your thoughts and allow them to be in subjection to God's thoughts toward you, your thoughts can transform your life ... because they will be God's thoughts whispering to your heart the way that you should walk.

CHAPTER SUMMARY:

- The primary method God uses to communicate with people today is through the sense of the inner ears, the "still, small Voice of the heart."

- There are primarily four "inner voices" that come in the form of thoughts that affect our conscience:

  - The voice of your reasoning

  - The voice of your flesh

  - The voice of the devil

  - The voice of God

- Your conscience is a part of your soul; it is the place where you recognize the difference between right and wrong. It's also the place where you establish moral and spiritual values.

- Your conscience will fall under one of the five following categories:

  1. A weak conscience

  2. A seared conscience

  3. A defiled conscience

  4. An evil conscience

  5. A good conscience

- Ignorance of our original identity and our potential to function in the image and likeness of God is a primary culprit of an evil conscience.

- Any type of consciousness other than a "good" one needs healing, restructuring, or complete elimination. We obtain this by educating ourselves in how to acquire a Godly thought life and following through on those things we know we should do.

- God doesn't call the equipped; He equips those He has called ... and He calls those who are willing to follow. One of the best talents is simply being willing and available.

- The greatest lesson in life that each child of God needs to master is the art of learning to hear the voice of God.

APPLICATION:

1. A quote from the chapter states, "It is good to look at the "pros and cons" of a situation, but we must never fail to make a decision without first seeking the wisdom and guidance that only comes from God." Do you look to God before making decisions in your life? God wants to lead and guide you every step of the way and there is nothing too small to seek Him about.

2. God wants to speak to you of the thoughts and purposes that He has intended for your life. Determine to take time on a regular basis to hear these thoughts so that you can fulfill the purpose for which He created you.

3. Now that you have read about the four voices of the mind and the five types of consciences that are described in the bible, take an honest assessment and discernment of your current thought-life to see where improvements can be made. Make it your life-goal to work towards nurturing your mind to create more of a good conscience in order to hear the voice of God more clearly and consistently.

CHAPTER FOURTEEN:

How to Hear and See like Jesus

> "Jesus was a 'Father Impersonator.' Make this
> the goal for your life as well."
> – Julio Alvarado Jr.

Though prayer is taught in many ways by many different religious organizations, my primary focus for this chapter is to look into Jesus' prayer life and to use it as a model. As we follow and practice this model, our lives will be transformed in unprecedented ways.

I have spoken to God in various places and at many different times of the day such as in my car, at work, in the shower, while running on my treadmill, and even while on the toilet. What's more, God has also spoken to me at these times and places. I'm sure that Jesus heard the voice of God throughout His normal day as well.

Hearing from God alone can be prayer, even if you are not asking God for anything in your prayer time. However, if we are speaking to God and seeking His help, we should first hear from the mouth of God as to what we should be praying for and about. Then we will have the wisdom and knowledge to pray accurately. In other words, accurate prayer can be guaranteed if God initiates the conversation.

Though I can hear and talk to God at any time of the day, I want to focus on early Morning Prayer. Jesus prayed early in the morning and I believe this is the best time to consistently hear the voice of God. A study of Jesus' prayer life reveals the indisputable fact that He woke up early every day for the purpose of prayer. The most important activity of His day was what He did in His mornings, which prepared Him for the rest of His daily activities:

"And in the morning, rising up a great while before day, he went out, and departed into a solitary place, and there prayed" [Mk. 1:35].

How Jesus Positioned Himself to Pray

"The preparations of the heart belong to man, but the answer of the tongue is from the Lord" [Prov. 16:1].

One who is serious about hearing and learning from God through prayer should learn to prepare him or herself for such a sacred event. When Jesus taught on prayer, He was teaching from a perspective of what He was doing when He positioned Himself to practice the art of prayer:

"But you, when you pray, go into your room, and when you have shut your door, pray to your Father who is in the secret place; and your Father who sees in secret will reward you openly" [Matt. 6:6].

This "solitary place" was first outward, then inward. Jesus would position Himself by going to a place that was absent of distractions. Then He would posture His mind inwardly and enter into the place He called the secret place. This was His meeting place where the mysteries of God for His life were revealed to Him.

This requires a level of mental discipline where you clear your mind in order to meet with God in His environment. This "border crossing" is a mindset where you cross over and enter into the culture of heaven that is within you. It's an environment within you that is designed by God – a meeting place of spirit to Spirit. Very few people are aware of this place, yet it exists within every human being.

Though there are biblical accounts of Jesus praying at times of the day besides the morning (including an account where He prayed all night) the following prophetic scripture about Him proves that Jesus had a consistent habit of starting His day with Morning Prayer. This is a model for those that wish to truly follow in His footsteps:

"The Lord GOD has given Me the tongue of the learned, that I should know how to speak a word in season to him who is weary. **He awakens Me morning by morning, He awakens My ear to hear as the learned.** *The Lord GOD has opened My ear; and I was not rebellious, nor did I turn away"* [Isa. 50:4-5 NKJV].

In my opinion, the most important word in these two key verses is the word "by." The word "by" in this passage signifies consistency and priority. It would be safe to assume that Jesus would purposely go to bed early the prior evening in order to wake up physically and mentally refreshed, prepared to hear and learn from God. He sought the will of God for His life on a daily basis during His Morning Prayer sessions. Jesus' consistent Morning Prayer sessions set His life's priorities. They set in motion the fulfillment of what I believe was the most important mandate for His life: to seek first the Kingdom of God and His righteousness. This is also the most important mandate for every one of us.

As mentioned before, Jesus modeled this activity throughout His public ministry for about three and a half years. This would have been approximately 1,277 consecutive days of showing His disciples how He would start His day.

"But seek ye first the kingdom of God, and his righteousness; and all these things shall be added unto you. Take therefore no thought for the tomorrow: for the tomorrow shall take thought for the things of itself. Sufficient unto the day is the evil thereof" [Matt. 6:33-34 KJV].

It is impossible to seek the Kingdom of God, much less His righteousness, if we do not seek after these things through hearing from God in prayer. An in-depth study of Matthew Chapter six and a root word study of verse 34 gives evidence of the fact that we are not to approach God begging, anxiously pleading, or requesting things that people normally ask from God in prayer such as food, finances, clothing, shelter or other basic needs.

If we are to "take no thought" of such things, doesn't it make sense that we are perhaps not to focus our prayers on such things? The word "evil" (in the phrase "sufficient unto the day is the evil thereof") explains why our focus in prayer should never be about the things that we think we need. Interestingly, the Greek-to-Hebrew translation of the word that was originally used here for "evil" is the word *rââh*, which is the word for "vision."[164] In other words, don't envision or focus on such requests; doing so causes us to miss the mark or true purpose for prayer. What is that purpose? It is stated in the previous verse: "seek first the Kingdom of God and His righteousness for your life."

Even though this may contradict what others teach on prayer, if we want to pray accurately, we must go back to the model example – Jesus. He specifically said to not be anxious or worry about basic needs:

---

[164] *Strong's* G2549 - H7200: AHLB#: 1438-H (V)

"Therefore do not be anxious, saying, What shall we eat? or, What shall we drink? or, With what shall we be clothed? For the nations seek after all these things. For your heavenly Father knows that you have need of all these things" [Matt. 6:31-32].

Many people seek the handouts of God and have turned their prayer time into begging, "life survival" sessions, fix-this-in-my-life sessions, or "If you bless me I will bless you" sessions. A look into Jesus' prayer life proves that He never prayed for the things that traditional Christianity and other religious teachings on prayer say that you should pray for. Traditional Christian teachers and believers use the following verses to validate such requests, focusing on the word "whatever" – which of course could mean anything as long as you verbalize and invoke the name of Jesus to the request:

"Therefore I say to you, All things, whatever you ask, praying, believe that you shall receive them, and it will be to you" [Mk. 11:24].

"And whatever you may ask in My name, that I will do, so that the Father may be glorified in the Son. If you ask anything in My name, I will do it" [Jn. 14:13-14].

If we focus only on these, we miss the full counsel of the written word of God as it relates to prayer. The following key passage clues us in on the type of prayer that God will answer:

*"And this is the confidence that we have toward Him, that if we ask anything **according to His will**, He hears us. And if we know that He hears us, whatever we ask, we know that we have the petitions that we desired of Him"* [1 Jn. 5:14-15].

Petitioning God *according to His will* is the qualifier to having prayer answered and puts the term "whatever" into proper perspective. Not knowing the will of God for our lives makes the application of this verse difficult. If you do not know how to hear from God, how can you possibly pray according to His will?

Did Jesus pray using the written word of God? We have no record of Jesus taking scrolls of scripture with Him to pray. Today, it is commonly taught that you must use your Bible and use scriptures in prayer. Jesus never taught this practice, nor did He do it Himself. Biblically, Jesus never took scrolls of scripture to pray though He had access to them. He never taught His disciples or others to pray along the lines of scripture. The written word of God (the Bible) is a framework of the overall will of God. The detailed and specific will of God for your life is always found in His mouth; therefore using only written scripture limits your encounter with God.

Using scripture to hold God accountable or in a sense to try to twist God's arm to perform something for you is a prayer practice that did not originate in God. Even the rabbinic teachings that Jesus would have been taught – to repeat or quote scripture – was merely an affirmation back to God. It was never used in an attempt to manipulate God into answering a prayer.

Jesus was looking for another form of scripture, one that we have explored throughout this book. That "scripture" was the specific instructions for His life, which were found in the book on His life that followed the pattern of the following passage:

> *"All scripture is given by inspiration of God, and is profitable for doctrine, for reproof, for correction, for instruction in righteousness: That the man of God may be perfect, thoroughly furnished unto all good works"* [2 Tim. 3:16-17]

Though the reference in the above passage to "all scripture" is traditionally taught to mean the written Word of God – the Bible – let me introduce a fresh perspective to the meaning of "all scripture." The Hebrew root word for scripture in this passage is *kâthâb,* which means both "something written" as well as "the act of writing."[165] When we take the time to listen to and record daily instructions from God as He lets us know His will for our lives, this "something written" is the scripture for your personal life. This does not mean that you can't use the biblical scripture as a guide as long as it leads you to eventually hear the voice of God personally for your life.

When you take time to hear from God, He leads you according to the book that He has already written about you. The book that contains the doctrine for your life was written from "before the foundations of the earth" [See Ps. 139:16, Jer. 30:2].

The Doctrine Contained in the Book on Your Life

Jesus was exposed to the Kingdom doctrine for His life that came from the mouth of God in His Morning Prayer sessions. In other words, Jesus received a doctrine specific to His life during His times of Morning Prayer, which is the reason He made the following statement:

"Jesus answered them and said, My doctrine is not Mine, but His who sent Me. If anyone desires to do His will, he shall know of the doctrine, whether it is of God, or I speak from Myself" [Jn. 7:16-17].

Jesus got the doctrine for His life and the doctrine that He taught specifically from the mouth of God.

"Give ear, O ye heavens, and I will speak; and hear, O earth, the words of my mouth. My doctrine shall drop as the rain, my speech shall distil as the dew, as the small rain upon the tender herb, and as the showers upon the grass: Because I will publish the name of the LORD: ascribe ye greatness unto our God" [Deut. 32:1-3] *[See also Isa. 55:10-11].*

---

[165] *Strongs* #3789: AHLB#: 2295 (N)

Why would the heavens and earth have to hear the voice of God? This verse is not referring to heaven as an expanse of external space or to earth as globe of dirt; it is a metaphorical expression of the environment of Heaven that was in Jesus and is also within you: the Kingdom of God. Heaven and earth don't have ears, yet the Kingdom of God within you does. Of course, naturally on earth you carry another set of ears. What this verse is saying is that we need to inwardly perceive the sound of God's voice. This is a metaphoric expression of what is inside of us – Heaven – that came from God spiritually and what every human being is physically made of – the earth.

When Jesus positioned Himself to hear from God, His Spirit – clothed in an earthly body – was hearing with the ears of the spirit. Every human being has the Kingdom of God within them, which originated in Heaven [Lk. 17:21]. Every human being also physically came out of Adam, the first human that God created from the dust of the earth [Gen. 2:7]. Enclosed within every human being is a substance of Heaven that came out of God, which is your spirit. Your spirit has the ability to hear from Heaven through your inner ears in order to influence your soul.

Every human being has an environment that comes from Heaven, which is the meeting ground that God has built into us from before the foundation of the world. This is the place we are meant to reach through prayer. When God says, "Give ear, O ye heavens, and I will speak; and hear, O earth," He is telling us to listen with our spirits.

Concealed within Deuteronomy 32:1-3 is knowledge that – once understood and applied – will give us access to the greatest learning environment possible. This is prayer from a hearing perspective – praying not to speak, but to hear the voice of God. God is describing in these passages His ultimate desired result, which is heavenly "education" that comes from the environment where He becomes your primary teacher.

The word "publish" in this supreme passage of scripture is the Hebrew word *qârâ*. In this particular verse, it is defined as "a meeting where selected individuals are called out in order to give and proclaim a name over them."[166] It is important to point out that the selected individuals are the ones that choose to position themselves to learn to hear the voice of God in order learn from God. This is what Jesus meant by His words, "many are called, but few are chosen" [Matt. 22:14]. Though all of humanity is called to experience consistent encounters of learning directly from God, unfortunately very few people choose to experience it.

The key phrase, "Because I will publish the name of the LORD" is a figurative expression of God teaching you who you really are according the identity of who He is in order to permanently publish His name (authority, identity, mind, character and traits) within you! This was the desired result in speaking the "hallowed by thy name" portion of The Lord's Prayer, taught by Jesus, which ascribed greatness to God. Jesus experienced this learning through His Morning Prayer sessions. God the Father was teaching Jesus a daily "like father, like son" experience. Jesus understood that if He had not been consistent with these Morning Prayer/learning sessions, He would have been rebellious:

"The Lord GOD has opened My ear; And I was not rebellious, Nor did I turn away" [Isa. 50:5 NKJV].

According to this verse Jesus would have considered Himself a rebellious son if He had not gotten up early and positioned Himself to have His inner ear opened to the teachings of God. Though some may consider this a hard saying, this verse is teaching us the principle that rebellion is actually a position we take when we fail to hear from God in the beginning of our day.

To further understand the impact of Jesus' Morning Prayer sessions and the impact that such prayer sessions can have on your life, let's examine three key words from Deuteronomy 32:2: "doctrine," "speech," and "distil."

---

[166] *Strongs* #7121: AHLB#: 1434-E (V)

"My doctrine shall drop as the rain, my speech shall distil
as the dew, as the small rain upon the tender herb, and as
the showers upon the grass" [Deut. 32:2].

The word "doctrine" is the Hebrew word *leqach*. It is defined
as "a learning that comes from the speech of the one teaching."
It is a learning that is received specifically through the speech of
God.[167] In other words, the doctrine of the Kingdom for your life
that comes from God can only be taught by God since it comes
from His speech.

The word "speech" is the Hebrew term *'imrâh 'emrâh,* which
is simply defined as "an appointed saying that comes in the form
of words that form sentences."[168]

The word "distil" is the Hebrew word *nâzal,* which is defined
as "a consistent drip that creates a flow."[169]

Water distillation is a process where water is turned into a
vapor so that its impurities are left behind. It is then turned back
to pure water through the process of condensation. Spiritual
distillation is an internal *still*ness that is required in order for
a constant flow of God's speech into our spirits. His speech
comes in the form of sentences that remove the impurities of
any doctrine that doesn't line up with the Kingdom doctrine for
your life.

Jesus understood the significance of starting His day in this
attitude of stillness and focus on the Father. He continually
gained knowledge and understanding of who He was and the
responsibility of His life assignments. Jesus positioned Himself
in not just a called position but, more importantly, a chosen
position by choosing to hear the voice of God at the beginning
of every day. True spiritual maturity should eventually lead to
Morning Prayer as the most important activity of your day.

---

[167] *Strongs* #3948: AHLB#: 2319 (N)
[168] *Strongs* #565: AHLB#: 1288-C (N1)
[169] *Strongs* #5140: AHLB#: 2387 (V)

From an English perspective, terms such as "when you pray" [Matt. 6:6] and that Jesus "departed into a solitary place, and there prayed" [Mark 1:35] are terms that immediately bring an understanding that the one praying will be positioned to talk to God.

One needs only to browse through the Bible and see that when God was talking to someone personally, He was doing the majority of the talking ... sometimes all of the talking. Why is it that many of the prayer resources available today only view prayer from a "talking to God" perspective instead of "hearing from God" experience – which is true prayer at its core?

Many modern biblical study resources and dictionaries define the word "prayed" from Mark 1:35 as "to supplicate, petition, to ask, and to request." The *Ancient Hebrew Lexicon* defines the word "prayed" as "a coming to one in authority to intercede on one's own behalf or for another." These definitions are traditionally viewed and applied from the perspective of us talking to God. Yet a deeper study of this key word reveals that it is God who desires to do the supplicating, petitioning, asking, requesting, and interceding in order to produce a certain outcome. From an ancient Hebrew perspective, this outcome is described as "a distinct performance that is based off a judgment that sets something apart as special." It is a sacred and holy event where special information is dispersed through the revealed thoughts of God – thoughts described as wonderful and marvelous – that are classified as secrets or mysteries.[170]

The word "prayed" encapsulated an entire lifestyle of Jesus choosing to empty Himself of external and internal distractions in order to receive His Father's thoughts and will for His life, which were already written and predestined for Him. Any other result would have not fulfilled the intended purpose and impact of "prayed." This is the same mindset and result we must seek when we position ourselves to pray at the beginning of the day. Anything less than this opens the door for a day that is not truly

---

[170] *Strongs* #6419: AHLB#: 1380

guided by the thoughts and will of God and puts you in danger of living your life through the thoughts and will of man. We may erroneously assume that we are doing the will of God, yet be far from it.

It is impossible to do the will of God daily in your life if you are not hearing from God daily. Jesus did not live His "today" on yesterday's instructions. Every day, Jesus' mind was being renewed by what was already written and purposed for that particular day.

The key to understanding what Jesus experienced when He started each day in prayer is found in the root word understanding of the word "prayed," which is *palal,* found in the following passage of scripture.

"And in the morning, rising up a great while before day, he went out, and departed into a solitary place, and there prayed" [Mk. 1:35].

Its parent root is the word *pala.* All words related to prayer stem from this Hebrew word *palal.* For the purposes of studying Jesus' prayer life – which is a model of what our prayer life should look like – because of the magnitude of its importance, let's revisit this crucial understanding of prayer.

As mentioned in briefly in chapter two and in more extensively in my first book, *The Mystery of Iniquity Revealed,* ancient scriptural writings were written in pictographic writings. Through time these pictographic writings were then converted into the Hebrew letters that are more commonly seen today. In ancient pictographic writing, the vowels as we know them today were not used. They were added later to enhance the understanding of what was being communicated in modern Hebrew and other languages.

Instead of *Palal,* the pictographic script would have read PLL and pronounced as, *Pey Lamed Lamed. Pey* was pictorially illustrated as a mouth. The second letter, repeated twice, is *lamed*, which pictorially illustrated the shape of a shepherd's staff, representing authority, and a tongue, representing language or speech. Combined, they originally defined prayer as: "one authority speaking to another authority" and "to speak the tongue of tongues."[171]

In other words, to pray was a scenario of a meeting where one authority (God) was speaking to another authority (you) or vice versa; the dialogue that was spoken at these at these prayer sessions was the language of languages or the speech of speeches. "Truth" is the language of God in terms of the speech that comes out of His mouth. True prayer is communication between God and you, the purpose of which is for God to speak the truth of truths. When God speaks to you, each session is a "truth session" that forms the truths for your life. Most people don't view truth as a language, yet it was the language that Jesus spoke. Though the vernacular that He communicated was either Hebrew or Aramaic, His language or speech was always truth. "I tell you the truth" [Jn. 8:42-47, 12:49].

Pala – the parent root of the Hebrew word *Palal* – is a description of the type of information that is revealed in a true *palal* or "prayer" session. Through the ancient pictographic writings, *Pala* would have read "PL" or *Pey Lamed*. In other words, only one authority is doing all of the speaking. The language is truth and the authority is God. *Pala* is described as the content of information that is given in order "to perform great work through distinct actions as an act of intercession." This information revealed by God describes a specific performance based out of a judgment or decree that God has already purposed for your life. It further describes this information as "marvelous, wonderful and extraordinary."[172]

Scripturally, whenever the word *Pala* is used, God is primarily mentioned as the one expressing His thoughts and ways in order

---

[171] This is not to be confused with speaking in tongues, which we explored in a previous chapter.

[172] *Strongs* #6381: AHLB#: 1380-E (V)

to produce His desired outcome. Fundamentally, the substance of *Pala* is knowledge of the good works that God has predestined for your life:

> *"For we are His workmanship, created in Christ Jesus to good works, which God has before ordained that we should walk in them"* [Eph. 2:10].

The following passage brings to light the vital importance of learning to hear from God at this level in order to get this type of information:

> *"And I saw the dead, small and great, standing before God, and books were opened. And another book was opened, which is the Book of Life. And the dead were judged according to their works, by the things which were written in the books"* [Rev. 20:12].

Every human being is going to be judged by God according to the works found in the book that has already been prewritten about you. This verse is traditionally interpreted to mean that the books are the 66 books of the Bible. This is not an accurate understanding of this verse for a couple of key reasons. Many of the sections of the Bible were letters at the time and thus cannot be classified as books.

As mentioned in a previous chapter, the term "books" in Revelations 20:12 is the dual word Hebrew expression called a *Sêpher Siphrâh*.[173] *Siphrâh* is the act of writing based on an account that is given. *Sêpher* is the book or document that is produced from that writing. Combined, *Sêpher Siphrâh* describes "the act of writing a book based on a specific account given to you by God." God first writes the chronicle for your life, and then desires to give you the information contained in it so that you can produce the works given in this crucial book.

It is once again important to note that Jesus Himself had such a book on His life:

---

[173] *Strongs* #5612: AHLB#: 2500 (e1), (N)

"Then I said, Lo, I come in the volume of the Book it is writ-ten of Me to do Your will, O God" [Heb. 10:7].

This is a crucial point that cannot be stressed enough. When Jesus was in prayer, He was experiencing a "reading" from God the Father of what was already written about Him. There was a book on Jesus' life, there is a book on my life, and there is a book on your life as well.

The word "volume" in the passage above is the Hebrew word *megillâh*, which means "a second time around of a time or event."[174] When God wrote the book on our lives, He saw the events of our lives played out the first time. The second time that these events come to life is when we copy or act out the script of what is already written about us. When we do this, we are not doing our will but the will of the Father, just like Jesus did.

God will only show you what you are looking for. If you are not looking for the will of God from this detailed perspective, He cannot show it to you. What God shows you at this level of prayer comes with the responsibility to fulfill what He reveals to you. These assignments will always be related to the reason He created you.

An example of this in my personal life is my writing three books on the topics of iniquity, prayer, and the Kingdom of God from a perspective that transcends traditional religion. I never thought that I would write a book, yet after learning to hear God at this level, He began to reveal to me what He had already written or prescribed for my life. I began to understand that I am meant to help people by writing key books on these topics and teaching the principles found in them through different forums. God has personally told me that before my parents conceived me, I was sanctified and ordained from before the foundations of the world by Him to be a teacher to the nations [See Jer. 1:5, Eph. 1:3-5]. My life's purpose is to teach people how to hear the voice of God for themselves, how to discover, develop and

---

174 *Strongs* #4039: AHLB#: 1058

experience the greatest learning environment that is on the earth today – which is already in them. Jesus referred to this learning environment as "The Kingdom of God."

In Psalms 139 we see another verse to validate the fact that all of our lives are already recorded in a book:

> *"Your eyes saw my unformed body; all the days ordained for me were written in your book before one of them came to be"* [Ps. 139:16 NIV].

The problem is that many people, including Christians, have no clue of what is written in their book. The result of this is that many are writing their own life stories. Unfortunately, some of these end up being books of fiction and not true or – more accurately – "truth" stories.

Another aspect of the root definition for the word "volume" is connected to the word "redeem," which in this case is defined as "to restore one to their original position."[175] Wow! This tells me that if I want to live the preordained Kingdom of God life that God has already established for me, then I must have pure and unhindered access to the library of the Kingdom of Heaven through prayer so that I can "check out" the book of my life. Like Jesus, I can then become a "Father impersonator" of all that God the Father has to say and show me through the Spirit of Truth.

The content of this book are the thoughts that God thinks towards you, derived from what He has already written about and thus seen for you. These are the thoughts of peace (wholeness, completeness), and not of evil (any other will that is not God's), to give you an expected end in which you can put your hope [Jer. 29:11]. Not hearing from at God this level will make you prone to creating your own works and story for your life.

Jesus was faith- and purpose-driven, yet His drive in these areas was fueled by His ability to first and foremost be "truth" driven. He found that drive in what was already prewritten

---

[175] *Strongs* #4039: AHLB#: 1058-D

and prescribed for His life. Today too many people attempt to be faith- or purpose-driven without being first truth-driven by hearing the voice of God. It is impossible to be driven from a godly perspective without learning to consistently hear the voice of God.

Imagine learning to hear from God unhindered and consistently recording such events. What you would end up with is a book or a document that contains the full scope of God's thoughts for your life. This book would contain your life's purpose, what you are supposed to have faith in and for. It would contain the detailed assignments for your life that God has already willed. These are all wonderful and marvelous assignments that transcend your ordinary thoughts about life and purpose. All faith and all attempts to live a purpose that doesn't originate from the mouth of God is sin [Rom. 14:23].

God is the creator of faith and purpose. "The purpose" of God for your life is synonymous with His will for you. It is impossible to have a Godly purpose if God hasn't told you why He created you and what you should believe in.

"Your testimonies also are my delight and my advisers. ...
I have more understanding than all my teachers; for Your
testimonies are my prayer" [Ps. 119:24, 99].

The word "testimonies" used in these two verses from Psalms is the Hebrew word *êdûth*. It describes the knowledge that comes out of a "witness as an event or person's testimony recounting another event or person."[176] God is the witness that testifies, through the disbursement of knowledge, what He has already seen for your life!

"Blessed are those who keep His testimonies, who seek Him
with the whole heart! They also do no iniquity; they walk
in His ways" [Ps. 119:2-3].

---

[176] *Strongs* #5715: AHLB#: 1349-A (N) L

Iniquity – which is the topic of my first book in this three-book series – is akin to a spiritual cancer and is the root cause of what keeps you from truly pursuing God wholeheartedly in order to truly hear from God at the level that Jesus did so that you can walk in God's ways for your life. Iniquity is responsible for many of our *assumptions* of the will of God rather than *accurate knowledge* about the will of God.

Breathing the Breath of God

Naturally, the most important ability that we have is the subconscious act of breathing. Spiritually, the most important ability that we need to learn is the act of breathing the inspiration of God. A child does not have to be taught to breathe. This occurs instinctively once the child is transferred from the environment of the womb to the environment of his new world. Spiritually, the same principle applies. This is the one of the most important revelations and foundational teachings that should accompany a genuine born-again experience.

The new believer should be taught how to breathe the breath of God, which happens when someone learns how to hear the voice of God. Once someone learns to breathe the breath from the environment where they originated, they become inspired with the presence of that environment. In His Morning Prayer sessions, Jesus was being inspired with the environment from which He originally came, which sustained His spirit. Every human being has this same origin, which means we also have the opportunity and ability to experience this.

This deeper understanding of prayer brings light to one profound fact that has remained a mystery to many. First of all, God created and desires to possess your inward parts, which include the spiritual environment of the Kingdom of God:

"For You have possessed my inward parts; You have covered me in my mother's womb" [Ps. 139:13].

Second, this environment is fearfully and wonderfully made and is where the marvelous works of God for your life are first revealed:

"I will praise You; for I am fearfully and wonderfully made; Your works are marvelous and my soul knows it very well" [Ps. 139:14].

"How precious also are Your thoughts to me, O God! How great is the sum of them!" [Ps. 139:17].

Jesus knew the sum of God's thoughts about Him because He positioned Himself inwardly and outwardly to get them. This is why He received daily readings from the book on His life [Heb. 10:5-7]. The problem is that most souls don't know it very well because they never discover and develop the prayer life that produces this type of mindset:

"Behold, You desire truth in the inward parts; and in the hidden part You shall make me to know wisdom" [Ps. 51:6].

This inner environment is where truth is revealed. It is that secret place where mysteries are revealed that Jesus referred to [See Matt. 6:6, 13:11. Lk. 8:10]. Since God is a God of Truth [Deut. 32:4], this is the only environment where He can reveal His wisdom for your life. This is the secret place where the wisdom of God is revealed for your life. It is an inward environment where "prayer" is much more heard than spoken because these revelations can only come from hearing from God!

We must capture two foundational realities when understanding Jesus' prayer life. The first is that He was hearing the thoughts of God from the mouth of God for His life. These thoughts are called "truth," which is original information that came from the only originator of all truth – God. Jesus' prayer life was more a hearing session than it was a speaking session. Every time that Jesus would depart to a solitary place, He was having a truth session with God. In other words, Jesus was always truth driven.

The second reality is that the truth from the mouth of God produced the faith or the belief structure that Jesus had, which caused Him to produce the works in His life. Jesus' prayer life resulted in actions. Like faith – which if not accompanied with works is dead – prayer that doesn't result in some type of action is also dead [See James 2:14-26].

"So then faith comes by hearing, and hearing by the word of God" [Rom. 10:17 NKJV].

"Word" in this passage is the word *Rhēma* in Greek. It means "an utterance through speech." In Hebrew, the root word is *emer*, which means "something said." The parent root of *emer* is *emet*, which is the Hebrew word for truth. If we are faithful to listen to the voice of God, we will discover what we are to have faith in and for. Any other source that we allow to produce our faith than what comes out of the mouth of God is susceptible to error.

Imagine living a life that is this precise. It's possible for you if this is the type of prayer life and lifestyle that you desire. Truth produces faith. Truth also reveals the purpose in which you are to put your faith. This is when you know that you are getting the thoughts of God. They are marvelous and wonderful thoughts that introduce more clarity to a vision or dream that you have, or they introduce a vision that becomes an assignment for your life. They are more illustrated, more intense and more doable because they come with instructions on how to fulfill them. Jesus received and practiced vision every day of His life based on what was told to Him that morning. In other words, He was able to take the words that He heard and formulate pictures or scenarios of those words taking place. This is what made Jesus so "futuristic."

God will only show you what you are looking for. If you're not looking for this type of experience in prayer, then traditional prayer according to the doctrine of men will be the extent of your prayer experience. This is the reason why Jesus preferred not to pray with groups or in what are called prayer meetings today. He never wanted to have His prayer time influenced by any source other than God. An encounter or meeting with God at this level like this requires an unhindered Presence (the Mind of God) to our present environment (the mind of man).

This is a level of God consciousness that very few people get, primarily because so few understand prayer from a hearing perspective. The majority of teachings on the topic of prayer today, teach content and practices that lean toward busying the mind versus how to quiet the mind in order to hear and learn from God. We lessen our experience with God by continually being dependent on humans to teach us about prayer and God. "Hearing from Heaven" prayer is necessary in order for each one of us to reach our maximum potential. It is the environment where Jesus was taught by God Himself and the environment where you and I can also be taught by God Himself.

Inside every human being is the greatest learning environment possible, yet it seems to be the least discovered. This is the place where you will discover the greatest and most intelligent Teacher that truly is a "Know-it-all." This is what Jesus was exposed to every morning. A person who disciplines him or herself to prepare inwardly and outwardly and who purposes to take this time will see amazing results. I am constantly being shocked at what I am learning at this place in my life.

Most people dread these three words: Early-Morning-Prayer. Prayer of this kind takes discipline, and early Morning Prayer increases the need for a life of discipline. Jesus said to "seek first the Kingdom of God" and early Morning Prayer puts that emphasis on "first." It takes a great deal of sacrifice and discipline to get to bed early and to rise up early. Personally, the discipline that has entered my life as a result of waking up early to hear and learn from God has benefited me tremendously in my spiritual life. I have discovered that God will speak to me whenever I position myself to be spoken to.

When consistently done, there's nothing quite like getting up early and hearing the voice of God before anything else is done that day. It is the key to accomplishing the greatest things for God – the things He would have me do each day.

CHAPTER SUMMARY:

- If we are seeking God's help for things in our lives, we should first hear from Him as to what we should be praying for and about; accurate prayer can be guaranteed if God initiates the conversation.

- It is impossible to seek the Kingdom of God, much less His righteousness, if we do not seek after these things through hearing from God in prayer.

- God will only show you what you are looking for. If you are not looking for the will of God from this detailed perspective, He cannot show it to you.

- Today too many people attempt to be faith- or purpose-driven without being first truth-driven by hearing the voice of God for their lives. It is impossible to be driven from a godly perspective without learning to consistently hear the voice of God.

- God will only show you what you are looking for. If you're not seeking this type of experience in prayer, then traditional prayer according to man's denominational perspectives, philosophies and practices will be the extent of your prayer experience.

- Inside every human being is the greatest learning environment possible, yet it seems to be the least discovered.

APPLICATION:

1. Though each one of us is called to experience consistent encounters of learning directly from God, unfortunately very few people choose to experience it. Write down some reasons why people might not choose to experience these encounters – such as a lack of faith, insufficient desire or a lack of accurate and effective teaching. Write down the reasons that most apply to you. Keep that list handy so you know what to work on as you seek to hear God's voice for your life.

2. A quote from the chapter states,

   "Spiritual distillation is an internal stillness that is required in order for a constant flow of God's speech into our spirits." Do you take time for stillness in your life? It is not easy in the mad rush of these current times, but is necessary to hear the voice of God. Determine how you can take time for stillness.

3. Waking up early for prayer takes discipline, but it also shows that you are serious about "seeking first the Kingdom of God." Think about whether this is the "missing link" in your life and consider making Morning Prayer times a part of your daily schedule.

CHAPTER FIFTEEN:

How Does It Work?

> *"Prayer is man giving God the legal right and*
> *permission to interfere in earth's affairs."*
> – Dr. Myles Munroe

After reading the previous chapters and expanding your understanding of prayer, you may be wondering where to start. How can this information work for you to change your life?

Over the past 24 years, since becoming a born-again believer, I have tried numerous techniques –some that I had been taught and some that I developed myself. I want to share with you details of my personal prayer life that I believe will help give you ideas of where to start and how to apply the things you have read.

I have tried praying at different times of the day to see what time would be most effective or fit best according to my schedule. I have also used numerous tools to aide me in prayer: books on prayer, reading the Bible before or while praying, prayer wheels, prayer books that outlined specific methods, soft instrumental or gospel music, personal prayer lists, and scriptures related to my prayer topic.

Though all of the techniques and tools that I used served me well for that particular season in my life, I have to admit that I still struggled in one way or another, often with distractions that would throw my focus away from prayer, or with thoughts of whether or not God was pleased with how I prayed that day. Though I believe that God honored my attempts, deep within myself I knew that there had to be a better way to pray.

One thing was certain: through all of these prayer sessions I was doing the majority of the talking and not learning to listen. Throughout my experiences I learned to hear the voice of God to a certain degree, yet I still felt as though there was a disconnection between God and me. At times I would question whether the thoughts that I got were my thoughts, God's thoughts, or perhaps even the devil's thoughts.

When God began to take me on that journey deeper within His heart (mentioned in the first chapter), I finally began to understand where the disconnection originated. It was because I was doing all the talking, without understanding that God wanted to show me His heart and His desire for my life.

Iniquity's Effect on a Prayer Life

During this same season in my life, I began to study the Bible from a Hebraic root word perspective. During one of my studies, in preparing for a class that I was about to teach at church, I came across the word "iniquity." Once I saw the definition of the original Hebrew word, the question that arose in my mind was, "Why hasn't anyone told me what iniquity truly means?" This discovery was a starting point that grew toward writing my first book in this series, titled *The Mystery of Iniquity Revealed.*

The presence of iniquity in my life had perverted my understanding of prayer and my relationship with God. That day I finally began to ask the right questions. I started by asking, "Lord, what must I do to get inside of Your heart?" He responded by beginning to reveal the iniquity in my life and what I had to do to root it out. I must admit that some of things God revealed to me, I had been convicted of before; however, instead of dealing with those sins, I had either ignored them or justified their existence, which led to my heart being hardened in that issue.

Iniquity is the root cause of all that hinders a relationship with God, especially in learning to hear His voice clearly. Unbeknownst to me, I was being affected by this thing called iniquity from the day I was naturally born and it continued into my born-again life without me knowing it.

The removal of iniquity and the constant maintenance of my heart and soul to ensure that iniquity doesn't gain a root in me again has been the most monumental factor in leading me to place where God began to teach me how to pray. If you haven't done so already, I encourage you to read *The Mystery of Iniquity Revealed* to gain a full understanding of iniquity and how it might be affecting your life and relationship with God.

A quote that I recently heard synchronized with what God was attempting to teach me about prayer and Him. This quote stated, "There are over seven billion people on the earth today yet there is only one mind; what we have are over seven billion on and off switches." The moment I heard this, a light went on within me. Though this person wasn't specifically talking about the mind of God and was using to the quote to convey another idea, at that moment God spoke to me and asked, "What are your thoughts about what that person just said?" Immediately I knew where God was going with His question.

Originally all humanity came out of God – beginning with Adam and Eve. When God formed Adam from the dust of the ground and then breathed life into him, He was inspiring Adam with His own mind. Unfortunately, Adam and Eve chose to "switch off" the mind of God and welcome the ideas of another mind – Satan, who came in the form of a serpent and tempted them to sin. It is important to note that they both chose to take on the actions of a mind that wasn't God's. Satan introduced the first "off switch" to the mind of God and Adam and Eve chose to use it.

Unfortunately, when it comes to prayer, many other minds throughout the ages have also influenced its original purpose and practice. Though many may disagree with what I'm about to say, I believe that Satan is still influencing the practice of prayer by "turning off the mind of God" as it relates to the original purpose and practice of prayer. Proof of this is found in the vastly different ways that prayer is taught and practiced by different religions and beliefs.

Iniquity is a mind-altering substance. In addition, it alters your connection with God through prayer. Iniquity disconnects the power that we have within us to live by and reproduce God's predestined will. Iniquity "switches off" the potential of our original connectivity to God; it has produced many manmade attempts to reconnect with God, but these attempts only create an artificial or limited experience with God. A void remains in the heart of the believer that only an iniquity-free life can fill.

When our thoughts and ways are not lined up with God's thoughts and ways, it is literally impossible to "let this mind be in you that was in Christ Jesus" [Phil. 2:5]. Jesus would have been taught to pray through His rabbinical education – which primarily consisted of the memorization of scripted prayers and quoting specific scriptures – yet He chose to be taught by God and practice what He was taught as it related to prayer.

Though there is nothing wrong with learning from other humans how to pray, all such teaching should eventually lead you to a place where God becomes your personal prayer Teacher. As the student matures, there should come a time when he or she steps over the threshold to embrace the ultimate Teacher and the best learning environment possible. One of the revelations that I got through learning from God was that I had acquired a massive amount of knowledge *about* God but I didn't have knowledge *from* God. Much of what is being taught on prayer today is either limited or tainted with the traditions and philosophies of men rather than the original purposes and practice of prayer. The

Lord's Prayer lesson that Jesus taught outlines the framework of this original purpose.

Statements that Jesus made such as, "As I hear my father speak, I speak" [Jn. 12:49] and "My doctrine is not my own" [Jn. 7:16] are clear indicators that everything Jesus taught and practiced came primarily from God – including His prayer life and how He practiced it.

This brings up what I believe is the most important request that you can ask of God: "Lord, teach me to pray." This was a request from Jesus' original disciples and should also be the deepest desire of our hearts, because it will lead us to know His heart. This request has caused me to unlearn prayer philosophies and techniques that had "switched off" my mind to the prayer lifestyle that God wanted to teach me.

Wouldn't it make sense that learning to pray from God Himself takes the mystery out of prayer?

My Morning Processes and Experiences

As I share with you a glimpse into my personal prayer life, please understand that my intention in sharing what I have learned about prayer is not to say that this is the only way to pray. This is what works for me, but your current situation and your guidance from God might lead you to a different plan. This is to give you some ideas of where or how to start. As you follow His voice whispering to your heart, you will come up with a prayer plan that works perfectly for you.

Let me start off by saying that the morning, for me, has been the best time of the day to pray. The first reason for this is that when I wake up before anyone else in my family, I have no one to distract me. Second, my mind is fresh after a good time of rest. Third and most important, I saw in the scriptures that the mornings were Jesus' primary time to pray and I wanted to duplicate His prayer process.

I currently pray in my living room next to the fireplace. I turn it on in the cooler seasons to add a pleasant ambiance to my time with God. When there are others awake in the house, I sometimes go down to my basement. For a season in my life, I would pray in a walk-in closet because it was the only place that I could pray without distractions.

I start my morning time with God by sitting in a comfortable place and clearing my head of all thoughts that relate to my day at work, family matters, finances, my to-do list, or any other thoughts that attempt to occupy my mind and meeting space with God. The practice of meditation has been the catalyst in being able to still myself inwardly. I use meditation to clear my mind of my thoughts in order to position my mind to hear and learn from God.

My morning sessions are the place where I gain access to spiritual intelligence and higher learning. The #1 goal of my Morning Prayer sessions is to always hear from God first; there are times when I will initiate the conversation by simply asking God something similar to the following requests:

- **Lord, what is Your will for me today?**

- **Please read to me what have You already seen and prewritten and about my life.**

- **What thoughts do You want me to convert into Your ways today?**

- **Where do You want to start our conversation today?**

- **Lord, teach me about You and the Kingdom that You have placed inside of me.**

Based on what I hear, my conversation takes a particular direction with God from that point on. My experience has been that, when God speaks to me, He primarily stays within the framework of The Lord's Prayer that Jesus taught, which I have outlined in detail in this book. Allow me to give you some simple examples.

Our Father who art in Heaven.

These are the conversations that God has with me informing and reminding me that He is my original source and sustainer. This may also be a time when He teaches me about His character and traits that I need to develop in my life in order to function in His likeness and image.

Hallowed be thy Name.

This is where God teaches me in-depth concepts about His identity and how it relates to me. It is also where He shows me how to properly apply His Name into my life.

Thy Kingdom Come, Thy will be done in earth as it is in Heaven.

This is where God informs me about His predestined purpose and will. This may include detailed knowledge and instruction about my purpose and His vision for my life. This is primarily where God tells and shows me overall how I can be an answer to a world problem.

Give us this day our daily bread.

This is where my personal book is read to me, where I get the thoughts of God for my life as to what I should be doing that day or in the near future.

Forgive us our debts, as we forgive those that are indebted to us.

This is where God speaks to me about whom I have wronged and how to correct it when possible. He also shows me how to love those that have unintentionally or intentionally brought harm or hurt into my life.

And lead us not into temptation, but deliver us from evil.

This is where God takes me into the depths of iniquity removal and maintenance. He gives me root causes and remedies for anything that is wrong in my life – morally, mentally, spiritually and physically.

For yours is the Kingdom and the power and the Glory forever and ever.

This can be where I affirm what God has told me about what is in me, and where I make commitments in order to fulfill the full measure of what He is through me.

Depending on the direction that God speaks to me, I don't always go through all seven of these components of prayer. For example, I am currently in a season of the "Your Kingdom come, your will be done" component. The majority of what I'm hearing from God is related to the building of material such as books, videos, and other teaching resources that enable me to share with others the information He has given me.

Personal Prayer Process

My morning times are not negotiable. I intentionally turn down late evening events in order to go to bed early so that I can wake up early the following morning. The most liberating and exciting times of my days are my early Morning Prayer sessions with God.

Taking that time in the early morning hours has helped me to remove the clutter of extraneous activities and even some relationships that I had no business attaching myself to because God never told me to get involved in them. It also removes all assumptions of whether or not I did the will of God that day. I believe that Jesus would have preferred to go into a private room or rooftop – which was a common place of prayer in that culture.

He chose places where there was no opportunity for distraction because of the importance and sacredness of His morning times with God.

I normally keep a journal of my times with God. I do this for a few reasons. First, it serves as a reminder of what God told me that morning so that I can refresh my mind with it throughout the day. Second, the continual recordings serve as a script of the book on my life. Third, these recordings become the detailed, God-breathed scripture for my life that serve me in the areas of doctrine, reproof, correction, and instruction in righteousness [See 2 Tim. 3:16]. God's specific teachings, or doctrine, enlighten me; He reproves me when needed; He corrects all that is out of order in my life; He instructs me in the ways of righteousness.

I currently use computer journaling software to take note of my morning sessions with God. In the past I have used notebooks and even created my own journal. Once in a while I will use an audio recorder and then transfer the audio file to my computer journal software and replay it when necessary.

I have approximately 10 years of these written or audio recordings and I review them from time to time. A few years back I was going through a season of depression because I simply did not like where I was at in life. That morning God told me to get my old journals and to read through them. The first entry that I saw was one from exactly one year before. That entry contained words of affirmation and promises of some things that God was going to do for me – things that had all came to pass within that year. That day, God showed me how far I have come as well as how close He is to me. I quickly realized that the reason I was going through that brief season of depression was because I had lost my focus of what God had done for me. I had simply failed to trust in some of things that He had recently spoken to me about.

Personal Prayer Experiences

I've had sessions that began with God telling me to look at a specific verse or passage, with Him asking me, "What do you see?" This is where I may do a root study of key words found in these scriptures. Once I have put forth the effort to study and get what I believe He wants me to see, I go back and ask Him to give me His interpretation or what He wants me to see in that passage.

God asking me questions like this has taught me the art of asking the right questions. Some of my most profound experiences with God have been when I ask Him detailed questions that primarily deal with what He has said to me. The art of asking God questions and keeping a clear mind to hear His detailed answers have brought some of the most illuminating experiences of my life.

There have been times when God has counseled me on my marriage in areas that I am failing or where I need to develop or implement key actions to strengthen my relationship with my wife.

If I'm invited to speak or teach that particular morning, I will envision what I am about to experience and get any final adjustments or instructions from God for what I am about share with people that day.

I will also use my mornings to get specific instructions from God as to what I am supposed to work on. This is where I may create my to-do list for that day. I might ask Him, "What am I supposed to write about today?"

God has even counseled me on diet and exercise. In a sense, God has become my personal trainer. I have changed my diet to a much healthier one by making important lifestyle choices. This education from God brought me awareness in how addicted I was to certain foods that were not healthy for me. It is one area in my life that has caused me to view self-discipline as mandatory skill. Doesn't it make sense that if God is concerned with our whole being (which He is), that we should be hearing from Him about our physical condition if we are not taking care of ourselves?

I, of course, use my Morning Prayer time to ask God for specific things that relate to my life purpose. This is also the time that I will intercede and pray for my family or others. I will seek instruction on how to deal with something or what choice to make if options are available to me. This is where I ask God for healing of my body if I find myself ill in any way.

If I find myself not knowing what to pray for, I will primarily pray in tongues. After doing so, I always quiet myself in order to listen for the interpretation of what my spirit just prayed.

I want to be a "Father Impersonator." I want to be able to say, like Jesus, "As I see my Father do, I do likewise." My morning sessions with God give me the opportunity to get all the instructions that I need, to envision myself doing them, and finally to follow them with actions that cause them to come to pass.

I am currently disciplining myself to spend time with God in the evenings as well, to serve as a "thank you session" towards God and a review of how my day went. I have also used these evening sessions to review anything I had been instructed to do that morning yet failed to do, and make any necessary adjustments.

CHAPTER SUMMARY:

- Iniquity is the root cause of all that hinders a relationship with God, especially in learning to hear His voice clearly.

- Though there is nothing wrong with learning from other humans how to pray, all prayer teaching should eventually lead you to a place where God becomes your personal prayer teacher.

- The most important request that you can ask of God is, "Lord, teach me to pray." This should be the deepest desire of our hearts, because it will lead us to know His heart.

- As you follow God's voice whispering to your heart, you will come up with a prayer plan that works perfectly for you.

- The #1 goal of my Morning Prayer sessions is always to hear from God first.

- The art of asking God questions and keeping a clear mind to hear His detailed answers can bring some of the most illuminating experiences of your life.

APPLICATION:

1. Reread the practical ideas in the chapter and take note of things that could work for you. Make a "prayer plan" for this current season of your life. (Remember to seek the counsel of the Lord about it as well!)

2. If you are struggling in developing a prayer plan, seek out a mature and disciplined believer whom you may ask for advice and who will hold you accountable in becoming a disciplined praying person.

3. Subscribe to my website in order to get updates to tutorials on prayer and other important topics that I will making available soon: **www.julioalvaradojr.com**

Conclusion

Prayer is at the same time a mystery and the means whereby we can solve all life's mysteries. It is our medium of connecting with God – the Source of all life and the Maker of all things good and pure.

If you had to write a research paper and could choose to ...

a) Write the paper based on existing knowledge you have in your mind,

   or

b) Use books and the internet to find the information you need

... what would you choose? Your answer is simple, right? It didn't take much effort to decide "b" because we know that our own knowledge is limited. It's the same with prayer. We can choose to devote all our prayer time to asking God for any number of things – to supply our needs, to heal our children or spouse, to help that job come through – but our prayers would be limited to our own narrow and finite understanding of the situations. Yet if we take time to remove our sandals and cross over the border, to hear from God as to His desires for each of the things on our heart, we will pray powerful prayers. What's more, we will in essence be an answer to those prayers because we will know what steps we are meant to take to bring about the solutions. When the prayer of our heart is, "Lord, teach me to pray," we will come to know God's heart and enter that beautiful paradise of the secret place of prayer.

If the only thing you remember from this book is the important of mastering the art of learning to hear the voice of God, you will be in a better position to see miracles in your life and see your heart transformed as a result.

May the prayer of your heart be to seek first the Kingdom of God and His righteousness for your personal life. As you come to know the will of God for your life, your prayers will be answered in the best way possible – God's way. He will also enable you to become an answer to the problem you face, and the problems that others face. As you hear from Him, you will grow in faith that God has a special and unique predestination for you, a life of purpose that only you can live for Him.

Are you ready to learn a new language – the language of God, which is Truth? Are you ready to become intimately acquainted with the greatest prayer teacher in existence? Are you ready to experience God in a new way every day by receiving His will for your life and fulfilling it? Are you ready to partake of the highest form of learning, knowledge and teaching available? All this and more is available for you now through the avenue of prayer and hearing from God.

Open your life to the mystery of God's will today. Open your heart to your true spiritual inheritance that will be revealed from the mouth of God. Determine to live your life according to the prayer Jesus taught by listening and receiving God's truth and enacting it day by day. As you do so, you will grow in faith and ability to change the world around you. You will be empowered to establish God's Kingdom "on earth as it is in heaven."

Utilize fasting, meditation, praying in tongues and receiving the interpretation, and your soul will be fertile ground to hear the "still, small Voice of God" in your heart. The greatest learning environment possible is waiting to be activated within you. Discover it today by connecting with God through prayer and receiving His directions for your life. You will find that your life and the lives of those you love will never be the same again.

Such is the power of prayer!

Appendices

Appendix 1:

From footnote # 15

A list of sites where the charts of the ancient Hebrew script can be viewed:

www.ancient-hebrew.org/28_chart.html

www.hebrew4christians.com/Grammar/Unit_One/Pictograms/pictograms.html

Appendix 2:

From Footnote #22

The Lord's Prayer in Aramaic:

Abwoon dâbwashmaya (Our father who art in heaven)

Nethquadash shmakh (Hallowed be thy name)

Teytey malkuthakh (Thy kingdom come)

Nehwey tzevyanach aykanna dâbwashmaya aph bâarha (Thy will be done on earth as it is in heaven)

Hawvlan lachma dâsunquanan yaomana (Give us this day our daily bread)

Washboqlan khaubayn (wakjhtahayn) aykanna daph khnan shbwoqan lâkjayyabayn (And forgive us our debts as we forgive those who are in debt to us)

Wela tahlan lânesyuna, ela patzan min bisha (And lead us not into temptation, but deliver us from evil),

Metol dilakhie malkutha wahayla wateshbukhta lâahlam almin, ameyn (For the kingdom, the power, and the glory are yours, now and forever, amen.)

Appendix 3:

From Footnote #88

Examples of books that were commanded to be written for a specific purpose:

- Genesis 5:1

- Exodus 17:14, 32:32-33, 34:27

- Numbers 5:23

- Deuteronomy 17:18, 31:24

- Joshua 10:13, 24:26

- 1 Samuel 10:25

- 1 Kings 11:41, 14:19, 29, 15:7, 23, 31, 16:5, 14, 20, 27, 22:39, 45

- 2 Kings 1:18, 23, 10:34, 12:19, 13:8, 12, 14:15, 18, 28, 15:6, 11, 15, 21, 26, 31, 36, 16:19, 20:20, 21:17, 25, 23:28, 24:5

- 1 Chronicles 29:29

- 2 Chronicles 9:29, 12:15, 13:22, 16:11, 20:34, 25:26, 27:7, 28:26, 32:32, 33:18, 35:26, 36:8,

- Esther 2:23, 10:2

- Ezra 4:15

- Isaiah 30:8

- Jeremiah 51:60

- 2 Thessalonians 3:17

- Revelation 1:11, 19, 21:25

Bibliography

Benner, Jeff A. *The Ancient Hebrew Lexicon of the Bible: Hebrew Letters, Words and Roots Defined within Their Ancient Cultural Context.* College Station, TX: **Virtualbookworm.com**, 2005. Print.

Benner, Jeff A. "Word of the Month - Pardes." **Ancient-hebrew.org**. Ancient Hebrew Research Center, July 2008. Web. 23 Sept. 2013.

"Eisegesis." *Wikipedia.* Wikimedia Foundation, 17 Sept. 2013. Web. 23 Sept. 2013.

"Historical-grammatical Method." *Wikipedia.* Wikimedia Foundation, 16 Sept. 2013. Web. 23 Sept. 2013.

"History of Education in Ancient Israel and Judah." *Wikipedia.* Wikimedia Foundation, 16 Aug. 2013. Web. 23 Sept. 2013.

"Kabbalah." *Wikipedia.* Wikimedia Foundation, 21 Sept. 2013. Web. 23 Sept. 2013.

Payne, Smith R., and Smith J. Payne. *A Compendious Syriac Dictionary: Founded upon the Thesaurus Syriacus of R. Payne Smith.* Winona Lake, IN: Eisenbrauns, 1998. Print.

Seekins, Frank T. *Hebrew Word Pictures: How Does the Hebrew Alphabet Reveal Prophetic Truths.* Phoenix, AZ: Living Word Pictures, 2012. Print.

Strong, James. *The Exhaustive Concordance of the Bible: Showing Every Word of the Text of the Common English Version of the Canonical Books, and Every Occurrence of Each Word in Regular Order, Together with a Key-word Comparison of Selected Words and Phrases in the King James Version with Five Leading Contemporary Translations, Also Brief Dictionaries of the Hebrew and Greek Words of the Original, with References to the English Words.* Nashville: Abingdon, 1980. Print.

Thayer, Joseph Henry, Carl Ludwig Wilibald Grimm, and Christian Gottlob Wilke. *Thayer's Greek-English Lexicon of the New Testament: Coded with Strong's Concordance Numbers.* Peabody, MA: Hendrickson, 2003. Print.

About the Author

Julio and his wife Ivette have been married for 21 years. In their blended family, they have three adult children and two grandchildren. Julio has been an employee at the Harley Davidson Motor Company for 24 years. Ivette is a licensed professional counselor with advanced clinical training in marriage and family therapy and sexual addiction.

Julio has overcome drug addiction, alcoholism, financial ruin, divorce, suicidal tendencies, depression and many other negative lifestyle issues.

In February of 2006, after being a traditional Christian for over 15 years, Julio experienced a unique encounter with God. His life journey has taken him from times of great emotional, physical and spiritual difficulty to a new life of experiencing God in an authentic and unique way. This experience birthed in him a hunger that changed the direction of his life. Through the many things he has overcome and the wonderful truths he has been blessed to discover, Julio is now on an inspiring and focused place in his life's journey.

He began to pursue the truth about who God predestined him to be from a true "Kingdom of God" perspective. The vital discoveries Julio made have resulted in the discovery of his God-ordained purpose: To help people learn how to hear the voice of God in a dynamic way, empowering them to discover, develop and "do life" from the greatest learning environment possible – the place within them that Jesus called "The Kingdom of God."

Julio follows God's original, Kingdom-of-Heaven-oriented personal development plan, which is to **Build One's Life from the Inside Out.** He has a passion to help others do the same.

Julio was recently awarded an Honorary Doctorate Degree in Philosophy from KME University of Alabama, an affiliate of Freedom Bible College of Arkansas for his in-depth research of key biblical topics. Julio is currently starting a ministry, which involves public speaking and teaching, creating books and other resources that transcend traditional religious teaching on key topics. These resources focus on rooting out iniquity from one's life; learning how to hear the voice of God; and how to position oneself inwardly through a meditative mindset in order to learn from God on a personal and highest level possible.

If you have questions or comments or would like to invite Julio to speak or teach on the topic of this book as well as other life-changing topics you may contact him through his website at **www.julioalvaradojr.com** or email him directly at **julio@julioalvaradojr.com**.

Made in the USA
Charleston, SC
18 July 2014